GUARDIAN OF THE GODS

An Inside Look at the Dangerous Business of Music

Mark Rodgers

D1262478

Design and production: Lee Tse & MacPros, Inc.
Introduction page and back cover photography: Jim Conway

Library of Congress Catalog Card Number
99-64025

ISBN 0-9671288-0-3

Photo acknowledgements appear on page 265, which constitutes a continuation of the copyright page.

Printed in the United States of America by Copy-Mor Inc.,
Chicago, Illinois, USA

Guardian of the Gods
Mark Rodgers
Monkey Boy Media, Inc.
122 Green Bay Road - Suite 9
Thiensville, WI 53092
1-888-Monkey-0
414/512-2688 (area code will change to 262 after Sept. 1, 1999)
414/512-1708 (area code will change to 262 after Sept. 1, 1999)
www.monkeyboymedia.com
info@monkeyboymedia.com

This book is dedicated to friends, family and faith.

To my family, who supported this project, and my partners, who made it a reality; to the artists who inspired it; and to Andre Augustine, for helping make my writing dreams come true. Special thanks to editor Michael Popke, whose guidance, skill and enthusiasm made this project come together.
To my wife, Amy: because of you, everything is possible.

– Mark Rodgers

ACKNOWLEDGMENTS

EXTRA SPECIAL THANKS

Thanks to God: With Him all things are possible. To Heather, Hamilton, Harrison, and Hugh, who have endured the most. To Mark Rodgers, who saw it all coming before I did. To Amy Rodgers, Ken and Yvonne Ostermann, Michael Popke, and the entire MacPros staff, for keeping the dream alive. And to Lee Tse, for the great cover design.

To my mother, who always kept me laughing and always told me I could; and to my father, who always reminded me to treat people the way you want to be treated.

Thanks also to Jackie Hickman, my other mom; Ingrid Hutt, my little sister; and Jim Hutt, my brother.

Plus: Kenny Martin; Chris Lee; Greg Tillman; Ronnie Davenport; Kevin Harbour; Henry's Tacos; Beverly & Elouise Martin; Mike McCoy; David Wooldridge; Earl Rezac; Jerry Browne; Charlie Williams; Cecil Stockdale; Keith Lee; John, Lori, Heather and Jamie Schmidt; Rick "RJ" Jones; Dotty Gundlickson: Rest in Peace; Chester Caddis; Dave Sidwell; Mike Ackerly; Sark Arcelanian; Dennis Greer; Billy Stennis; Tony Morehead; Al Lewis; Ron "Bear" Jones; Jeff Hamilton; Rich Guberti; Nigel Shanley; Lonn Friend; Gerri Miller; Russell; Mike; Lisa; Keith "Ice to Eskimos" Leroux; Tracy Jett@Nike; Angelo@Adidas; and Ole Ostergard@Adidas.

THE FIRST CREW

Thanks to Ron "Big Ron" Scoggins; James "JD" Daniel; Lamont Williams; Dave "DC" Coley; Lee Douglas; Andy "Gomeo" Gomes; Charles Bayfield; Garo Amerian; Pete Kranzke; Damon Zumwalt; Mama and Papa Z; Rick Sandoval; Steve Gemza; John Tracy: Rest in Peace; T.J. Tracy; Mark Zelman; Jerry Landrum; Dave "Double D" Davis; Jerry Crutcher; Warren Kaye; John Gordon; John Greenstreet; and Earl Paysinger.

Thanks also to Jam Master Jay; Run; D.M.C.; Big D; Russell Simmons; Lyor Cohen; Eric Moskowitz; Chuck D; Flavor Flav; Professor Griff; The S1Ws; The Fresh Prince & Jazzy Jeff; L.L. Cool J.; The Beastie Boys; Eric "Eazy-E" Wright: Rest in Peace; Dr. Dre; Ice Cube; MC Ren; Yella; K.J. Fierro; Atron Gregory; Speed; Laylaw; Mr. & Mrs. Richard Wright; Jerry Heller; Gary Ballen; Tomica Wright; George & Marla; Billy Blough; Jeff Simon; Hank Carter; Robert Allen; Irish Mike Donahue; Bill Hutchings; Steven and Teresa Tyler; Joe and Billie Perry; Joey and April Kramer; Tom and Terri Hamilton; Brad and Karen Whitford; Thom Gimbel; Bob "Tour Manager Extraordinaire" Dowd; Steve Cox; Jeff Krump; Tim Collins; Keith Garde; John David Kalodner; Tim Rozner; Mike "Big Mike" Henry; Otis Thrasher; Tom Rogers: Rest in Peace; Tres Thomas; John Bionelli; Mike Verge; Karen Linehan; Burt Goldstein; Jimmy Eyers; Peter "I've got a shoe in my eye" Mertins; Matthew and Gunnar Nelson; Bobby Rock; Joey Cathcart; Bret Garsed; Paul Mirkovich; Gary Grosjean; Greg "Grit" Frederick; Charlie Hernandez; Steve Wood; Larry Mazer; Fred Coury; Stephen Pearcy; Frankie Wilsex; Michael Andrews; Donny Syracuse; Gene $immons; Paul Stanley; Eric Singer; Bruce Kulick; Peter Criss; Ace Frehley; Doc McGhee; Paco Zimmer; Tommy Thayer; Melissa Madden; Sandy Rizzo; Angus Vail; Jon Bon Jovi; Richie Sambora; Dave Bryan; Tico Torres; Hugh McDonald; Scott Bellone; Dave Davis; Paul Korzillius; Matt Bongiovi; Patrick Prendergast; John "Bugzee" Hougdahl; The Artist and Mayte; Ian Jefferies; Earl Gabbidon; Aaron Liepens; Big Coco Chilton; Michael Bland; Morris Hayes; Sonny Thompson; Duane Nelson; Kim Berry; Pat and Neil; Mick Mahan; Ray Brinker; Suzie Davis; Madonna; George Michael; Donna Deitz; Melody Vincent; Mr. Seijiro Udo; Take Takahashi; Tommy Shigatomi; Ossy Hoppe; Arnie Granat; Ross Zapin; Mark Burger; and Loren Cornelius.

Thanks To All The Road Warriors:

Andy "The Prince of Methuen" Gilman; Franklin Felder; Jim Survis; Julie Petersen; Rocko Reedy; Bobby Carrell; Curtis Battles; Orris Henry; Billy Head; Mike "Spike" Rush; Dave Romeo; Todd "T Boy" Confessore; Brian Gazo; Tony Bird; Kenny Barr; David Mathews; Karen Hughes-Mathews; Suzanne Seidel; Jon Cordes; J.J. Liberato; Kevin Sapanski; Jim Schroder; Mike "Hoss" Keifer; Wes Leathers; Tyler Lockett; and Max Stauffer.

– Andre Augustine

TABLE OF CONTENTS

Rockers, cont.

"People don't know I exist. But I'm there,
all the time ... watching you."

Andre Augustine

OPENING ACT

Guardian of the Gods tells the incredible story of Andre Augustine's career in the music industry. As security director and road manager for some of the most famous musicians of the Eighties and Nineties, Andre is an "industry type" whose name you rarely hear, but he has fascinating experiences and insights to share.

Andre began working with Run-D.M.C. when the seminal rap group first started to break big in the mid-Eighties. He later teamed up with Run-D.M.C. and controversial Public Enemy for the groups' first tours of Europe. Soon, Andre found himself in charge of security for N.W.A. on the infamous rap group's troubled U.S. tour – the one in which the song "Fuck Tha Police" drew nationwide attention from the media, local authorities and reportedly even the FBI.

Transitioning to the world of rock 'n' roll in 1988, Andre spent the next decade working for such musical giants as George Thorogood, Aerosmith, Bon Jovi and Kiss. His involvement with these artists came during some of the most engaging periods of their careers.

Thorogood, for example, proved a perennial drawing power in the United States long after "I Drink Alone" hit the charts. Bon Jovi released two albums in the Nineties to critical and commercial acclaim, establishing itself as one of the few rock bands of the Eighties to survive the decade. Both Aerosmith and Kiss reached the pinnacle of their careers for the second time – some might say for the third time, in Aerosmith's case.

All of these rappers and rockers achieved the status of superstardom and firmly cemented their place in music history. They are living legends ... gods, if you will. *Guardian of the Gods* takes you beyond what you see on the stage, hear in the music and read in the press to give you insight into these artists' lives and work that only an insider like Andre Augustine can bring.

How the Story is Told

Guardian of the Gods employs several story-telling techniques. Re-creations make the reader a proverbial "fly on the wall," detailing events as Andre remembers them. Whether receiving death threats while working with N.W.A., leading Aerosmith onto a stage in war-torn Czechoslovakia, being on safari with Bon Jovi or flying out of storms in a private jet with Kiss, Andre's and my objective when using re-creations is singular: We want to take you there.

Another technique is the inclusion of Andre's present-day insights about these events and experiences. It's amazing to see the clarity of his hindsight. Through this blending of techniques, we've attempted to accurately tell Andre's story.

Sources

The bulk of the information used for this book was garnered from hundreds of hours of personal interviews with Andre. During these interviews, Andre and I have explored every facet of his life, psyche and career – probably more than Andre really wanted to share.

In an attempt at objectivity, we've also spent time interviewing some of the people who have worked closely with Andre – fellow security guys, band technicians and other colleagues from the road. Their observations proved invaluable to rounding out this project.

When possible, supporting documentation and research from other sources also are included. Comments from the Internet, books, newspapers, magazine articles and television-award shows are used to help reinforce or amplify particular points. We do this for two reasons: 1.) So you get a sense of how others may have perceived these events, and 2.) So you have the facts to make up your own mind as to how significant some of these events are to music history. When available, sources are always credited.

This Work is Not an Exposé!

Although we are aware of some artists' negative offstage behavior, we have endeavored to portray all of them in a favorable light. This is not an attempt to sugarcoat reality, but rather to accentuate the positive. It would be impossible to say this work is impartial. As the author, I make no apologies for being biased. These musicians have created the soundtrack of my life – and probably part of yours. Their work has been there for us in good times and in bad, adding emotion to our existence. To the artists mentioned in this book – speaking for myself, my friends, and millions of fans – I humbly say, "Thank you."

It's also important to see this story in its larger context, and to reflect on the social issues that gave rise to gangsta rap and to contemplate the behavior that led to the tragedy befalling Eazy-E. Also inspiring is to observe the strength of the human condition, which enabled Aerosmith to triumph over addiction and a fallen career. And endlessly fascinating is the consumer mind-set that drives hordes of seemingly insatiable Kiss fans to spend millions of dollars on concerts and merchandise showcasing four adult men wearing Kabuki-style makeup and costumes while playing four-chord rock songs.

Andre and I hope we've captured a sense of these artists' personalities and enabled you to perhaps see their world from the inside. We hope this book entertains you, informs you and enlightens you. The one outcome we wish for is that, as a result of reading this book, rock fans will explore rap and rap fans will explore rock. And through music, we all might gain an alternate perspective of our world.

Andre's musical journey begins in the developing rap world of the mid-Eighties.

– Mark Rodgers

June 1999

RAPPERS

1

TOUGHER THAN LEATHER

Run-D.M.C.

June 19, 1987: San Diego, California

"Warning: if you are carrying knives, guns or any other object that could be used as a weapon, discard it immediately. You will not be allowed access into the arena. Any persons attempting to bring weapons into the arena will be arrested."

THIS ROBOT-LIKE, AUTHORITARIAN VOICE BOOMED REPEATEDLY over the loudspeaker system at the San Diego Sports Arena. The announcement greeted concertgoers there to see Run-D.M.C. and the Beastie Boys.

The message sounded even harsher as it bounced off the cement sidewalk and landing areas leading to the arena. As hordes of people moved towards the building, the scene at dusk became more surreal.

Fans not only endured the usual pat-downs as they entered the hall, but security officials asked them to empty their pockets, too. Olde English 800 40s, dime bags of dope and all kinds of paraphernalia could be found on the sorting tables. People in line shouted to the security people to hurry up the process. They wanted in. Those discovered holding contraband now pleaded their cases.

A second checkpoint also was set up. Walk-through metal detectors, hand-held wands and nothing less than full-blown airport-style security were in use. Most people made it through with no problem; others were arrested on the spot.

The crowd became increasingly aware that Run-D.M.C.'s security team – headed by Andre Augustine and executed by his crew at Contemporary Services Corporation – wasn't kidding around. These guys meant business. Andre watched it all unfold, exactly according to plan.

Standing well over 6 feet tall and weighing in at around 300 pounds, Andre wore short black hair, a headset and a laminated pass. His solid arms and shoulders were forged from years of weight training and football, and the black jeans, a black T-shirt and black Adidas sneakers only added to his intimidating appearance.

Many people were thrilled that this plan was working. Run-D.M.C. had hit a critical juncture in its career. Only a few short months ago, the group's camp didn't even know if this tour would happen. And it had nothing to do with the popularity of Run-D.M.C. and rap. It had to do with security. Run-D.M.C. needn't worry; Andre Augustine had big plans. And the high-profile clients didn't faze him one bit.

In the Beginning...

Celebrity contact – even at an early age – wasn't uncommon for Andre. He grew up playing basketball with Tina Turner's kids. In fact, they spent their time shooting hoops over at the Charles' place. That's right. Ray Charles' place. But none of this seemed unusual to Andre. Didn't then, doesn't now.

When asked if he and his friends thought it was strange to be playing basketball at the famous entertainer's house, Andre responds quickly. "Why would we? The Charles' had the best court."

Andre Augustine was born in Los Angeles on January 25, 1958. He and his parents lived in Compton, California, until November 1964, when they moved to the Baldwin Hills area, near Los Angeles. Andre's father was a counselor for the California Youth Authority, where his mother also worked.

Andre enjoyed sports but excelled at football. He played for Pierce Junior College for two excellent seasons. The scouts from big-time schools with great football traditions showed interest; Nebraska, Arizona, Arizona State, Colorado and Kansas made inquiries. But in the end, Colorado State University became Andre's choice.

During Andre's senior year, Colorado State went 0-12, setting a college record for most losses during a season. That kind of notoriety hardly launches a pro career. Fortunately for Andre the pro scouts were paying more attention to his personal ability, rather than team performance.

New York & Out

Andre remembers the 1979 National Football League draft vividly. "All my teammates were sitting around drinking coffee, taking No Doz and watching the draft on TV," he says. "They were expecting the phone to ring at any moment."

Not Andre. He went to the library, turned in reports and ran errands. Andre came back to the apartment around 1 p.m. to check in. The draft was into the ninth round, and everyone was still glued to the TV. "Did anyone call?" Andre asked excitedly.

"No," came the lifeless response.

So Andre left to run more errands. When he returned, the draft had concluded. The stunned group sat around, staring at the walls. "What's up?" he asked.

"Al called," came the response from one dejected teammate, referring to agent, Al Vacanti, who represented several of the players in the room.

"Oh yeah? What did he say?" Andre asked, half-thinking someone else had gotten an offer.

"He said for you to call him back. Some teams want you."

A quick phone call to Vacanti confirmed the news. The Oakland Raiders, New York Jets and Miami Dolphins all were interested. Vacanti didn't have much more information. "I don't know what the deals are," he said. "I'll know in the morning."

After all the negotiating, Andre signed with the New York Jets. He packed his things and flew to the Jets' training camp on the East Coast, scared to death.

"I was just thankful to be going," he recalls. "I kept thinking, How many people ever get this chance? I felt very fortunate."

The fact that he continued to train and work out during the off-season while still at Colorado State also turned out to be a good thing. Training at high altitudes put him in top condition, and he was tearing it up, making the coaches take notice. There was just one problem. Or rather, four: Mark Gastineau, Joe Klecko, Abdul Salaam and Marty Lyons.

Andre played defensive end, shifting between the left and right sides. But in 1980, the defensive line of the New York Jets was among the best in the league. Unfortunately, no matter how well Andre played, there was no chance of him starting instead of these guys.

Unfortunately, Andre didn't see as much playing time in New York as he would have liked. During the four years he was on the Jets' roster, Andre estimates he played "one full game." Restless, he needed a change.

Disgusted with professional football's politics and little playing time, Andre left the game in 1985 and returned to California.

He hooked up with Pete Kranzke (ironically, during a Jets/Raiders game) a rough-and-tumble entrepreneur, who was also no stranger to a weight room. Kranzke owned Contemporary Services Corporation, a crowd-management firm in Los Angeles. Andre got to know him while working during the off-season as a "yellow jacket" guy at various Los Angeles sporting events. Kranzke liked Andre's work and asked him if he would return to work with CSC as a supervisor. Andre agreed.

And so began his music-industry journey. Andre's first job as a CSC supervisor was to work on CSC's new high profile clients: Run-D.M.C. Andre quickly found himself thrust into the volatile and developing world of rap.

Run-D.M.C. Rising

Music fans and insiders alike praised this emerging new musical genre called rap. And everyone appeared galvanized by Run-D.M.C. The Adidas-wearing trio – Run (Joseph Simmons), D.M.C. (Darryl McDaniel) and Jam Master Jay (Jason Mizell) – definitely led the charge.

Their electrifying Live Aid performance on July 13, 1985, at Philadelphia's now-defunct JFK Stadium exposed more than 162,000 concertgoers and a worldwide television audience estimated at 1.5 billion to their explosive brand of spare beats set to heavy-metal samples. In the name of African famine relief, and perhaps to promote this new form of music, Run-D.M.C. and all artists that day performed without pay.

Radio stations started spinning rap, the fledgling MTV started airing it, clubs started playing it and record stores started selling it.

Run-D.M.C. moved rap from a singles-oriented genre into an album-based one. Considered by many rap observers to have paved the way for even more volatile groups, such as Public Enemy and N.W.A., Run-D.M.C.'s album *Raising Hell* broke the Top 10 on the pop charts and went platinum. The group also became the first rap act to gain major airplay on MTV, appear on the Grammy Awards and headline *American Bandstand*.

In March 1986, Run-D.M.C. remade Aerosmith's "Walk This Way" on *Raising Hell* and invited the band's singer, Steven Tyler, and lead guitarist, Joe Perry, to film the song's video – thus endearing the rappers to rock fans and greatly increasing Run-D.M.C.'s exposure.

The recording sessions for "Walk This Way" took place on March 9, 1986, at Magic Ventures Studios in Manhattan. The video production took place two weeks later in Union City, New Jersey. The song peaked at No. 8 on the Black Singles charts and reached No. 4 on *Billboard's* Hot 100. MTV played the video twice an hour, giving an incredible boost to both groups.

One *Creem* magazine reviewer commented, "As the 'Walk This Way' video cleverly and humorously points out, both sides benefit when the walls come tumbling down. ... Run-D.M.C. are on the cutting edge of a sound and a scene that will affect generations of music still to come."

But in late summer 1986, just as Run-D.M.C. was starting to gain incredible popularity, the violence broke out. Followed by the bad press.

A front-page headline in the August 18, 1986, edition of the *Los Angeles Times* proclaimed "30 Injured at Long Beach Concert; L.A. Show Off." The accompanying story, written by George Ramos, detailed the events:

> Long Beach, CA - At least 30 people were injured and four others were arrested when sporadic fighting - apparently provoked by Latino and black street gangs - broke out during a "rap" music concert Sunday night at the Long Beach Arena, Long Beach police said today.
>
> Fearing a recurrence of the violence, officials at the Hollywood Palladium today canceled a concert scheduled for tonight that was to feature some of the same entertainers. "In view of the incidents last night, we just felt it was prudent to take precautions against any further problems," Palladium Manager Dick White said.
>
> The show Sunday night ended about 10:45 when 60 helmeted police officers swept through the arena and forced spectators outside after authorities stopped the show. Police Cmdr. Al Van Otterloo said fighting continued outside the arena.

"I'd never seen anything like it," said one concertgoer, Blaine Austin, 18, of Eagle Rock. "The gangs were just running all over the place causing havoc."

Some witnesses said innocent bystanders were struck with metal chairs, wooden sticks and, in one instance, a fire extinguisher during the brawling that continually marred the three-hour concert.

A spokeswoman for Run-D.M.C., the show's lead act, which is currently on a nationwide tour, said the group was "very upset because the police didn't protect fans" from the gangs. A statement issued by the group said Run-D.M.C. will "refuse to play Los Angeles until police and the authorities take sterner measures to protect Run-D.M.C. fans against local gangs. The gangs stand for everything rap is against. ... "

The big gang fight at the Long Beach show injured dozens of fans, damaged property and scared promoters – who were now hesitant to book Run-D.M.C. because of the violence associated with the group's shows.

But perhaps it wasn't Run-D.M.C's fault at all. It's important to note that this particular California arena already had a 16-year history of violence. In 1970, 46 people were arrested at a Jethro Tull show. In 1971, 21 were arrested after fighting with police during a Ten Years After concert. In 1972, 31 people were arrested on drug charges at a Led Zeppelin show. And in 1985, a young concertgoer was seriously injured when he fell from a balcony during a Deep Purple performance. But no one in the media bothered to comment on the history. Their message was clear: Run-D.M.C. spelled trouble.

2
TOGETHER FOREVER
Run-D.M.C. & Beastie Boys

As a result of the negative publicity, Run-D.M.C.'s
managers feared they would miss out on the momentum garnered with *Raising Hell*. Timing was critical. Another New York rap act, the Beastie Boys, was gaining in popularity. Their song "Fight For Your Right (To Party)" was receiving a lot of airplay on MTV and college radio stations.

In a brilliant move, management of both groups paired the two upstarts. The double bill of Run-D.M.C. and the Beastie Boys offered a chance at attaining the music industry's most beloved word: crossover. Crossover acts expose music to larger audiences, thus creating a larger market opportunity. The Together Forever Tour could be a promoter's dream.

In spring 1987, New York's Rush Productions issued the following press release announcing the event:

> Rush Productions
> 298 Elizabeth Street
> New York, N.Y. 10012
> For Immediate Release:
>
> Together Forever
>
> The two most prominent bands in street music will join for a tour that is almost certain to set new standards in controversy. Run-DMC, the first rap act ever to go triple platinum, will join The Beastie Boys in a summer-long, forty-city tour guaranteed to make parents of every nationality tremble.
>
> Run-DMC and the Beastie Boys' Together Forever Tour will kick off in Hawaii June 12. The Hawaiian date will include a special appearance by Aerosmith's Steven Tyler and Joe Perry, who performed on Run-DMC's top-five remake of the Aerosmith classic "Walk this Way."

The Together Forever Tour will be one of the few in music history to co-headline a black and white act of equal stature. Run-DMC have compiled a spectacular string of firsts: they were the first rap act to go platinum, the first to go multi-platinum, the first to reach the pop top five and the first to have more than one LP go platinum. The trio has won over 25 awards in the last two years. *Rolling Stone*'s readers voted them the top male R&B act of the year. The *New York Times* and the *Los Angeles Times* both named their "Walk This Way" the top single of 1986. And *Newsweek* and *People*, noting the storm of headlines that often pursues Run-DMC, called them one of the most riveting phenomena of the last year. Run-DMC are the subjects of a full-length biography due out in July, and the stars of a feature-length film entitled *Tougher than Leather*, due out in August.

The Beastie Boys - some of whose music is written by Run-DMC - have also been the center of a tempest of attention. They've had the fastest-selling debut album in the history of Columbia records. Their *Licensed To Ill* LP spent seven weeks at Number One on *Billboard*'s Top Pop Albums chart. Their spring '87 Licensed to Ill Tour was denounced for lewdness in an op-ed piece in the *Washington Post* and praised for its fun-filled rock and roll power in the *Los Angeles Times* and *Rolling Stone*. Heublein Inc. has reported that the Beasties' song "Brass Monkey" has doubled the national sales of the beverage. Following the conclusion of the Together Forever Tour, the Beasties will begin filming their first feature film, *Scared Stupid*.

Russell Simmons, Run-D.M.C.'s manager and Run's brother, saw a huge opportunity in pairing the two acts. Combining Run-D.M.C. and the Beastie Boys would mean almost certain financial success and at the same time help rap music evolve. The last barrier to success remained the threat of violence at the live shows. Enter Contemporary Services Corporation and Andre Augustine.

CSC was the brass ring of the crowd-management industry. If the groups' management wanted Run-D.M.C. and the Beastie Boys to tour together, they had to guarantee promoters there wouldn't be any security problems. CSC came as close to such a guarantee as anyone.

Andre and CSC owner Pete Kranzke worked diligently to come up with concert security measures that were unheard of at the time. Airport-type security tactics, local gang member research and pre-show preventive measures, which until now were never even considered in

the music industry. Their plan, considered state-of-the-art at the time, gave the groups'
managers and event promoters the peace of mind they needed. After reviewing CSC's
strategy, Rush Productions secured them for the tour and then issued another press release.

Rush Productions
298 Elizabeth Street
New York, N.Y. 10012
For Immediate Release:

Together Forever - Security

Security at the Run-DMC and Beastie Boys shows has always been
impressive, and effective. On last year's Raising Hell Tour, for
example, 64 out of 65 shows were trouble-free.

This year, the safety of fans will be ensured by a carefully-
conceived set of security measures. Crowd-control barriers will be
used to create a "snake" effect for incoming patrons. Security
personnel will use ten Phillips walk-through metal-detection units
augmented by a battery of hand-held metal detectors. Anyone who trips
off the units will be searched in privacy in a screened-off tent
area.

Security men and women will be unobtrusive and friendly. But
their ability to communicate will be enhanced by the use of two-way
radios. The stage and the fans near it will be protected by a double
barricade system. An 80' barricade will stand in front of the stage
backed by an additional 60' padded barricade to alleviate crowd
pressure.

The security staff will be headed by a team from Contemporary
Services Corporation, which has handled massive events like The
Jacksons' Victory Tour and the Super Bowl.

In the past, Run-DMC and Beastie Boys concerts have been as safe
as the average professional football game. When *Billboard*'s Nelson
George investigated widespread reports of crowd control problems at
Run-DMC performances, he discovered that the incidents cited usually
had nothing to do with the presence of Run-DMC. For example, in New
York, muggings, which occurred at Times Square - eight blocks away
from a Run-DMC show at Madison Square Garden - were cited in stories
about violence at the Run-DMC performance. But there was no evidence
that the muggers had been anywhere near the Run-DMC show.

In Pittsburgh, where street violence over a mile from a Run-DMC concert was reported in one local newspaper (whose account was repeated in stories across the country) as a Run-DMC problem, the rival paper checked with the police department and found that there had been LESS violence after the Run-DMC show than normally occurs at that hour on a weekend night.

"After the Long Beach incident, Run-D.M.C.'s management called us in," Andre recalls. "Our whole strategy was to stop the problems before they started. This was my first touring gig, and I wanted everything to go well. I had done my homework. We hired the best guys, worked with local law enforcement and used airport-type security procedures. I certainly wasn't going to let anything happen on my watch. At least nothing that could be prevented."

> *"... I certainly wasn't going to let anything happen on my watch. ..."*

As the crew supervisor for the tour, Andre knew to be effective he would have to learn as much as possible and communicate throughout his team. One part of Andre's strategy included getting to know the intimate details of gang life. He spent time with the Los Angeles Police Department's CRASH unit – the L.A.P.D.'s name for gang detail at the time.

CRASH officers go into gang territory and find out who's who. They befriend local gang members and engage them in friendly conversation, discussing problems and offering such solutions as going back to school or getting involved in sports activities. In return, officers become familiar with the gang-bangers and their habits.

"We went on a ride-along with an officer and ex-CSC supervisor by the name of Ron Cade as he made his rounds," Andre remembers. "In plain clothes, he patrolled Crips territory in an unmarked car. He made three or four contacts with different factions of Crips in South Central L.A. Gang members knew who he was and seemed to like talking to him."

On a typical ride-along, CRASH officers approached gang members hanging out on street corners, at liquor stores or even just walking down the street. Their objective? To create a dialog and get a sense of what's happening on the street. That particular night, for example, Cade investigated a shooting that occurred a few days earlier.

The time Andre spent with the CRASH unit helped make him more aware of the street element and mentality of the audiences most likely to attend Run-D.M.C. and other rap concerts. He also established relationships with other officers, so that wherever the Together Forever Tour went, he could hire off-duty officers to help identify local gang members.

Andre even went back to school, attending L.A.P.D.-sponsored classes. "The L.A.P.D. really helped me understand how to recognize gang members, their leaders and how to develop a strategy for managing their attendance, ensuring a successful event," he says.

Andre found the basics of gang identification most helpful. Blue is worn by Crips, while Bloods wear red, he says. These colors can be found on many articles of clothing but the most telltale items are hats, handkerchiefs and bandannas. Hats turned a particular way or bandannas hanging out of a particular pocket carry hidden – even deadly – meanings. Another key to success is identifying how gang members move through the crowd.

"When you get a big crowd in front of the stage, it's important to look around on the floor and see what kind of activity is going on," Andre explains. "If you see 10 or 12 guys hanging around together, all wearing the same color, that's a dead giveaway that trouble's coming."

Other times, the actions would be more subtle. "There might be individuals or pairs who would be moving around the crowd," Andre continues. "These might be people communicating messages or conducting 'business.' Typically, when people go to a show, they may hang out in the lobby for awhile, then get something to eat and drink and then go to their seats to watch the show. When you've got someone who is moving to all different areas of the arena, they are either the biggest social butterfly you've ever seen or they are up to something."

The preferred security method was making contact with gang members before they even entered the building. Working with local gang-patrol officers, Andre and his crew identified and approached gang members.

"The local officer would walk up and call the leader by name and usually start with a simple, 'Hey, what's going on?'" Andre says. "We would then continue the conversation, trying to determine what the mood of the day was, whether the gang-bangers were in party mode or retaliation mode. Sometimes we would get a hard time from the members. But our bottom line was, 'Want trouble? We'll give it to you. Hey, we're here to have a good time and you guys aren't going to come in and ruin it. We refuse to let you spoil the event for

15,000 people.' Some people say the problem with rap music is that the problems outside the arena get carried into the arena."

That night in San Diego proved that Andre's plan worked. Now, four dates into the tour, the problems remained outside. Kids emptied their pockets into dumpsters. Girls yelled at their dates to leave the dope at home. Gang members took off their colors. If there was one thing these kids wanted, it was to see Run-D.M.C. and the Beastie Boys!

No colors or gang insignias were allowed inside. If the gang-bangers gave the cops any attitude, Andre and his crew simply took them out, sometimes literally. They deferred to the disclaimer on the back of all tickets that read, "We retain the right to refuse any patron, for any reason." It was that simple.

Today, such disclaimers are common. A 1996 study by *Performance* magazine, a touring-industry trade publication, revealed that one of the biggest concerns of crowd-management companies is liability. Security-staff training, as well as increased support from and better planning by promoters and facility employees, have lessened the burden in recent years. But problems still exist, especially with acts who encourage moshing and violence. As one employee of Staffpro, a respected crowd-management firm, told *Performance* in 1996: "Things like radio spots and announcements printed on the tickets of what is expected are used and needed. Things seem to be getting worse. It's not safe all the time, and we can't guarantee anyone's safety."

That night in San Diego, the Beastie Boys opened the show. They revved the crowd to a fevered pitch and then turned it over to the boys from Queens.

As Run-D.M.C. took the stage, they opened with their trademark medley. The crowd of 13,000 went crazy as the trio played to the kids like old pros – even though the group itself was less than five years old.

Andre and his crew stayed alert. Although they had done all they could to prevent disturbances, they wanted to keep a serious eye on crowd dynamics to quell any problems during the show. After almost three hours, the gig ended without a hitch.

The crowd was gone. The floor was littered with empty cups and cigarette butts, but no blood. No one got hurt and nothing was damaged. A new attitude emerged in terms of crowd management, at least on this tour: No BS. Period.

And Andre, proud as could be, was at the helm. "I like rap," he admits. "That was my music. Sure, we listened to Aerosmith and Kiss, but for a black guy born and raised in Los Angeles, rap was where we found ourselves. And Run-D.M.C. was huge."

"Run-D.M.C. are the bonafide superstars of rap, the ultra-urban mix of industrial-strength beat and rhyming slang," declared *USA Today.* *People* magazine said, "Pop pundits who dismissed rap as a penny-ante phenomenon look less than prophetic [in the wake of Run-D.M.C.'s successes]." The *New York Post* reported that the concert its staffer attended was " ... welcomed by a louder, more intense reception than any rock or heavy-metal show in recent memory."

But perhaps *Rolling Stone* said it best: "Run-D.M.C. has more than mainstream credibility. It is one of the hottest groups in America."

And it was the masterful combination of Run-D.M.C. with the Beastie Boys that critics say really gave rap a leg up. The tour was unforgettable.

In the music industry, security people for a long time were not really noticed and were considered more of a necessary evil rather than a business asset. Andre began to change that. Anxious to prove himself, he worked incredibly hard. Everyone started to talk about the "new guy" over at CSC. Andre's affable personality and professional behavior made him one of the best in the business.

Andre remembers that he and his four-man crew were distanced from the groups, especially Run-D.M.C. "Because of the job we were performing, we really didn't have that much personal contact with the band. My crew and I were at the venue all day and we didn't know anything other than when the artists were in the building or when they left the building."

But then things changed. "They really began to understand we were there because of the danger associated with rap concerts," Andre continues. "They knew we were filling a necessary role, and because of that, they were able to do shows."

3
THE KINGS FROM QUEENS
Run-D.M.C.

AFTER ONLY A FEW SHOWS, D.M.C., RUN AND JAM MASTER JAY
began talking to Andre and the guys on his crew. After all, if you see someone around
enough, you start to get friendly with each other. And the guys in Run-D.M.C. knew that this
tour was happening thanks largely to the excellent CSC security and the work of Andre's team.

Andre remembers his initial impressions of rap's originators: "These guys were more
down to earth than a big, established rock 'n' roll act might be, or even an older R&B band.
You could say hi to them and not worry about breaking some protocol. They were street kids
– homeboys from the neighborhood. They were more approachable."

Born and raised in Hollis, Queens, New York, the trio has been friends since childhood
and grew up within blocks of each other. They also were classmates attending St. Pascal's
Catholic School. Run and D.M.C. knew each other first. Run met Jam Master Jay when they
played basketball together at St. Pascal's in the fourth grade. They later attended Andrew
Jackson High School together.

Run got started in music at an early age. His now famous brother, Russell Simmons,
managed music acts back in 1977, including Kurtis Blow. Through this connection, 12-year-
old Run began deejaying for Kurtis and soon began grabbing the mic. Even early on, Run
made great rhymes like: "DJ Run, son of a gun/Always plays music and has big fun/Not that
old, but that's all right/Makes all other emcees bite all night."

Run made tapes of these performances, and he and D.M.C. would take turns rapping
and deejaying with them. Thirteen-year-old Jay meanwhile, was doing his own thing, playing
bass and guitar in local bands. He quickly switched to turntables and began to deejay in the
neighborhood crew, Two Fifths Down.

After graduating from high school in 1982, Russell agreed to produce a record for Run, D.M.C. and Jay. In March 1983, "It's Like That/Sucker M.C.s" was released on Profile Records. An immediate hit, it was followed by the release of the group's first album, *Run-D.M.C.*, in May 1984. "Rock Box/30 Days" and "Hollis Crew" followed, and in 1985 they released the *King of Rock* album, the second of the Simmons co-productions to go gold.

Halfway through 1986, *Billboard* magazine ran a full-page ad placed by Profile Records announcing that Run-D.M.C.'s third album, *Raising Hell*, had sold two million copies. The caption for the accompanying photo of the group read, "The Year of Run-D.M.C. continues."

"When I first met Run, I couldn't believe it," Andre comments. "His personality is like his name – he just talks all the time. He never stops talking. And he talks about anything. Whatever he sees – streetlights, taxicabs, mailboxes – he's got something to say about everything. That's one of the things that makes him great on the mic."

Andre suddenly becomes more serious. "I'll tell you one thing about Run. He's real. They all are. All three of the guys in Run-D.M.C. are real people – not like the West Coast guys now who are trying to be gangsters. The guys in Run-D.M.C. were groomed by Russell to be larger than life."

And they were. Run-D.M.C. impacted many people at the time – not just Andre.

The group not only set musical trends, but fashion trends, as well. Offstage, they wore exactly the same clothes they wore onstage: monochromatic fashions consisting primarily of black or blue shirts with black or blue Levi's. And, of course, don't forget the trademark Kangol hats and gold chains.

"They might have owned ten or fifteen pairs of jeans, all in one color," says Andre. "It was what they wore every day. And they didn't do laundry. I think their clothes were always new. They would just pull clean clothes out of their bag, and it would be black Levi's or blue Levi's."

Perhaps that's why they insisted on having new socks and underwear, every day. Not just clean, but new – in the package, every day.

"When we started traveling with them, it was my responsibility to get everybody going in the morning," Andre says. "I can remember knocking on D.M.C.'s door, going in and seeing socks and underwear in the trash can. I didn't think too much about it. I did my thing and then went to get Run up. I went to Run's room, knocked on the door, went in, I gave him the quick rundown of when we would be leaving and whatnot, and there were socks and underwear in *his* trash can. At this point, I started to wonder what's going on. So I went to Jam Master Jay's room. Same thing. I ran into a crew guy named Garfield. He was the guy who carried the turntables, mixers and records for the group. Garfield was considered the 'keeper of the craft.'" He explained it very simply. "The guys like new underwear and socks every day."

"They were always revved up to hit the stage," Andre says. "Part of that was their affinity for Olde English 800."

Run-D.M.C. brought with them a supply of underwear and socks for the tour. If inventory started to run low, Garfield or Runny Ray, another Run-D.M.C. crew member, would get them more.

Clean socks were probably a necessity because of the apparel deal that Run-D.M.C. cultivated with athletic shoe manufacturer, Adidas.

Run-D.M.C. legend has it that the Adidas connection can be traced back to a June 21, 1986, concert at Philadelphia's Spectrum Arena during the Raising Hell Tour. As the crowd of 20,000 watched the trio explode into their hit single, "My Adidas," the fans thrust an estimated 5,000 pairs of Adidas sneakers into the air.

Not wanting to miss the moment, Russell Simmons videotaped the event and sent a copy to the German footwear manufacturer. Impressed, the company made an endorsement deal with the group and manufactured four Run-D.M.C. styles: the Eldorado, the Brougham, the Fleetwood (after the group's favorite models of Cadillacs) and the Ultra Star.

In 1985, Run-D.M.C. got so big so fast that the group toured for almost four years before taking any kind of a break.

"They were always revved up to hit the stage," Andre says. "Part of that was their affinity for Olde English 800. They didn't get drunk before a show, but they definitely had one or two for medicinal purposes, to take the edge off of the pre-show anxiety. They were very brand-loyal. I remember when we went to Europe, we took about 50 cases of Olde English 800 with us. They had to have one or two 'eight balls' (bottles of Olde English 800) before hitting the stage. It was like the magic formula, and they weren't about to experiment with other brands."

And it worked. Run-D.M.C. never let their fans down.

Andre and his crew never let the band down, either. Both Run-D.M.C. and the Beastie Boys liked them, and not one incident of violence broke out during the seven-month Together Forever Tour.

Word got out. Promoters, venues and artists all looked to Contemporary Services Corporation and Andre Augustine to help make their tours safe and successful.

But Andre wasn't like other security directors; he had a human side. Take Memorial Day 1988, for example, when he invited the Run-D.M.C. gang over to his house for a cookout. Not just the guys in the band, but the group's entire entourage, which consisted of about 40 people. Being on the road for so long and under such pressure changed the dynamic between the artists, employees and co-workers to a family relationship.

"It was a great afternoon," Andre remembers. "Jam Master Jay took over the duties of grilling burgers, while the others ate, swam and played dominos and cards. Everyone felt right at home."

Perhaps that's because Run-D.M.C. recognized the importance of family. Later that month, when Andre and his wife, Heather, were expecting their first child, Run-D.M.C. played Las Vegas. Heather came to see the show, and Run, D.M.C. and Jam Master Jay all took turns rapping to the unborn child backstage.

Two months later, the group was playing in the Midwest when Andre got the call that Heather was in labor. Run-D.M.C. wasn't going to let anything get in the way of Andre being there for the birth of his first son. But there was one problem. The nearest airport was a small facility with very limited flights, and nothing was leaving for the next twelve hours. So Run-D.M.C. found a solution.

The group transported Andre to the next town, where he could catch a commuter "crop duster" back to L.A. On July 19, 1988, Andre's first son was born.

Thanks to Run-D.M.C.'s efforts, Andre made it to the hospital to share the experience. The doting "uncles" wasted no time sharing their love, affection and advice with the new parents. And even though they were far from the commercial success that would arrive later, they were quite generous in contributing to the infant's college fund.

Andre rejoined the tour a week later. One afternoon, Andre showed pictures of his new son to several of the crew members and Jam Master Jay.

"What's his name?" Jam Master Jay asked.

"His middle name is Jason," Andre replied.

"Say what?"

"His middle name, its Jason. I named him after you."

The rapper stood there stunned. A moment passed and then the man whose birth name is Jason Mizell broke into a smile so wide all you could see were teeth. He stood up and threw his arms around Andre.

"I think he was shocked at first," Andre remembers now. "It was pretty cool. You have to remember, the rap guys don't usually show emotion because they consider it a sign of weakness. It was a special moment."

There were many reasons why Run-D.M.C. sold so many records and filled so many concert halls in the Eighties. Their strong social conscience resulted in such songs as "It's Like That," "Hard Times," "You're Blind," and "Proud to be Black," which were positive influences for many young listeners. Run-D.M.C.'s participation alongside Bruce Springsteen and other superstars in the anti-apartheid "Sun City" record and video also contributed to making the band a social force. Its members were very active in civil rights, anti-violence and anti-drug movements. Humor, great beats and a willingness to take a stand made Run-D.M.C. approachable and popular.

Run-D.M.C.'s influence can still be seen today. From the podium at the 1997 MTV Video Awards, L.L. Cool J. thanked "the true pioneers of rap: Run, D.M.C. and Jam Master Jay, for making it all happen."

Andre remains close to the guys in Run-D.M.C. and occasionally gets a chance to hang out with them, especially Jam Master Jay. Both Run and D.M.C. are born-again Christians, a conversion they proclaimed on their 1993 album *Down With the King*, and they still tour, much to the pleasure of old and new fans alike.

The other side of the Together Forever bill also is still together and making records. The Beastie Boys found themselves on the covers of *Rolling Stone* and *Spin* in summer 1998, marking the release of the group's long-awaited and widely acclaimed *Hello Nasty*. That record, which harkened back to the days of *Licensed to Ill* and *Paul's Boutique*, put the Beasties back on the charts and introduced them to a whole new generation of listeners.

In fact, *Rolling Stone* readers – which skew younger these days – named the boys Artists of the Year for 1998, the same year the Beasties sponsored their third successful Tibetan Freedom Concert.

But a decade earlier, rock and rap fans didn't know quite what to think of the Beastie Boys.

4
WHIPPED INTO A FRENZY

The Beastie Boys

"The first time I met 'em, I thought I was on Candid Camera."

- D.M.C. (Darryl McDaniels), on the Beastie Boys

BEING THE NEW GUYS ON A TOURING BILL HAS ITS PROS AND CONS. And the Beastie Boys found that out all too well while on the road with Run-D.M.C. in 1987.

All natives of New York, Ad-Rock (Adam Horovitz), MCA (Adam Yauch) and Mike D (Michael Diamond) began playing together in 1981 and cut their first record (released on the Rat Cage label) later that year.

"Beastie" reportedly is an acronym for "Boys Entering Anarchistic States Toward Internal Excellence."

In 1983, inspired by Carvel Ice Cream's creation, the Beasties recorded "Cookie Puss," which showcased a young hoodlum hassling a real-life Carvel Ice Cream employee while trying to make contact with "Cookie Puss." The B-side featured a track called "Beastie Revolution," which is prophetic when you realize that in 1985, the boys opened for Madonna and were booed nightly. "It was a terrible idea!" Ad-Rock told *Spin* in September 1998. "But it was great for [Madonna] because we were so awful that by the time she came onstage, the audience had to be happy." Madonna, quoted in the same article, has a different opinion. "I couldn't understand why everyone hated them – I thought they were adorable," she said.

After an opening-act stint on the 1986 Raising Hell Tour with Run-D.M.C., the three Beastie Boys found themselves invited back to do the race-barrier-breaking Together Forever Tour. All in their late-teens or early-20s, the Beasties were enjoying great success with their debut album, *Licensed to Ill*, and they found themselves living the lifestyle of famous musicians. But that didn't mean things always went as planned.

Backstage at Oakland's Shoreline Arena one night, the Beasties invited some female concertgoers to spend a little time with them. Eventually, the girls snuck away from the Beastie Boys' backstage area.

Discovering their "guests" had slipped away, the boys – all in various stages of undress – dashed out of their dressing room chasing the women. But the cagey fans proved too quick, running out of the backstage area and disappearing into the crowd, taking with them a little bit of the Beasties' pride and several pairs of Run-D.M.C.'s coveted Adidas tennis shoes.

At another show, this one at the Starplex Amphitheater in Nashville, Tennessee, the Beastie Boys were enjoying the lull between their opening set and Run-D.M.C.'s performance by cooling down a bunch of groupies.

Andre prowled the backstage area, checking on last-minute details before Run-D.M.C.'s show. Nothing seemed out of the ordinary, just the usual backstage scene. A few girls, a few suits and lots of tired-looking crew. Andre turned the corner and headed for the Beasties' dressing room. They had their own security guy, but he was new and not very experienced. For that reason, Andre liked to check in on the boys every now and again to make sure that things were cool. Inexperience and big-time touring never go well together.

As Andre approached the Beastie Boys' dressing room that night, he heard it. "There were literally dozens of voices, most of them female, yelling, shrieking and making a huge commotion," he remembers.

Andre quickened his step, not knowing what he was about to discover. Who was involved? Was someone hurt? Could there be a fight? Was Run-D.M.C.'s crew inside?

With a twist of the knob and a push of the door, Andre entered the room in one fluid motion, and for a second, all the noise stopped. Everyone turned and looked at him.

"There I am, worried about whether I'm suddenly going to be thrown into some sort of battle protecting the band's honor, and I walk in on this scene," Andre laughs.

Fighting couldn't have been further from the activities going on. The large square dressing room housed about 30 teenage girls – some topless, some skirtless – with their backs to the dressing-room walls. Girls lined three of the four sides of the room and all were in the process of being hosed down by the Beastie Boys with Olde English, shaving cream, whipping cream and whatever else the young rappers could find.

"When I burst into the room, the Beasties stopped for a second, and you could have heard a pin drop. The guys looked at me, smiled and then it was like someone turned the volume control back up. They continued with their antics," Andre remembers. "I just shook my head, laughed and went on my way. What else could I do?"

With *Licensed to III* selling so well, plus the pressures of a major tour, who could blame the boys for blowing off a little steam? Other than the occasional off-stage antics, the Beastie Boys often seemed humbled by their success, Andre says.

Girls lined three of the four sides of the room and all were in the process of being hosed down by the Beastie Boys ...

"They really were amazed," he recalls. "Walking onstage and getting the reactions they were getting at that age had to have been mind-blowing. They always were a little unsure of themselves during the opening moments of the show, but then fueled by the energy of the crowd, they looked like old pros in no time."

Andre and his team were becoming old pros, too.

5
ALMOST BROTHERS

Ron Scoggins

ANDRE HAS WORKED WITH DOZENS OF PEOPLE THROUGHOUT HIS career. Many became friends; Ron Scoggins he considers family. Scoggins, also a CSC employee in 1987, worked with Andre on those early rap tours. Together, Andre and Scoggins learned many things about the business and life.

The two got to know each other when they both worked at CSC on the 1987 Run-D.M.C./Beastie Boys Together Forever Tour and later on the Def Jam and Dope Jam gigs, as well as on Run-D.M.C.'s European House Tour.

"Man, we loved working with Run-D.M.C.," remembers Scoggins, who is still in the security business. "It was a real exciting time. And once we got over the shock of what was going on with these guys, in terms of their popularity, we settled down and really did some great work.

"And that's how we both got started," Scoggins continues. "Andre and me, we went dang near everywhere together."

And 'dang' just about sums up Scoggins' character. Andre refers to him as "the original black cowboy." A big guy with a deep voice, who often wears a cowboy hat and boots, Scoggins has been a Nevada resident for over a decade.

That cowboy persona came in handy one 1987 night in Philadelphia when he and Andre encountered some hopeful entrepreneurs selling bootleg Run-D.M.C. T-shirts in the parking lot of a concert hall.

Andre and Ron kept the two bootleggers – discovered by Run-D.M.C. manager, Russell Simmons – in sight as they crept closer, moving between parked cars and small groups of people partying. Andre got there first.

"What up, fellas?" Andre popped up from behind a parked van.

Shocked at his size and appearance, the pair took a minute to assess the situation. To hide his identity, Andre had tucked his laminated passes and radio inside his shirt. The bootleggers couldn't tell he was there to bust the business.

"Yo, we ain't got no shirts *that* big, brother," said one of the young bootleggers, dressed as a Run-D.M.C. wannabe in black jeans, black T-shirt, unlaced Adidas sneakers and a gold chain.

"Really?" Andre said, enjoying his final moments of anonymity. "I guess I'll just have to take them all."

"What, mothafucka?" shouted the other bootlegger, moving to pull something out of the waistband of his jeans. Just then Scoggins appeared. The two "businessmen" looked at the two Run-D.M.C. security guys and broke into a dead run. Andre caught the one with the bag of shirts, while Scoggins nabbed the other.

"Let's just say we got the product," Scoggins laughs. "And Andre was particularly persuasive that night."

So persuasive that the local authorities came looking for Andre later in the evening. On a trumped-up charge, the two criminals had turned the tables and claimed that Andre assaulted them. He unsuccessfully pled his case, and Andre was a guest in the Philadelphia city jail for a few hours until the situation was rectified by Run-D.M.C.'s management. After a quick explanation and payment of a small fine, Andre was back with the guys. Andre doesn't like to remember the event and doesn't think it's funny.

"I don't want to talk about it," he says.

"All I know," Scoggins laughs, "is that those guys should be glad Andre didn't find them when he was released."

"I still don't want to talk about it," Andre says firmly, not sharing Scoggins' amusement.

6

DEF & DOPE

Will Smith

HE WAS SURROUNDED. RUN, JAM MASTER JAY, D.M.C., GARFIELD
and Runny Ray – all older, bigger and definitely more combative – took turns making
intimidating remarks and talking trash.

"What'cha think you're doing here, punk?"

"I think we oughta kick your ass."

"Yeah, maybe you should just run home to your momma."

"Oh!" said the wide-eyed 17-year-old, making sweeping movements with his arms,
causing the group to take a half-step back. "So you're gonna talk about my momma, now?"
The air was filled with tension. He was cornered and there was nowhere to go. But up.

The boy continued. "Well, if you're gonna bring my momma into this, we should talk a
little about your momma. Your momma is so low ... your momma is so low, she's got to play
handball against the curb."

The five who surrounded him stopped, looked at each other and then burst into
laughter. This kid from Philadelphia had done it again. In the face of peer intimidation, Will
Smith – the artist formally known as Fresh Prince – came out a winner.

After the Together Forever Tour, Andre's next assignment found him running security
crews on the U.S. Run's House and Dope Jam tours. Crews on this tour consisted of four or
five guys from CSC who would travel with both tours and be responsible for building
security. Andre switched back and forth between the tours every few days.

Both the Def Jam and Dope Jam tours resembled the old rock 'n' roll shows of the early 1950's, in that there was a host of talent playing on the bill. Run-D.M.C., the Beastie Boys, L.L. Cool J., and DJ Jazzy Jeff and the Fresh Prince were just some of the performers.

Artists on the Dope Jam tour participated in the daily game of "dozens," the verbal art of put-downs and a common practice with many of today's urban youth.

K. Maurice Jones, in his 1994 book *The Story of Rap Music*, describes dozens: "A ritual of urban African-American boys, the dozens was a good-natured vocal competition in which a boy made disparaging remarks about an opponent's mother. The dozens was always played with an audience, which encouraged the two opponents to outdo or 'cap' each other."

"Will Smith was young and so squeaky clean," Andre says. "I can remember standing around backstage between sets, and the other guys would gather around him and talk shit to him. They would play dozens, and he would just stand there and give it right back to them."

Dozens wasn't the only skill Will possessed. He also did pretty well for himself on the stage and in record stores. He and his deejay, Jazzy Jeff, sold records at an amazing pace under the moniker of DJ Jazzy Jeff and the Fresh Prince and turned a lot of people onto their brand of life-affirming rap music. He was also one of the few rappers who wasn't from New York.

"The rest of the guys on the tour were in their early-20s," Andre says. "With the exception of L.L. Cool J., Will was the youngest guy. But L.L.'s from New York, so that gave him a kind of immunity. Will is from Philadelphia. In addition to him being younger, there was this New York vs. Philadelphia dynamic between them. Plus, when you add the type of music he was doing into the mix, he *really* used to get hassled."

Will's music may have been more innocent than other rappers' songs, even soft. But it had mass appeal. Young children liked it, he had a large female following and both black kids and white kids danced to it. Some of the Fresh Prince's early hits included "Girls Ain't Nothing But Trouble" and "Parents Just Don't Understand."

Will's universal musical appeal continues today. His 1997 album, *Big Willie Style*, is a record the rapper has said he's proud to play for his young son, Trey. In fact, it experienced a chart resurgence in summer 1998 – months after its initial release – thanks to "Just the Two of Us," a tribute to Trey.

Fewer things make promoters smile more than an artist with huge mass appeal. The Fresh Prince may have been one of the first rappers to really cross over in a significant way.

Will's positive demeanor wasn't just a facade, Andre claims. That really was his personality. "For one thing, Will could tell a joke," Andre says. "For another, it was corny and completely different from what everybody else was saying. He had a different style, a different way of saying things. His delivery made a stupid joke hilarious. You'd listen to him and think, *This kid is funny, he's clean-cut, and he's got this enormously appealing look about him. He's good-looking, he's tall, about 6 feet, 2 inches, and he has an aura about him.*

"I just knew he was going places. And that's why his name was the Fresh Prince. That's why he was able to cross over. In fact, a lot of performers on those Def Jam and Dope Jam tours eventually crossed over. Run-D.M.C., L.L. Cool J. and Public Enemy all crossed over, but those were more like underground crossings. The Fresh Prince did it in front of a national television audience."

The Fresh Prince of Bel-Air starred Will and premiered on NBC on September 10, 1990. The series was about a streetwise young man from Philadelphia named Will, who gets sent by his mother to live with his aunt and her family in upscale Bel-Air, California. The character had to adjust to a completely new lifestyle and relatives with entirely different backgrounds. The show aired for six seasons and is currently syndicated in many markets.

The cast included another person Andre knows well, Alfonso Ribeiro, who played Carlton Banks, Will's nerdy and straight-laced cousin.

Years earlier, when Andre worked for CSC, two employees were contracted to work with Ricky Schroeder on the set of the television show *Silver Spoons*. Once in awhile, Andre would fill in for them. At the time, Schroeder experienced death threats and stalkers, so security on the set was tighter than usual. Ribeiro had played Schroeder's friend on that show.

Schroeder and Ribeiro were at that age when they thought it was cool to talk back to adults. Some observers might even have called the duo spoiled. On the set, as is the norm in Hollywood, crew members tried to cater to the boys' every whim and would tip-toe around them. But Andre and the others from CSC let the two budding actors know right away who was in charge.

"I think they respected us for that," Andre says. "They loved us, in fact, for that reason. We wouldn't let them get away with stuff. And so throughout the years, I have seen Alfonso grow from this little kid on *Silver Spoons* into an industry veteran."

The Def and Dope Jam gigs proved challenging for Will, Andre says. Perhaps that's one of the experiences that helped develop his strong character.

"Will was taking punishment every day because of his squeaky-clean image," Andre says. "These audiences wanted to hear Run-D.M.C., L.L. Cool J. and the Beastie Boys. Then here comes Will, who was wet behind the ears. It had to have been tough for him."

But Will Smith succeeded while most of his Def and Dope Jam colleagues disbanded or – until recently – hit bottom. Andre still gets a chance to see him occasionally.

"These audiences wanted to hear Run-D.M.C., L.L. Cool J. and the Beastie Boys. Then here comes Will, who was wet behind the ears. It had to have been tough for him."

One time, a mutual friend invited Andre and his wife, Heather, to a party to celebrate the 100th episode of *The Fresh Prince of Bel-Air* at the House of Blues in West Hollywood.

The couple could hear the celebration the moment they walked into the club. The animated conversation, laughter and dance music floated throughout the room. People gathered around the main attractions, Will and Alfonso, who were dancing as Andre and Heather made their way to the edge of the crowd.

The moment Alfonso spotted Andre at the club, he sprinted towards him, leapt in the air and landed straddling Andre, hanging from the big man's neck.

"Dre, Dre, what's up, man?" he asked excitedly, using Andre's nickname.

"The next thing I know, Will was standing next to us and chanting, 'Dre! Dre! Dre!'" Andre recalls. "And then the whole crowd started chanting. 'Dre! Dre! Dre!' It was a weird scene. All of a sudden, I was the center of attention. And I'm not sure I wanted to be."

Even today, Will Smith, remains one of Andre's personal favorites.

Years later, Andre, returning from a New York business trip, stopped at an airport newsstand for something to read on the long flight back to Los Angeles. He found a copy of that week's *People* with Will and his new wife, Jada Pinkett-Smith, on the cover.

He had met Jada just briefly and thought she was a spectacular woman. Andre smiled as he paid for the magazine. It would be interesting to see what the media was saying about the couple.

As Andre boarded the plane, he was shocked to see, laughing and snuggling in the first-class section, Will and Jada!

Will immediately recognized Andre.

"Dre, man! How are you doing?"

"Great, Will. How are you?"

"You know Jada, don't you?"

The three of them talked and laughed for several minutes. The flight attendant mentioned to the group that the plane would depart soon. Then Andre remembered his issue of *People*.

"Well, I'm gonna find my seat *in the back*." Andre joked as he started towards the coach section.

Then he stopped and turned. "Oh, yeah, I thought you two might want something to read."

With that, Andre dropped the magazine – cover up – on Will's lap. He and Jada looked at each other, smiling, before Will broke out into one of his trademark guffaws. Andre grinned and left to find his seat.

"It's nice that he remembers me and takes the time to be interested in what's going on in my life," Andre says. "He is one of the few all-around good guys to reach superstardom and keep his feet on the ground. If more people were like Will Smith, the world would be a better place."

But back in the concert halls of the 1987 Def and Dope Jams, Andre's attitude wasn't quite so charming.

7
CROWD COMPLICATIONS
Dope Jam

As Andre looked out over the sea of humanity, which tonight was an audience for a St. Louis stop on 1988's Dope Jam Tour, he knew there was going to be trouble. Andre has a sixth sense for such things. Ron Scoggins, also working the show, felt it, too.

"Did you know it was GA tonight?" Scoggins asked.

"No. I don't think the promoter wanted us to know."

"GA," or general admission, shows mean there are no assigned seats. The purchase of a ticket gains fans entrance to the arena. Then their strength and determination gets them close to the performance.

Defended by promoters as part of the concert-going social experience, GA really is a way of maximizing ticket sales. Without reserved seating, promoters can oversell an arena and watch kids jam themselves as close as possible to the stage.

It was a GA show that night in St. Louis, and Dope Jam had come to town with no assigned seats for the thousands of kids pinned across the front of the stage. The air smelled like cigarettes, dope and sweat.

Suddenly, Andre saw a kid disappear into the crowd. Typically when this happens, a hole is created and a concertgoer will disappear. Moments later, the hole reappears, as the crowd around the downed person helps him or her back up. This time, though, the kid went down and the hole never reappeared, which meant trouble.

"I didn't know whether this kid passed out, got stabbed or bent over to tie his shoes," Andre says. "All I knew was that if I didn't see him in two more seconds, I was going in after him."

Two seconds were up. Andre shot out from behind the barricade and took off into the crowd. Relying on his football skills, he cut a path in a hurry. He mentally marked the kid with several people who were wearing Adidas jackets. When he got there, he couldn't find the downed fan.

Trying to find a spot in a crowd is like trying to mark a fish in an ocean. Crowds ebb and flow and constantly move. The other problem is a person's perspective. It's one thing to look at a crowd from a higher elevation and quite another to be at floor level, seeing just a mass of faces. By the time Andre got to the spot he marked in his mind, the crowd had shifted slightly.

"Where is he?" Andre shouted over the thumping bass.

"Who?" a stunned fan shouted back.

"The kid that went down."

"He's over here," yelled a young girl, in her early 20s.

Tight and loose spots are also common crowd traits. Fans will be pushed together more tightly in some areas than others. The girl who identified the location of the downed kid called out from one of the floors tighter areas.

Andre made his way to her, and with the help of several surrounding people picked up the young man who went down. He apparently fainted and was just starting to come around when Andre quickly scooped him up, flung him over his shoulder and made his way back through the crowd. He took the fan to the arena's first-aid station, passing the show's promoter on the way.

Greedy bastard, he thought. Andre hated GA seating.

The scrutiny around general admission seating first gained national attention when 11 people were trampled and killed and another 22 injured at a 1979 general admission concert by The Who at Cincinnati's Riverfront Stadium.

The practice virtually became extinct after three deaths at a January 18, 1991, AC/DC show at the Salt Palace in Salt Lake City.

In that case, the January 22, 1991, edition of the *Los Angeles Times* reported:

> The heavy metal rock band AC/DC continued playing as three fans were being crushed to death, despite chants of "stop the concert," witnesses in Salt Lake City said. Two 14-year-old boys and a 19-year-old woman died and another woman was hurt after

thousands of fans rushed the stage Friday at Salt Palace arena. Witnesses said at least one security guard tried to get the lead singer's attention and stop the band. Police turned the investigation over to Salt Lake County after determining no crimes had been committed.

That security person may have been Andre's friend Bob Wein. "Bob was really impacted by the AC/DC incident," Andre says. "We knew each other from being out on the road. When you do what we do, it's like a small fraternity. We all know each other. Bob is a great guy who cares about his job and his fans. He's nicknamed 'Pit Bull,' because he's small, strong and very outgoing. But the last time I saw him, he didn't seem the same. He was quieter and not quite as rambunctious. I asked others what was up, and they said he still wasn't over the AC/DC thing. The role of a security director comes with a lot of stress and mental anguish. The lives of people on both sides of the barricades can change in an instant."

Today, GA seating is rare at stadiums and theaters. The North American Concert Association estimated in 1991 that the policy was implemented in 15 percent of the 6,000 rock shows presented around the country each year. GA seating is still alive and well, though, in such 2,000- to 4,000-capacity places as the Hollywood Palladium, the Aragon Ballroom in Chicago, and the Roseland Ballroom in New York City. But it's not always the seating that impacts safety.

The musicians themselves play a large role in the dynamics of the crowd. When they play a fast song, the fans push and bodysurf more. Then when they play a ballad or a slower song, the crowd relaxes, people take a step back and they're off of each other for a little bit.

"There's always a struggle between the security director, the production manager and the band," Andre elaborates. "If the artists aren't happy with what they see, as far as how close they can get to the audience to let them work a crowd, then they're going to have a 'bad' show. They hassle the production manager, the production manager hassles me ... you get the point."

When it comes to staffing a venue, the degree of difficulty of the security director's job depends on a particular building crew's degree of enforcement. "If a building crew has got a crowd trained, then my job is easy," Andre explains. "But on nights when you've got a shitty security company whose people don't know what they're doing or may not be very aggressive, you've got people all over the place. That's when I really have my work cut out for me. If you've got aisles clogged from the front of the stage all the way to the back, the crowd has just overrun the ushering staff. Then you've got people from the last seat in the house way in the back suddenly down in the barricaded area, and the guy who paid for front-row tickets is pissed. No one can enjoy the show."

The bottom line for any security guy should always be safety, Andre contends. "There are two things that you think about on the job: You think about the safety of the artist and you think about the safety of the people in the building. It's almost like you are protecting them from themselves," he says.

Another concert phenomenon is the "reflection" of a particular city through the crowd. If a city is undergoing hard times or is densely populated, for example, crowds usually act more aggressive. If times are good – employment is up and crime is down – the crowds usually prove to be more mellow. This helps Andre anticipate problems.

"Some of the most aggressive cities are in the Northeast," Andre notes. "Certainly Philadelphia and New York. In the Midwest, it's Chicago, and down south, it's New Orleans. People are looking for outlets, and that's what entertainment is. People want to escape from their day-to-day humdrum. They want to be entertained. They want to forget for a couple of hours what it is they had to do that day or that month or that year. You can tell on a nightly basis how tense people are, how much they drank. It's all tied into society and what people are going through in their own little corner of the world."

In Andre's own little corner, as his professional reputation continued to precede him, he and Scoggins made perhaps the most important move of their young careers after the conclusion of the Dope Jam and Run's House tours.

8
TIME TO GO SOLO

September 1988: Los Angeles, California

"**RUN-D.M.C. SOLD OUT THE GREEK THEATRE IN L.A. CSC** management wanted to come see the show and check on their employees," Scoggins laughs, remembering an incident involving company owner Pete Kranzke and a colleague. "They didn't know how tight we had gotten with the band. Jam Master Jay had asked me to look after his girlfriend, to keep her with me at the front of the stage during the show and bring her backstage immediately afterward."

Run-D.M.C. had just taken the stage, and the audience was going crazy, leaning over the barricade in front of the stage.

"Hey, Ron! What's with the girl?" Kranzke shouted from his spot near the left speaker towers.

"Get her out of there," ordered his partner, jerking his thumb.

Scoggins turned. "She's got a ticket and a pass. And she's staying. If you have a problem with that, you better talk to him." Scoggins pointed to the stage, where Jam Master Jay busily scratched away.

To this day, Ron can't believe what happened. "It became a big ordeal," he says. "The management of the venue and the owners of the company were wondering why this girl was in the pit. I let them know that they weren't always in charge."

That didn't sit too well with angry CSC officials. They wanted to set the matter straight and told Andre to let Scoggins go. "Fire him," Kranzke ordered.

"So there I am," Andre picks up the story, "being told to axe my boy. There was no way that was going to happen."

Andre gathered enough courage to tell Scoggins that CSC wanted to terminate him. Then the two went straight to Jam Master Jay.

"I'll tell you what we're going to do here," Jam Master Jay said definitively. "We're going to have a meeting, and we're going to let the rest of the crew go, and you're going to stay, and whoever wants to stay with you guys can stay."

Jam Master Jay went to the rest of the group, set the deal and offered to hire Andre and Scoggins independently of CSC, giving them the chance to call their own shots and make a little more money.

"For me, it was an easy decision." Scoggins says. "For Andre, it was another matter."

"I didn't want to just leave CSC hanging," Andre recalls. "But I wanted to talk to them about time off. They had been working us for months without any time off, and this gave me some leverage."

Leverage that didn't work.

Andre had worked for a year and a half straight. Wanting to stay with CSC, but having Run-D.M.C.'s offer on the table, he walked into Kranzke's office in September 1988 and asked for some personal time. Andre's decision-making process was simple. If Kranzke gave it to him, Andre would stick with CSC. If not, he'd take the position with Run-D.M.C.

"Hey, Pete. What's going on?" Andre asked, making small talk.

"Everything, Andre, everything."

"I wanted to come in and talk about the schedule."

"Great, me too. We've got a lot happening."

"Well, Pete, do you realize I've been working for more than a year with no time off?"

"I know, Andre. And you've been doing a great job, too."

"Well, thanks. I'd like to get a little time off."

"Time off?" Kranzke acted as if he'd never heard the term. "Andre, I can't give you any time off. The Raiders games are just about to get into full swing. We've got the music stuff. We can't afford to have you taking any time off right now."

Kranzke couldn't help. CSC's business was booming, and he faced more work than he could handle.

"Maybe you could have some time off in February."

Then again, maybe not.

Andre turned and walked out of CSC's offices for the last time. He called his contact with Run-D.M.C. and sealed the deal, going into private business with Scoggins. This was a new beginning for Andre as an independent security director.

During those early tours, artists took notice of Andre's professionalism. He and his crew carried themselves differently and were organized much better than many of their security counterparts. This was a departure from rap groups' first security people, who initially were hired friends. The criteria back then was simple: If you were big, could fight and came from the group's 'hood, you were hired.

Artists quickly realized professional crowd-management strategies and tactics were essential. Run-D.M.C., so continually impressed with Andre's skills and abilities, asked Andre if he and Scoggins would join the group on an upcoming European tour as independent security contractors.

Andre and Scoggins accepted the positions of security directors on Run's European House Tour, which would showcase Run-D.M.C. and the politically charged Public Enemy.

Little did Andre know that this would be a watershed moment in his life, one that would change the direction of his career for more than a decade.

9
PUBLIC ENEMY NUMBER 1

THE FED EX PACKAGE ARRIVED PROMPTLY AT 10 A.M. ANDRE opened it quickly and found the necessary paperwork to obtain a passport and international work visa. It also contained plane tickets and a preliminary itinerary. His first gig as an independent: Run's European House Tour.

Andre went about making all of the necessary arrangements and preparations. In addition to his good friends in Run-D.M.C., Andre also would get a chance to spend some time with another unforgettable group of rappers who would leave an indelible impression on both him and the music industry at-large.

"Public Enemy was on the bill for many of those first Rush Productions outings, but because I was going back and forth so often between the tours, I didn't spend much time with them until we went to Europe," Andre says. "There were three main guys: Chuck D, Flavor Flav and Professor Griff. When they initially started this group, it was a way for them to communicate their political ideas. And they didn't hide any intentions about why they started performing."

Public Enemy – named after a popular anti-drug song, "Public Enemy Number One," by James Brown – was the creative concept of Chuck D (Carlton Ridenhour). The intent was to form a rap group with great rhymes and a strong black-nationalist message.

Like Run-D.M.C., Public Enemy formed in 1982 and hailed from Long Island, New York, which the guys quickly renamed "Strong Island."

Considered by many critics as the definitive rap group of all time, Public Enemy picked up where Run-D.M.C. left off, combining street-style beats and rhymes with hardcore social commentary. The group's production teams created dense sounds of samples, sirens and pervasive beats with funk that turned on rock and rap fans alike.

It Takes a Nation of Millions to Hold Us Back appeared in 1988, sold more than 1 million copies and became arguably the best rap album ever recorded. Then in 1990 came *Fear of a Black Planet,* which featured the controversial "911 is a Joke" and the homophobic "Meet the G That Killed Me."

Public Enemy also followed Run-D.M.C.'s cue by recording a song with a rock band. Headbangers Anthrax were enlisted in 1991 to re-record "Bring tha Noize" for *It Takes a Nation ... .*"

When Andre first met Public Enemy in 1988, the group was just beginning to fine-tune its creativity. "Chuck D, then 27, developed the concept behind the group," Andre explains. "Everyone served a particular function. Chuck was the mouthpiece, the strong black militant who says what he wants." In Jenette Beck and Bill Adler's 1991 book, *Rap,* Chuck D is quoted as saying, "It's about gold brains now, not gold chains."

On a lighter note, there was Flavor Flav (William Drayton), "one year older than Chuck D and always the court jester," Andre says. "He plays the black character of the 1920s and 1930s. You know, a step-and-fetch-it type. He's the clown, always smiling, saying 'yes sir,' 'no sir.' That's his personality."

The other member of note was Professor Griff (Richard Griff). "Griff was like the strong black-power, militant Panther of the 1960s – the original, black-gloved, fist-raised proponent of that movement," Andre says.

Andre describes Public Enemy's act from the other side of the stage: "Onstage, they wore military fatigues and did military maneuvers. They stood at attention and carried fake Uzis. At different times during the show, they performed military formations. The whole concept was put together by Chuck D. That was his way of getting his anger out about the state of affairs in America, as he saw them."

Public Enemy's performances were characterized by choreography featuring a stealthy stable of back-up dancers, who were recruited by Professor Griff and dubbed the Security of the First World, or S1W. Group infighting and anti-Semitic comments from the stage and in the press eventually doomed Public Enemy, who opened several shows of U2's U.S. Zoo TV Tour in 1992.

That series of dates proved to be the group's last big hurrah until a new album, *He Got Game,* released in spring 1998, reinstated Public Enemy in the public eye. A soundtrack to the Spike Lee basketball film of the same name starring Denzel Washington, *He Got Game* teams Chuck D, Flavor Flav, Terminator X and Professor Griff with original P.E. producers, Hank Shocklee's Bomb Squad. The album came about because Lee himself asked Chuck D to contribute to the film's music. "Chuck is such an avid sports fan; I knew it would be a great opportunity to put his lyrical genius to work," Lee told *Rolling Stone* magazine in May 1998. "I felt it was important enough to get P.E. back together. And I'm glad that in some small way, the film was a catalyst to that. We need them."

"This is the one group I worked with that I could say, at least initially, for them it wasn't about the money," Andre says. "Everybody had regular jobs, so they didn't need money from the group to survive. They really didn't live off the money they made from the group until later on. The group was more of a platform for them to voice their political views."

Indeed, in Greg Tate's 1992 book, *The Devil Made 'Em Do It: Public Enemy*, Tate writes: "P.E. wants to reconvene the black power movement with hip-hop as the medium."

As Public Enemy rejoined Run-D.M.C. for a 1988 run of shows through Europe, they would soon fall under the spell of the man many rap observers consider the most powerful and greatest business mind of the genre.

10
FATHER OF A HIP-HOP NATION

Russell Simmons

AS THE OLDER BROTHER OF JOSEPH "RUN" SIMMONS, RUSSELL Simmons helped turn Run-D.M.C. and other performers into legends. Some insiders say he made rap music what it is today. Andre remembers Run-D.M.C.'s manager as a serious businessman who was comfortable both on the street and in the boardroom.

"They were all from the streets," Andre says. "But we knew early on that Russell Simmons was different."

He remembers his first trip to Europe on Run's European House Tour with Run-D.M.C. and Public Enemy.

Clouds covered London on a typical English day. The crowded Heathrow International Airport seemed like another world to the young rappers. Life had become hectic for the members of Run-D.M.C., who recently completed the successful Together Forever U.S. Tour, which left them exhausted but happy. And now Europe stared the rappers and Public Enemy straight in the eye – a frightening proposition for the rest of the entourage. But not for Russell Simmons.

A lengthy cab ride took them to Le Meridian, close to Piccadilly Circus. Fatigue and the long flight added to the sense of confusion. After checking in at the front desk and getting settled, the rappers, crew and Simmons all met in the hotel restaurant.

The scene, strangely symbolic of his future influence, found Simmons surrounded by all the members of Run-D.M.C. and Public Enemy, the tour manager, the road manager and Andre. As usual, Russell Simmons held court.

"What we have to do is turn these European crowds on," Simmons said, looking first at Run-D.M.C., then turning to Public Enemy. "We expand our market, we expand our earnings. And we carry our message to more people."

Everybody nodded seriously.

Much like his younger brother, Russell spoke often and moved quickly from topic to topic. That's how he got nicknamed "Rush" (and how his company, Rush Management, got its name).

"Watching Russell that day in London, I knew he was going to be very influential," Andre says. "Plus, he was the first person we ever saw who had a Platinum American Express Card. We were all very impressed."

Andre's initial impression proved on target. Russell Simmons has shaped rap music by identifying talent and providing opportunities and advancement for many people in the industry. And he's also not afraid to tell others how he sees things.

"Sometimes the Beasties were a little out of hand," Andre admits. "Young and on the road for the first time, they acted more than a little crazy. And Russell called them on it. In essence, he told them that the audiences came to the Together Forever shows to see Run-D.M.C. They were the stars who could get away with murder. Not the Beastie Boys."

Another time, Simmons spoke candidly to Andre. Frustrated with the questionable behavior of his younger brother, Run, Simmons didn't know what to do. At a hotel in Tennessee, Simmons confided in Andre.

"I can't believe he's even talking this way," Simmons told Andre.

Andre asked for specifics. "What do you mean?"

"He says he doesn't know if he wants to do this anymore. Can you believe that, man? Can you believe that?"

Run's life seemed out of balance. He loved his wife and family and loved the band, a tough combination for anyone. Eventually, the touring lifestyle really got to him.

Today, Andre realizes the struggle. "It's tough. Run saw the world as ceaseless touring and being away from his family. Russell saw that as the payoff – the result of hard work and tough negotiations. The gigs were gravy."

In the end, the traditional, fragile and careful dynamic of artist and manager gave way to the much more powerful dynamic of brotherhood. Run continued to tour, perhaps thanks to the watchful eye of big brother Russell Simmons.

And that watchful eye has proven profitable.

As the CEO of Def Jam Records, Simmons and his label earned a significant chunk of the hip–hop market share in 1998. His strategy for aggressive acquisition of new talent has him poised to keep him atop the industry for years.

In the past ten years, Simmons also has diversified. Under the Rush Communications umbrella falls the Def Jam label, Phat Farm apparel, an advertising agency representing Coca-Cola, and various film and TV projects. The Simmons empire billed almost $200 million in 1998, reported *The Source* magazine in February 1999.

All of this success was just beginning back in the late Eighties. As Run's European House Tour wore on, Public Enemy became more accustomed to Simmons' straight-up management style, and Andre became more familiar with the rappers. In fact, he even shared some tense moments with the boys in Public Enemy.

11
SKINHEAD SHOWDOWN
Public Enemy

October 1988: Germany

ANDRE LAID ON THE BED IN HIS GERMAN HOTEL ROOM EARLY ONE
Tuesday afternoon, staring at the ceiling and thinking about how the tour was progressing in its
earliest stages. During the long plane ride from L.A., he found the guys in Public Enemy to be
fairly approachable. The German hotel wasn't the fanciest he had ever stayed in, but he was
tired and thankful for the time to rest that afternoon. Andre thought about his family far away in
Southern California. He missed them terribly. The ringing of the phone broke his concentration.

"Hello," Andre answered quickly.

"Andre," came the voice of Chuck D. "The guys want to get something to eat."

"OK," Andre responded quickly. "I'll meet you in the lobby right away."

Andre remembers the event and laughs. "The guys in Public Enemy had pretty strict
diets. They were partial vegetarians, they didn't eat pork, and they ate very little red meat.
Their diet consisted of maybe some turkey or chicken and all kinds of vegetables. It was all
part of their military-like lifestyle. We didn't know where to go to get that kind of food. We
weren't familiar with Europe, so we figured we could survive at McDonald's by ordering
chicken sandwiches and salads. So everywhere we went, we had to go in search of a
McDonald's. Not always the easiest task. Anyway, I was the first person to reach the lobby ... "

Andre walked quickly to the registration desk. The hotel was located in the heart of old-
world Germany and was far from being modernized. But the people were friendly enough,
and as Andre approached, the sturdy middle-aged woman behind the desk smiled.

"Ma'am, could you please give me directions to the closest McDonald's?" Andre asked politely.

Her eyes widened as if she had just received awful news. "Undt, vhy do you vant?"

Andre, not knowing whether he had committed some sort of German faux pas, hesitated. "Uh, because we want to get something to eat?"

"Undt, leave zie hotel?" she replied in an almost accusatory tone.

"Uhh ... yeah. If that's all right with you," Andre became slightly more uncomfortable in this exchange.

"You must be careful," she hissed. "The skinheads are out."

Just then, another woman came to the desk clerk's side. She was about the same age and equally sturdy. She had overheard the conversation and wanted to add her advice.

"Be careful. Walk in a group. Be careful," she cautioned.

The two women quickly gave Andre directions to the local McDonald's. When they were through, Andre started to leave as the first desk clerk hissed again, this time shaking her finger. "Remember. Watch out for skinheads."

Andre nodded and smiled appreciatively. *Lady, have you seen the guys I'm with?* he thought, turning to discover his lunch companions, all seven of them, standing in a group, arms folded, watching him.

Chuck D, dressed in an Oakland Raiders' jacket and hat, stood with feet spread and shoulders squared. Professor Griff looked particularly imposing, as his shiny black combat boots flashed brilliantly, even in the dimly lit lobby. His camouflage pants looked freshly issued. The others were all dressed in similar military fashion, except for Flavor Flav, who was a good guy to have around if you wanted to know the time.

"Yo, Homes! You ready or what?" Chuck D asked.

"Ready," Andre replied.

As the eight men made their way onto the street, Andre wondered whether he should say anything about the desk clerk's warning. He decided against it, figuring it would just ignite another conversation about the group's political views. Although interested in their opinions, he really didn't feel like getting into such a heavy conversation during lunch.

"So we're walking down the street in search of a McDonald's. I look up, and here come about six skinheads," Andre remembers. "I saw them before anyone else did."

Andre tried to remain calm. The Public Enemy guys spotted the skinheads, and immediately shot determined glances at each other. *This ought to be interesting,* Andre thought.

Being the security man for Public Enemy is almost a contradiction in terms. This group of rappers – all trained in the martial arts – was as savvy about personal defense as the Navy S.E.A.L.s. They probably could list seven different ways to kill you with their bare hands. But, nonetheless, Andre positioned himself between Public Enemy and the approaching skinheads.

"They see these guys coming, and the hair is standing up on the back of their necks," Andre says of his clients. "They were like pit bulls ready to attack."

The skinheads making their way towards the rappers were no sweethearts, either. They all wore combat boots and leather jackets. Two of them sported particularly shiny heads and what looked to be swastika tattoos on their biceps. Andre readied himself for confrontation.

All trained in the martial arts ... they probably could list seven different ways to kill you with their bare hands.

The gap between Public Enemy and the skinheads closed. Fifty yards. Forty yards. Thirty yards. Andre clenched his fists, preparing for a fight. And then it happened.

One of the shaved heads snapped up. Another one turned. And yet another shot a fleeting look.

Andre laughs about the confrontation now.

"I kid you not. Those skinheads took one look at our group, their eyes got as big as silver dollars, and they put their heads down and crossed the street. They tried to not even look at us. They didn't say a word. It was the first time I felt I might have to protect the public from my artists! I don't know if they realized who they were, or if they thought we were like some American GIs, or maybe they just found Chuck D and the others intimidating. But for whatever reason, they tucked their tails between their legs and went to the other side of the street.

"The skinhead incident typifies the attitude of the Public Enemy guys," Andre continues. "They didn't take anything from anybody. They spoke their minds. They were always respectful. But they had their views, and you were going to hear about them. If you asked a question, you better be prepared to get the answer. The guys in Public Enemy weren't going to tell you what you wanted to hear, but rather what they wanted you to know. If you didn't like it, well, then that was your problem."

Andre remembers his time with Public Enemy fondly. Those were the days he learned about rap's political underpinnings and cut his teeth as an independent security director.

When Public Enemy reunited for *He Got Game*, Chuck D publicly restaked his claim in the rap world. "I'm like the Julius Erving of rap," Chuck D told *People* magazine in June 1998. "I'm as much as 20 years older than the kids coming in. Whatever they're going through, I've been there. But it's not like I'm decrepit. ... Having game is being able to deal with whatever is thrown at you. You're not looking from the outside in – you're in. And I'm in."

After returning from Europe, Andre found himself an "in" guy, about to sign on for the rockiest gig of his life.

12
WHAT'S NEXT?
N.W.A.

December 1988: Los Angeles

THE TV DRONED. AN NFL GAME FLICKERED ON THE
screen, but neither man watched. Ron Scoggins and Andre, just back from Europe with Run-D.M.C. and Public Enemy, sat in Andre's living room planning their future. It looked anything but certain.

"What are we gonna do, Andre?" Scoggins asked.

"I don't know," Andre replied, drumming his fingers on the coffee table. "Something will turn up. It's got to."

Andre remembers the uncertainty. "Ron and I went independent at the same time. We took the Run-D.M.C. and Public Enemy tours, but we didn't have any other work lined up. We didn't really have a client roster. We were just starting to learn the business, and not lining up second and third moves. We didn't have anyone to turn to and say, 'Hey, we're available. What's next?' It was a little frightening."

As anyone who has ever started a business knows, getting new clients is never easy. And not knowing where your next paycheck will come from is a scary proposition. So Andre did what many new entrepreneurs do. He counted his money and determined how long he and his young family could live on what they had saved. The next task was to brainstorm ways to drum up business.

Over the next couple of weeks, Andre and Scoggins pondered their futures. "We were lost. We didn't know what to do. We didn't know how to get jobs. We didn't know who to contact," Andre says. "We had no networking other than our Def Jam or Rush Management

(Public Enemy) contacts. And they only toured in the summer, one or two tours per year that were only two or three months long."

And then came an unexpected break – something that has since become standard in Andre's life. This one appeared in the form of a phone call.

"We had an old friend in the business, a guy known as K.J.," Andre explains. "We remembered him being pretty active in the industry, but we hadn't seen or heard from him in a long time. Then one day, out of the blue, K.J. called my house and said, 'Hey, what are you and Ron doing these days? We need some more security for a thing we're working on. Why don't you come over and meet the tour manager and we'll see if I can get you guys hooked up with some work.'" Andre quickly agreed and set a time to meet K.J. over at Cole Studios in West Hollywood.

Andre pulled his metallic-blue 1987 Honda Civic wagon into the parking lot of Cole Studios late one afternoon in late 1988. He and Scoggins were familiar with the studio – an older and square building, a bit run down but with a great history.

As the sun set, Andre and Scoggins, who had no idea who they were about to meet, made their way into the rehearsal studio, taking in the gloomy, dark wood interior and the Seventies-style shag carpeting. The walls reverberated with bass. Then they heard it:

> Straight outta Compton/Crazy muthafucka named Ice Cube
> From the gang called Niggaz With Attitude.
> When I'm called off/I got a sawed off
> Squeeze the trigger/And bodies are hauled off.

Andre and Ron exchanged rather serious glances. Coming out of the largest rehearsal room in Cole Studios were the rhymes of N.W.A., short for Niggaz With Attitude.

The group's album *Straight Outta Compton*, had just been released (and would eventually sell more than 2 million copies), and N.W.A. was gaining enormous popularity by developing into the most notorious of rap acts – even more so than Public Enemy. And for good reason: the group's breakout song from *Straight Outta Compton* was called "Fuck Tha Police."

N.W.A. consisted of Eazy-E (Eric Wright), Dr. Dre (Andre Young), Ice Cube (O'Shea Jackson), DJ Yella (Antoine Carraby) and MC Ren (Lorenzo Patterson). Their music, fueled by unapologetic violence and sexism, set the stage for rappers like the late Tupac Shakur and Notorious B.I.G.

Ultimately, many of N.W.A.'s members would go on to successful solo careers after the group's unfortunate and nasty demise in 1992. The group's lyrics celebrated criminal life – blunt language and all. "Fuck Tha Police" forced the FBI to warn Ruthless Records and Priority Records, the group's labels, about taking the act too far.

The group dressed differently than other rap acts, preferring the baggy black and silver apparel of the Los Angeles Raiders, thereby setting fashion statements for a new generation of gangsta rappers. Yet N.W.A.'s core audience included both urban African-American youth and suburban white kids.

"Eric's money started the whole thing," Andre says. "He had a bunch of money from an inheritance and he and Dr. Dre did the very first demos. Then Eric found [soon-to-be N.W.A. manager] Jerry Heller, and they got it all together."

Eazy-E, an ex-drug dealer, started N.W.A. with the goal of creating and ruling a successful rap empire. Although some critics would say he never built that empire, he certainly made history.

Hailing from Compton, California, N.W.A. originated a new form of rap, initially called "West Coast gangsta," that would evolve into simply "gangsta rap." Many critics considered this to be an abrupt about-face to what was happening on the other side of the country. One reviewer described the East Coast lyrics as "Afro-centric with politically conscious tendencies." N.W.A.'s lyrics, on the other hand, consisted of straightforward and violent life-on-the-street stories.

Everyone in N.W.A. played an essential role. The lyrics came from Ice Cube, the music from Dr. Dre and the concept from Eazy-E. Yella handled the deejay activities, as well as some producing and engineering tasks. MC Ren was strictly a rapper with a great voice. Together these guys hit their niche and went from nothing to platinum sellers.

"There they were in Cole Studios in 1988, trying to put this tour together to capitalize on their instant fame and popularity," Andre says. "They sold a million records before they even toured. And trust me, these guys weren't getting radio airplay. It was the buzz on the street that drove these sales."

Upon entering Cole Studios that day, Scoggins and Andre bumped into N.W.A.'s tour manager, Atron Gregory. Standing about 6 feet tall, of medium build and with short curly hair, Gregory told the two that K.J. had highly recommended them. "K.J. was there," Andre recalls, "and we were just standing in a small circle, talking. We were really used to a slightly more sophisticated and professional setting. But we needed work, so we weren't complaining."

The small hallway gathering eventually adjourned to a cramped, but well-lit office. As Andre and Scoggins settled themselves on an old leather couch, the members of N.W.A. appeared, one by one, as if part of a police lineup, to introduce themselves.

13
BOYZ-N-THE-HOOD
N.W.A.

EAZY-E ENTERED FIRST, SPORTING BLACK LEVI'S, WHITE NIKES, AN oversized Los Angeles Raiders nylon jacket and a matching Raiders baseball cap. He always wore his hat straight, rather than cocked.

Eazy was a little guy making a big name in the music business. Andre was shocked to see just how small he really was. "He must have been about 5 feet, 3 inches, sort of stocky and muscular. Eric probably weighed 140 or 150 pounds." Andre always refers to Eazy-E by his given name.

With the money he made from life on the streets of Compton, Eazy-E started Ruthless Records and produced the group's first single, "Boyz-N-the-Hood" from 1987's *N.W.A. and the Posse.* With the financial foundation in place, he then gathered all of the local talent he could muster: Dr. Dre, Ice Cube, MC Ren and DJ Yella. He put together a dream crew and was now ready to take on the world.

Eazy-E's next step was to get a little managerial assistance from Heller, who had worked with acts as diverse as Pink Floyd and Elton John. Heller knew how to get things done. Eazy paid a mutual friend $750 in cash, which he reportedly pulled out of his sock immediately after the introductions were made, just to meet Heller.

At the time of his first meeting with Eazy-E, Andre knew very little about him or N.W.A. But he eventually learned a lot of things about the rapper, including his huge affinity for women.

"I think he was addicted to sex," Andre says bluntly. "Every day, there had to be a conquest. He would leave the office four, five, sometimes six times a day. He didn't get up and announce where he was going, but we all knew. And Eric knew we did."

Heller, who knew Eazy-E since 1987, told *Vibe* magazine in its June/July 1998 issue that, "I always said [women] would be his downfall." Eazy also lived, by the code of the street. That is one of the keys to why N.W.A. eventually split up.

Andre explains: "Rap groups are notorious for hangers-on. I mean cousins, neighborhood buddies, everybody. And everybody had a job. Even if they weren't getting paid, they were on the road. They had something to do, and they had a good time doing it.

"One interesting guy was Laylaw," Andre continues. "He was more like a fringe member of the group. Laylaw contributed because he was a songwriter and a deejay – plus he was a childhood friend of the group members. 'Laylaw' was his nickname. I'll let you figure out how he got it."

One day on the tour bus, Laylaw had an idea he wanted to share with Eazy. However, his approach needed some work.

At about 1 p.m., the bus neared the venue for that evening's show. Everyone had been awake for only a short while, and the artists and crew were just starting to show signs of life from the night before.

"Hey, man, we need to change that section after the second song in the show. It's weak, man," Laylaw announced to Eazy.

The rapper, as the leader of the group, responded quickly, "No."

"I think we need to change that section," Laylaw repeated, louder.

"Laylaw, I'm telling you, we ain't changing it." Eazy said purposefully. Either subconsciously or consciously, he was sending a subtle message to Laylaw that the discussion was about more than a piece of constructive criticism.

Laylaw was the type of guy who liked to discuss things thoroughly – and who usually didn't take no for an answer. Eazy, on the other hand, considered the topic a dead issue.

"But why not, E? It's better if we do."

By this time, the exchange had captured the attention of everyone on the bus. It was quickly escalating beyond a conversation.

This dose of reality served as a sobering reminder of what life used to be like. Gone was the quiet laughter that filled the bus only moments earlier. It had been almost a fantasy ride for this bunch of guys from the streets of Compton – selling records, filling concert halls, a non-stop party. And now came a harsh nod back to the violent life on the streets.

"I said no."

Eazy dropped his hands to his sides and squared off to Laylaw. His nostrils flared as his breathing quickened like a bull preparing to charge.

Now the matter was out of Eazy's hands. Now 'street rules' dictated his actions, Andre recalls. As the leader of the group and the label, his position of authority was being challenged in front of the rest of the group.

"No," Eazy-E repeated.

"What'cha gonna do, little man?"

Laylaw, who was much larger than Eazy, crossed the line. Not only did he challenge Eazy's

"You gonna shoot me? What'cha gonna do, little man?"

authority, he challenged his physical stature. Although Eazy never took comments about his size too seriously, his eyes flashed with anger when he heard this one.

Eazy responded succinctly. "Fuck you!"

"No. No. No. I wanna know," Laylaw insisted. "What'cha gonna do? You gonna kick my ass?"

Laylaw poked him in the chest and continued his questioning. "You gonna shoot me? What'cha gonna do, little man?" Again, he poked.

The situation was like a Wild West gunfight. The only sound on the bus was that of the highway, the occasional shifting of gears or the hissing of air brakes from a passing tractor-trailer. All eyes were on Eazy-E and Laylaw.

"What'cha gonna do, little man? What'cha gonna do?"

Eazy threw a solid right–handed roundhouse, landing it squarely in Laylaw's face.

Laylaw, after recovering from the blow, went after Eazy. That's when Andre and company stepped in to stop the fight. They weren't about to let the fastest-rising rap act in the country get derailed as a result of some flared tempers.

Eazy possessed a real "kill or be killed" demeanor. Laylaw quickly realized he'd made a mistake. Eazy proved his dominance and, at least for now, kept his position as the leader and decision maker of the group.

"That's just the way he was," Andre remembers about Eazy-E. "It was a power thing. If Laylaw had come to him one–on–one, Eric might have been more receptive. But he didn't. He brought up the situation in front of everybody. That forced Eric's hand. Even if Eric thought the idea had merit, he said no in front of everyone. And then he couldn't back down. We talked a lot – Eric and me. I tried to get him to change that street mentality, but I was unsuccessful. Black folks have a saying: 'You can take the nigga out of the ghetto, but you can't take the ghetto out of the nigga.' At some point, you will always revert back to the street. And in some situations, if you can't talk your way out of or into something, you'll revert to physical violence out of frustration."

Back at Cole Studios that January day, the next person to introduce himself to Andre and Scoggins was Dr. Dre. As usual, he wore a black T-shirt, black jeans and white Nikes. "Dre is just a fun-loving guy," Andre says. "While Eric acted more casual and very subdued about meeting Scoggins and me, Dre seemed very upbeat. He has a great outgoing personality, loud and gregarious."

He's also much larger than Eazy, standing just over 6 feet. Dre loves to be the center of attention, a trait that became magnified when he left N.W.A. in 1992 over financial issues and a very public feud with Eazy.

Dr. Dre pursued a solo career and founded Death Row Records with Suge Knight. His first solo album, *The Chronic*, also came out in 1992, and he has since become one of the premier hip-hop producers of the Nineties.

"Dre isn't really a musician by the classic definition," Andre continues. "But he can take songs, decipher them, cut them up and put them together in a way that makes sense. It's pretty unusual. He can hear layers of music in several different songs. He takes a melody line out of this, a bass line out of that, a horn section out of something else and creates a musical track for guys to rap over. That's his expertise."

In many ways, Dre's personality can be compared to that of Will Smith, Andre says. "He has a big heart and he's a nice guy who would do anything for you. He likes to laugh and have fun. But he has a business side to him, as well. A positive business side with the street edge."

Ice Cube entered the room next. "Ice Cube is a serious, serious guy," Andre recalls. "On tour, he wasn't trying to be involved in all of the outside-influence stuff. He was serious about his music and his career. He had a vision about where he wanted to go. Ice Cube used to walk around with this bag. In there he kept notebooks of material he was working on. Whenever he would have a creative thought, he made sure he captured it. And it showed. He just keeps coming out with more and more material. He is incredibly creative and was the thinker of the group. He had his sights set on being a superstar, and he didn't spend his time getting chemically altered or trying to be seen by everybody or running after women."

But Cube's seriousness contributed heavily to N.W.A.'s demise, Andre contends. "You could see the trouble brewing onstage. Battling for position, battling for who had the most lines in the song, who had the most impact and who was the most popular. Ice Cube was destined for greatness because he had the hardcore image. He's the one who performed 'Fuck Tha Police.' He's got the look. He's got the stare. He's got the menacing face and the mean persona. Rap audiences identified with him. He was the one who had the deep voice. He was the one who cursed the most. He was the one with the scowl. Look at any of the pictures he's in. Eric will have a peaceful, blank look on his face, but Ice Cube is always scowling, always!"

But most of that was an act, Andre claims. Ice Cube wasn't that hard core off the stage. He perpetuated the image, though, because that's what he did best. And he wanted to get paid for what he did so well.

"If Eric wasn't going to give him what he wanted, then he was going to get it some other way," Andre continues. "And he laid it on the line. He went in and said, 'Hey, I need more money. I'm contributing more than I'm getting paid for.'

"When Eric said, 'No,' Cube just said, 'I'm gone. I'll see you later. What's it going to cost to get out of this contract?' So that's what happened. He got a manager, had N.W.A.'s books checked and that was it. He just wanted to make sure that he was getting paid what he should have been, per the original agreement. If Eric had been smart, he would have worked out a deal and kept both Dre and Cube."

Cube left N.W.A. in 1989 over the financial squabble and dissed the group's management on his 1991 *Death Certificate* album in the song "No Vaseline."

Ice Cube has continued with a successful career as a solo artist and record-label executive, releasing Volume I of a planned two-part *War & Peace* project in late 1998. He starred in such movies as *Anaconda, Dangerous Minds* and most notably, 1990's *Boyz in the Hood.*

During the final introductions at Cole, Andre met DJ Yella and MC Ren. "DJ was a real quiet, nice guy – not really a street guy at all," Andre says. "Plus, he's a light-skinned black guy. That's why he's called 'Yella.'"

By contrast, MC Ren was the group's darkest and youngest member. Still in his late teens at the time, MC Ren boasted N.W.A.'s most recognizable and best voice with a deep baritone, Andre argues. "Unfortunately, they never really let him do much," he adds. "He was from the same neighborhood, but they didn't really give him much responsibility performing."

Andre's initial meeting with N.W.A. that December day in 1988 signaled the beginning of perhaps his most dangerous stint in the music business.

14
RUTHLESS BUSINESS
N.W.A.

THE DEF JAM AND DOPE JAM TOURS BOASTED A PRODUCTION
company that provided lighting, sound and all other necessities of life on the road. Andre
and Ron thought that was the way all tours ran. Not only was there no production company
this time around, but the N.W.A. camp didn't even seem to have the basics covered.

"Where are we going?" Andre asked Atron Gregory during their initial meeting that
January day at Cole Studios.

"We don't know yet," the tour manager said.

"How will we be traveling?"

"We don't know that, either."

Andre remembers the tension. "We must have looked a little concerned, because
Gregory and K.J. kept trying to reassure us by saying things like, 'I don't have any answers for
you on any of those questions. But in the very near future, all those questions will be
answered.' So we took their word for it." Andre and Scoggins agreed to do the tour.

At the time, *Straight Outta Compton* had just gone platinum, and "Fuck Tha Police" was
generating a lot of mainstream media attention. The 200,000-member Fraternal Order of
Police and a representative of the FBI officially condemned the track.

N.W.A. made Public Enemy look like New Kids on the Block. And the group knew it.
During a photo shoot at Eazy-E's mother's house for *L.A. Weekly*'s May 5, 1989, issue,
someone asked Eazy, "What? No A-K?"

"This is my mother's house," the rapper replied. "All that stuff is over at my place." Then
he disappeared into the house and came back moments later carrying a canvas duffel bag,

which he emptied on the grass. A pile of 9mm pistols, 12-gauge shotguns, a couple of small-bore rifles and a ton of ammunition poured out of the bag.

"Public Enemy uses plastic guns, you know," Ice Cube told the reporter.

Meanwhile, things were getting a little sticky as N.W.A.'s tour bus rolled across America. Take, for example, the St. Louis stop on N.W.A.'s 1989 U.S. Straight Outta Compton Tour. Andre was the first one off the bus as it pulled into the St. Louis Civic Center. Immediately, he saw four squad cars and quickly got the guys organized and headed for the building. This was getting to be a routine drill.

"Normally, when you go into these buildings, you have the support of the building management, local police and everybody else," Andre explains. "Well, if your hit song is 'Fuck Tha Police,' you're guaranteed you don't."

Once inside, Andre sought out building officials and local authorities. Usually he worked hand in hand with police, but this time he now didn't have that luxury. Because of negative publicity from "Fuck Tha Police," cops were less than enthusiastic toward N.W.A. Andre made his way to where two uniformed officers stood, just outside the production office. Usually four or five met with Andre.

"You with these guys?" the cop – white, about 6 feet, 4 inches tall and 250 pounds – asked. His partner, an equally large black man, wasn't giving Andre any warm vibes, either.

"Yes, sir." Andre said.

"Look, we know about the song," said the black officer. "Wanna tell us more about it?"

Andre proceeded to give them the party line, just as he had done dozens of times on this tour.

"Well, it's all about black kids getting unjustly hassled by less-than-professional police officers." Andre started. "It really is meant to raise public awareness."

His explanation didn't win any points.

"Huh," the first officer grunted, sarcastically. "And we just thought you guys hated cops. Well, here's the way this is gonna work. You guys say the F-word, you're gonna get arrested."

The second cop, as if on cue, jumped in. "You guys grab your crotch onstage, you're gonna get arrested."

"If you do that song verbatim, you're gonna get arrested," came the first cop.

"If you start to incite what we interpret to be a riotous situation ... "

"Let me guess," Andre interrupted. "We're gonna get arrested?"

"Wise ass, huh?"

"No sir. Just starting to get the picture of how this is gonna work. You won't have any problems from us." Andre thanked the officers for their time, turned and headed down the corridor toward N.W.A.'s dressing room.

"What did they say?" Scoggins anxiously asked upon Andre's return, hoping the authorities in this town would be different from every other city on the tour.

"They're pissed." Andre said flatly. "Just like everyone else."

In another routine exercise, Andre took a list of the officers' conditions to Gregory, who then assembled the band to review them. They were used to these demands by now.

N.W.A. crafted an ingenious response, one that Andre says separated them from the East Coast rap scene. "The East Coast guys would have just said, 'We don't care. We're doing it like we want to do it. If we go to jail, we go to jail. We're not backing down,'" Andre explains. "They would try to buck the authorities. The West Coast guys, even though they were from South Central L.A., were smart enough to know that this is their business and their livelihood. They knew if they got arrested, it might make for good headlines. But down the road, it was just going to cause them more problems they didn't need. They were businessmen, as well as artists."

If we can't say, "Fuck Tha Police," maybe the audience will say it for us, the group members reasoned. *They can't arrest us for what the audience says.*

And that's what N.W.A. did. When they reached the point in the show when it came time to perform the infamous song, the guys simply held their mics out to the audience, who fervently filled in the blanks. N.W.A. knew what they could and could not get away with. When they were given artistic constraints, they worked around them.

"It was a complicated situation." Andre remembers. "Crowds were volatile because several rival gangs might be attending. And there was more pressure from the establishment, because people thought the music was less than appropriate. We really didn't know what we were getting into. We signed on for this tour and met more civic leaders, church groups and local police than you can imagine."

But the attention from government agencies and volatile crowds wasn't the most frightening part. That came during a short break on the tour.

N.W.A.'s entourage was given a few weeks off. Being at home served as a welcome break from life on the tour bus. One weekday afternoon, Andre was enjoying a little peace and quiet at home with his wife when a phone call interrupted their respite.

"Andre," a concerned Heller said into the phone. "I need you to come to the office right away."

"What's wrong, Jerry?"

"Just get down here as soon as possible."

Andre heard the receiver click. He looked at Heather. Her eyes told the story. As an exhausted parent married to a music-industry guy, she was used to last-minute changes in plans. But it certainly didn't mean she liked it.

"Sweetheart ... " Andre began.

"Just be home soon," she smiled.

Andre kissed her forehead and then headed for Heller's Woodland Hills offices. Upon his arrival, he pushed open the door and saw Heller sitting behind his desk, smoking a cigarette.

Eazy-E, Heller and other members of N.W.A.'s entourage were already there. All sported grim looks on their faces. These were tough times for N.W.A. Ice Cube had just split over money, and dissension was in the ranks. There were no exchanges of pleasantries.

"Andre, listen to this," Heller said.

He hit the play button on the answering machine. The group fell silent. After the message finished, the tape clicked off. It was a death threat. Heller looked at the group.

"Well, what do you think?" he asked. Immediately, the most logical comments started.

"It's got to be some sort of right-wing conservative group."

"Maybe it's the skinheads, or some neo-Nazi types."

"I still don't think the cops ever got over that song."

"Play it again." Andre said, not offering any opinions.

As the voice on the tape evaporated into the air for a second time, Andre knew he'd heard it before. But he kept it to himself – at least for a while.

"Something stinks, man. All this right after Cube bugged out?" someone added.

Nods all around the room.

"I mean, that guy on the tape doesn't sound like any neo-Nazi. He sounds like he could be a homeboy."

"I'm no voice expert," Andre offered. "But I have a good idea of who is on that machine."

Everyone, including Heller, leaned in close to listen to Andre's theory. After several minutes, it made sense to everyone in the room. The meeting broke up shortly thereafter.

Back home, Andre pulled into his driveway, put the car in park and turned off the ignition. But he didn't move; he just sat quietly. Eyes closed, he ran the scenario through his mind.

What the hell is going on? Is it gang-related? It's got to be about money.

Andre knew this was dangerous territory. No longer business, this was war. Street mentality with bank accounts. He knew he must leave the rap world – before things really got out of hand. The shows were no problem. The hotels were no problem. The fans were no problem. But being in an office or a car and getting attacked with A-K 47s wasn't something that could be controlled. And an intelligent person doesn't expose himself to that. He had bigger responsibilities than successfully seeing a controversial rap group through a troubled tour.

Andre wasn't about to risk the future of his family on a music-industry thug match.

"How was your afternoon?" Heather asked when Andre finally entered the house.

"Fine," Andre replied as he kissed her on the cheek.

"What was so important?"

"Nothing," Andre said. "Just some changes in the touring plans." Andre did not tell her about the death threats for several months. He didn't want to worry her.

The late-Eighties proved to be a strange time for Ruthless Records and rap music. Some individual members of N.W.A. hired their own security people, there were disagreements about money, and now being in the group featured an added element of danger to it. The threats could have come for any number of reasons – creative control, distribution, management roles, and of course, money – from any number of people.

Dre, at the same time, had gotten his fill of N.W.A. and Ruthless Records. Several other operators in the industry expressed interest in him, and some sources say he was entertaining all offers. But he was still under contract with Ruthless, and that contract would have to be bought out before he could make a move.

Even now, Andre won't say exactly whose voice he heard on the tape that day, or what it said. But you can tell by the look in his eye that he doesn't think it was any fanatical right-winger. He just nods and says, "It was much closer to home than that."

The June/July 1998 issue of *Vibe* magazine sheds a little more light on the subject. In an article by R.J. Smith titled "It Ain't Eazy," Smith writes: "Back in 1991, when Dre was leaving Ruthless for Death Row, Suge Knight reportedly used baseball bats and pipes to persuade Eazy-E to release Dre from his Ruthless contract."

After Andre informed Heller of his decision to move on, some insiders say the band's manager overreacted in terms of security. Smith continues:

> It was Heller who brought the mysterious Mike Klein to
> Ruthless Records at a moment when Ruthless's future seemed at
> stake. Heller had known Klein since the mid-1980s, when Klein
> ran a garment business near Heller's office. ...
>
> ... Klein was a textbook in self-defense; he's probably the
> only one of the few people who can claim close friends in both
> the militant Jewish Defense League and the Nation of Islam.
>
> Klein did take Ruthless employees to firing ranges to learn
> defensive techniques. You can't really say he armed the label,
> however. "Everybody had their own guns, including me," explains
> Heller.

The markers indicating the end of N.W.A. had come and gone. The combination of the death threats and Cube and Dre leaving seemed to have irreversible negative effects on the group. After those events, neither N.W.A. nor Andre was ever the same. He often reflects on the group's downfall.

15

CODE OF THE STREETS

N.W.A.

"WHY DIDN'T N.W.A. STAY TOGETHER?" ANDRE ASKS TODAY, referring to the group's 1992 disbanding. "Power and greed. Who had it, who didn't. It all came from the street. You get a bunch of street guys doing business, and this is the way they do it. It's all about machismo. You have to realize that on the streets of South Central, only the strong survive."

Although Andre didn't grow up in the inner city, he had family who did. He spent a lot of time with them and learned the trials and tribulations of the 'street code.'

"Because he started it all with his money, Eric had the power," Andre continues. "And the way the street works is that occasionally the guy in power gets challenged. There will be some other guy who will say, 'Hey, man! I don't think you've got the power you think you do. You don't have the juice to back it up.'

"That's what Ice Cube did. He challenged Eric. Cube basically said, 'Here I am. Every song that is on both of these records, I wrote. You put your name behind mine, but I'm the one who wrote it. You put your name behind mine because it's your record label. You put your name on the record that says you're executive producer because you started the thing. That's fine. But I want to get paid. I'm not doing this for my health. I want to make money. How can you not pay me – after all I did? I'm the one who made this. If it weren't for my songs, you wouldn't have a record. If it weren't for Dre's music, you wouldn't have a record. If it weren't for your money, we wouldn't have a record. It's a partnership.'

"But instead of Eric saying, 'You're right. I'm going to give you more money,' he felt he couldn't give Ice Cube any more money than what they initially agreed on because it would make Eric look weak. If he gave Ice Cube more money, he would have to give all the other guys more money, too.

"So on one hand, the guys in N.W.A. were incredible entrepreneurs because of what they created and how they created it," Andre sums up. "But when it came down to it, they had too much street in them. It didn't allow them to be the businessmen that, say, Run-D.M.C. or the Fresh Prince could be."

Before the group fell apart, N.W.A. became a microcosm of inner-city life, representing both the good and bad aspects of black urban culture. "N.W.A. had demons to deal with before they could even get down to the business part of things," Andre says. "That was what ruled their lives. None of these guys were married. Some had kids out of wedlock. Some came from single-parent households. Everything that embodied the inner-city black youth was all there, inside that group."

Shortly after the release of *Straight Outta Compton*, Ice Cube exited N.W.A. But the group carried on, recording the lesser *100 Miles and Running* EP in 1990 and *Efil4zaggin* ("Niggaz 4 Life" backwards) in 1991, which entered the charts at No. 1 under the newly implemented SoundScan system.*

In subsequent years, Eazy-E floundered, Andre says. He produced and managed a few acts, but he couldn't recapture N.W.A.'s original magic.

*SoundScan is the computerized system for tracking music sales at midsize to large retail outlets. Before SoundScan, the most credible source for music sales was the Billboard charts, compiled primarily from subjective reports of bribable radio programmers and store managers. The switch to SoundScan was revolutionary. Popular genres like hip-hop, country, heavy metal and R&B scored on the new playing field, especially now that smaller record stores counted in the sales tallies.

16
HEART OF GOLD

Eric Wright/Eazy-E

DESPITE THE DISDAIN ANDRE HOLDS FOR EAZY-E'S STREET-CODE
philosophy, the man is one of the artists Andre remembers most fondly. "Eric Wright was a
good person with a huge heart," he claims. "I was between tours, poor, and our refrigerator
went bad. So there I am with a new wife, new baby and no refrigerator. I did what anyone
who has ever been low on cash does: I went to my employer."

The whole thing played out like a scene from the movies, Andre says. He walked into
Eazy-E's office and found him sitting behind his huge mahogany desk with papers and pictures
scattered on top. The office was equally oversized, making Eazy seem that much smaller.

"What up?" Eazy-E asked, looking up from his paperwork and dropping his pen.

Andre reached over the desk and shook hands with Eazy. He remembers the moment:

"Here is this little man sitting behind this huge desk, and here I am, coming to him like
he's Marlon Brando in *The Godfather*. Eric also had this tendency to suck his teeth, which
really added to the drama of the scene."

Andre said, "I really hate to do this, but I don't know where else to turn. I need to
borrow money to buy a refrigerator.'"

Eazy-E looked at him, and with both palms planted firmly on the desk, he asked, "Well,
how much is this refrigerator you want to buy?"

"It's $1,100."

Eazy paused, sucked his teeth, and gave a long and drawn out, "Wellll ... "

And then in one breath, he asked quickly, "When you gonna pay me back?"

You could tell Eazy was being playful and enjoying the role. Andre smiled a little
before responding.

"The next tour we go out on. I'll pay you back a little bit at a time. Unless I get another tour before then, and then I can pay you back sooner."

Another pause.

"I suppose I could give it to you."

And that was it. In one swift motion, Eazy picked up the phone, called the group's manager and said, "Jerry, Andre is coming to your office. I want you to write him a check for whatever he wants."

"To me, this was another side of Eric Wright that not enough people got to see," Andre says now. "And we still have that refrigerator. I can't bear to part with it."

Shortly thereafter, though, Andre parted ways with the rap world and plunged into the rock 'n' roll circus – an act he would continue for more than ten years.

ROCKERS

17

GOOD GUYS WEAR BLACK

George Thorogood

May 1989: Los Angeles, California

GEORGE THOROGOOD ALWAYS WORE BLACK. THE ONLY THING THAT changed in George's daily wardrobe was sleeve length. That was one of the first things Andre noticed when he shifted his client list from rappers to rockers. "Black proves that George is comfortable with himself and not trying to impress anyone," says Andre, who calls him a "man's man."

When Andre worked at CSC, he developed a great working relationship with a production assistant for Avalon Attractions, a large promoter in Sherman Oaks, California. Mike Donahue, George Thorogood's manager, called Avalon Attractions one day between tours looking for a security person.

With Andre's permission, the production assistant returned the call and made the connection, thus taking Andre to the next level of his career. George and his Destroyers would be an excellent opportunity to expand his contacts. And George's upcoming tour offered a great first step into the rock 'n' roll zoo.

On a typical bright and beautiful California day, Andre strode into the airy and contemporary lobby of the Santa Monica Hotel at precisely 1 p.m. His eyes scanned from left to right. He saw people checking out, two bellhops lazing against their stand and businessmen in suits talking into pay phones. Then he heard a familiar voice and spotted his potential employers sitting on a couple of couches across the lobby.

Although he had never met Donahue, Andre had spoken with him on the phone and knew his voice. And, of course, Andre recognized George Thorogood.

As Andre approached the two men, George immediately stood up. Andre extended his hand and said, "Mr. Thorogood, Andre Augustine. Nice to meet you."

George responded with a huge, toothy grin. "Mr. Augustine, we've heard a lot about you. I'd like you to meet Mike Donahue." Calling Andre "Mr. Augustine" is a formality George continues to this day.

Donahue and Andre shook hands, and then all three men took a seat.

The black leather couches sat opposite one another with a glass coffee table between them. Andre sat on one couch; Donahue and George occupied the other.

"Andre, George's popularity is really picking up," Donahue began quickly. "This is an important tour for us and we want to make certain there aren't any problems." Indeed, after a half-dozen albums in 10 years, George Thorogood and The Destroyers were enjoying a resurgence in their boogie-blues sound and heading out on a United States tour.

"I understand," Andre replied confidently. "There won't be."

"But it's equally important that we have a personality fit," Donahue added.

The band's previous security director, Andre learned, was better suited for Third World military intervention than touring with one of the coolest guitar players on the planet. He treated George's every move as a covert military action. He acted very hush-hush and stern, Andre was told. Jokes and casual conversation were not part of his repertoire. George felt uncomfortable around the security chief, and he didn't want that tension this time.

Donahue spent about 10 minutes explaining the dilemma. And then George took over.

"How long were you with the Jets? What was it like? What position did you play in college? Do you like baseball?"

As the interview in the hotel wore on, George and Donahue took an interest in Andre's previous clients. They also liked the fact that Andre had an athletic background. George and Andre clicked. They shared jokes, and George talked about how he taught himself to play guitar at age 14 and how his early years were spent much like those of real bluesmen, traveling from bar to bar and playing for food or beer money.

Andre discovered that George possessed a laid-back personality that should never be mistaken for apathy. Sometimes, however, George yearned for simpler times. In fact, George has told Andre more than once that he would be just as happy playing again for beer in a bar somewhere, without the pressures of success and money.

But playing bars or arenas wasn't George's first love. Originally, the man born on New Year's Eve 1952 in Wilmington, Delaware, was a minor-league baseball player.

After seeing a performance by bluesman John Paul Hammond, he switched his allegiance to the guitar and in 1973 formed the Delaware Destroyers, who eventually moved to Boston and earned a decent reputation playing originals and cover tunes on the bar circuit there.

The group released its self-titled first album in 1977 and worked its way into consistent FM radio exposure, where George's music remains today. Among his most popular songs are "Bad to the Bone," "Move It On Over," "I Drink Alone" and "Get A Haircut."

Andre got the gig. As he and Donahue took their first limo ride together to pick up George and start the new tour, he perused the itinerary. The plans were to fly from LAX to Florida. Conversation between the two was light and pleasant.

When they arrived at George's house, Donahue instructed Andre to wait in the limo, that he'd be right back. Donahue took a short jog up the stairs and rang the doorbell.

As Andre looked at the beautifully manicured lawn, he couldn't help but think about the difference between this gig and his rap tours. They seemed like worlds apart. Most rap artists he worked with didn't even have lawns.

Andre glanced at his watch. Ten minutes had already passed. He chuckled to himself. The N.W.A. boys would have been out and gone ages ago. Just then, he heard the front door open. Donahue emerged from the house, shaking his head.

"Well, you might as well go home," Donahue told Andre.

"What's up?" asked Andre.

"The deal with the promoter fell through. This one's not going to happen."

Andre was in shock. His first rock 'n' roll tour fell apart before it began. Donahue went back into the house to regroup with George. The driver eased the limo slowly out of the driveway to take Andre home.

"I couldn't believe it," Andre recalls. "There I was, all geared up to go, and no gig. It certainly made me think twice about my decision to move into the rock world."

Fortunately for Andre, his rock 'n' roll partnership with George began shortly thereafter. Unfortunately, Donahue and Andre got off to a rocky start.

Andre's first tour with George was the 1989 Badlands Tour. As with any new working arrangement, there is always a period of adjustment. Learning protocol, personalities, and how and when who likes what done happens over several weeks. But something didn't click this time. Andre had trouble falling into his usual "get along with everyone" pace.

"For some reason, Mike Donahue and I weren't seeing things eye to eye," Andre recalls. "I was new and figured I just didn't know all the nuances of this management team yet."

George noticed something was wrong, too. He asked Andre about it backstage one afternoon. Andre, as always, used the opening to receive feedback regarding his own performance.

"Am I doing everything to your satisfaction, Junior?" Junior is George's nickname reportedly given during his baseball days.

"Of course, Andre. Why? Is something bothering you?"

"Yeah. Mike and I seem to be having a bit of a disagreement regarding how some security issues should be handled."

"Do you work for me?" George asked pointedly.

"Of course I do."

"Well, I only hire the best. So if you're working for me, you must be the best. Mike manages business affairs. You handle security."

Andre remembers that conversation with a smile. "I was blown away. I was flattered, embarrassed, energized, proud ... everything!"

Several minutes later, George was in his dressing room, door open, casually riffing on his guitar. The riffing was typical; the open door was not.

Still carrying his guitar, George suddenly rose and stood in the doorway. He yelled loud enough for everyone to hear.

"Donahue!"

One quick-moving manager appeared seconds later.

"Junior, how's it goin'?"

George pointed at Andre, who tried to act as inconspicuous as possible.

"Donahue, see that man over there?" George pointed with his guitar toward Andre. The manager nodded.

Andre strained to hear the conversation. In a hushed tone, George made it clear who was to do what. "You do the business. He does the security. Leave him alone. Don't bother him. Let him do his job."

"OK, OK. No problem. Whatever you say."

Andre was floored. But the incident made him realize how seriously George took each of his employees. He hired people to perform certain functions, and he didn't want anyone's efforts or authority usurped.

Andre worked with George on several arena and theater tours. Through it all, the guitarist's obsession with baseball never waned.

One October evening in L.A., Andre remembers, George was required to attend a family function. Normally, this would be no big deal for George, as he enjoys spending time with his family. However, there also was a World Series game on TV that George didn't want to miss.

It was a Friday night, and George and his family were going to be dining out. George was familiar with the place and knew the owners would have a TV on in the bar.

To be safe, George sent Andre to the restaurant several days beforehand to give the bartender a significant gratuity to make certain the game would be on during Thorogood's visit. He did. It was.

In addition to watching baseball, George also enjoys a good cigar and a shot or two every now and then.

One night at the Windsor Court Hotel in New Orleans, George and his Destroyers were enjoying a well-deserved night off after a string of particularly hot shows on the Let's Work Together Tour. The rest of the entourage laid low in their hotel rooms, but Andre and George decided to a do a little sightseeing and shopping.

For George Thorogood, the position of security director is as important as that of business manager or accountant. When George is onstage, he gives everything he has. Offstage, he cherishes his privacy. Andre's task is to protect that privacy. Andre's position included now not only concert security, but also personal protection. More importantly Andre and the guitar man were fast becoming good friends.

The owner of the hotel, an avid foxhunter, adorned the lobby and pub areas with ribbons and trophies proving the owner's prowess in the field. An astounding number of original oil paintings depicting the traditional hunt covered every public spot in the hotel – even the restrooms.

"I just can't believe it," George said, as Andre escorted him into an elevator upon their return. "There are so many paintings of this foxhunting gig."

"Yeah, I know what you mean," Andre added.

"Come on. This is a little much. There are three in this elevator. Look at this one with the guys and the hats, and this one where the dogs are chasing the fox. This one has a horse that's out of control. I mean, I can see the guy being into it, but this is a little out of hand. He could have some paintings that might interest someone besides him."

> *Most young security guys working with a big-name artist like George Thorogood would have kept their mouths shut or crawled under the typical "yes-man" rock.*

"Like if you owned a hotel," Andre started.

"What?" George asked.

"Like if you owned a hotel," Andre wisecracked. "The paintings would be of a guy lying around on a couch."

Andre knew George's favorite pastime, other than playing the blues, was hanging out and watching a baseball game on his couch. But no other security director before now had dared to bridge the artist/employee gap with George.

It was a gutsy move, considering to whom the comment was directed. Most young security guys working with a big-name artist like George Thorogood would have kept their mouths shut or crawled under the typical "yes-man" rock. And for a second, Andre didn't know if he said the right thing.

After an uncomfortable (and silent) ride up the elevator Andre walked George to his room. George turned his back to Andre and slid the key in the door. As he turned and looked squarely at Andre, the security director braced himself for a reprimand. George broke out in his trademark ear-to-ear grin.

"Shots and cigars?"

Andre felt a wave of relief wash over him. "Absolutely," he replied quickly. "Ten minutes?"

Andre has enjoyed many such humorous exchanges with the artist he refers to as "the most stand-up guy" in the business – honest, hardworking and trustworthy.

On the Badlands Tour, for example, the band played Chicago and some members wanted to stay overnight and spend the next day in the Windy City. They were scheduled to play a show at Milwaukee's Riverside Theatre the next night.

George, on the other hand, decided that instead of waiting around, he and Andre would rent a car, drive to Milwaukee and relax a bit. It was only 10:30 p.m., and they could reach Brew Town by midnight. While George cleaned up, Andre got the black Lincoln Town Car ready for the journey.

Cruising to Milwaukee at close to 80 mph on Interstate 94, Andre slouched in the driver's seat, leaning over the armrest. George sat in a similar position on the passenger side, soaking up the peaceful luxury.

Suddenly, he looked over at the speedometer and deadpanned, "Uhhh, Mr. Augustine, the speed limit is 65, and you're going pretty fast. Don't you think maybe you should slow down a little bit?"

Andre shot him a look. "Junior, the faster I go, the faster you get there. The faster you get there, the faster we can get to the bar. The faster we get to the bar, the faster you can get that shit in you. The faster you get that shit in you, the faster you can start talking that shit you talk."

There was a pregnant pause. Then both men broke into hysterics.

"It was late and we were tired, so that amplified the laughter," Andre recalls. "People in my position usually don't make that kind of comment to their artist. But George will be the first guy to tell you that one of his favorite things is sitting in the hotel bar, having a few drinks and telling stories."

On some music-industry management teams, security directors and/or road managers are crucial to the success of an artist or act. Andre's security team enabled the early Run-D.M.C. and Public Enemy tours to be booked by guaranteeing promoters no problems associated with violence. For artists like Aerosmith's Steven Tyler and Kiss' Paul Stanley, proper security is essential for daily existence.

In addition to working with artists when on tour, Andre also works with them when they're off the road. He may be asked to provide his services on the set of a video shoot, accompany the artist to an awards show or drive someone to the health club.

In the early Nineties, George Thorogood wanted Andre to act as a daily escort. Even though they were at home, George's popularity demanded Andre be by his side. Part of these duties included accompanying George to the gym, to The Source for lunch and to the rehearsal studio for a little guitar workout.

Andre also served as communications liaison. George does not accept business calls at home. During that time, if someone wanted to speak with George when he wasn't touring, they called Andre.

Donahue lived in West Virginia while managing George, so most business was conducted over the phone. To get in touch with George, Donahue actually had to call Andre. Imagine the artist's manager needing to go through the security director to talk to his client. This is just one excellent example of the importance that some artists place on Andre's position.

But Andre's position was never more important than on the concert stage, physically protecting his artists.

18

YOU REALLY *CAN* SCARE SOMEONE THAT MUCH

George Thorogood

OVER THE YEARS, ANDRE'S ASSIGNMENTS HAVE VARIED. ON ANY given tour, he might oversee venue security, the band's protection or logistics. When working with the Delaware Destroyers his objective was simple: protect George Thorogood.

Before Andre goes on tour with an artist or celebrity, he usually gives them some tips and techniques about how to respond to threatening situations. Tip number one: if a person makes it onto the stage, keep eye contact, start backing away and put as much distance between you and the person as possible. It gives Andre time to get between the fan and the artist. The second piece of advice is to remain calm and not make any sudden moves or do anything unusual. This minimizes the variables. Andre then can concentrate on the actions of the offender rather than try to be aware of what the artist is doing.

As Andre continued to work with George, they played many places. One night, the venue boasted a huge fixed stage. Constructed with heavy wood and an ornate design, the stage was solid as a rock, but also more than 100 feet wide and unusually deep. Heavy black stage curtains draped both sides. It seemed more suited to a 1930s theatrical production than a George Thorogood concert.

Andre doesn't remember the city, but he remembers the setup. "It was just a dangerous situation," he says. "The stage was so wide that there was no way to protect all areas very well. Adding to the complexity were steep drop-offs all around the front and the sides of the stage. And this place got dark. When the house lights went down, you couldn't see a thing. Moving around was unusually tricky."

Three songs into the show, George addressed the crowd. He sounded like an auctioneer.

"Hell, yes, we're here! We're gonna try and throw a rock and roll program tonight, ladies and gentlemen, for your enjoyment, one like you've never seen before and one like you ain't going to see after tonight. Cause we're gonna do some funny things ... Some dirty things ... And some bad things ...

With that George and his Destroyers tore into their next song.

Seconds into it, a fan leapt onstage and headed for George. Andre clicked into action. From linebacker's set position, he launched out from the side of the stage. His mind slipped into slow motion as if reliving a football play. Hut one. Hut two. Hike! His body instinctively responded to the threat. His muscles acted out the fluid motions of a decade on the football field. Andre felt the switch into the brute-like mind–set necessary for survival in the NFL.

'I can't believe you're up on my stage ... When I get you outside of this door, I'm gonna kick your ass.'"

On this night, George did exactly as instructed. He saw the jumper and kept his cool. George stepped away from the front of the stage and started walking backwards, making no sudden moves. He just kept playing, walking backwards and never losing eye contact with the guy.

When Andre got to him, the fan was three feet from George. Andre threw his whole body between George and the fan, quickly grabbed the offender around the waist and gripped his belt.

"Uuuugggh" groaned the jumper, as the air quickly left his lungs as Andre hit him.

The stage jumper was a small guy, about 135 pounds and in his mid-30s. Smelling of sweat and alcohol, he went limp as Andre grabbed him. Recovering from the hit, he waved to George and the crowd as Andre turned him around and started walking towards the exit sign.

Maybe because it was early in Andre's career, or maybe because George Thorogood was the first artist Andre had worked with after the violent rap tours, or maybe it was because rap tours require a different mind-set. Regardless, Andre was sporting a nasty attitude that night.

Andre laughs as he remembers the scene. "I grabbed this guy by the waist and started walking him off the stage to the exit door. What can I say? I was in intimidation mode. I started whispering in this guy's ear, 'I can't believe you're up on my stage ... making me look bad in front of my artist. When I get you outside of this door, I'm gonna kick your ass.'"

Because of the wide stage, Andre and the jumper enjoyed an unusually long time to "chat." At the backstage exit, Andre kicked open the door and gave the fan a gentle push on the back, moving him outside the door. As if switching a television channel, Andre changed his demeanor. "Good evening, sir. I hope you had a nice time tonight," Andre said, smiling pleasantly. "But we have to say good-bye now."

The man spun around, shoulders squared. Andre thought he was about to get attacked. Then the look in the fan's eyes changed from anger to bewilderment. He started to stammer, then stopped and looked down at himself.

Once cocky and arrogant, the jumper, who had endangered himself and others, was drenched from the waist down!

Andre shook his head and closed the door, leaving the embarrassed fan outside. On the way back to his post, he chuckled and thought, *I guess you really can scare someone that much!*

Andre loved the time he spent during those early years on tour with George Thorogood. But all good things must come to an end. While Andre occasionally still works for George today, in 1989 he was ready to take the next step.

19

AERO-FORCE ANDRE

Aerosmith

May 1989: Phoenix, Arizona

ANDRE FOUND HIS WAY INTO THE AEROSMITH CAMP, STRANGELY enough, through the world of rap. (Similarly, Aerosmith found its way back into the public eye when Run-D.M.C. covered "Walk this Way" in 1986 and asked Steven Tyler and Joe Perry to appear in the video.)

When Andre traveled to Europe with Run-D.M.C. and Public Enemy in 1988, the tour accountant was a man named Jeff Krump. He was, in Andre's words, "a white guy traveling in a sea of darkness." Krump lived in Denver and was also the accountant on Aerosmith's 1987-88 Permanent Vacation Tour.

"We got to be friendly and started talking about each other's backgrounds," Andre recalls about the days the two spent with Run-D.M.C. and Public Enemy. "Jeff commented to me that he liked my personality and the way I handled my end of the business. It was early in my career, and not wanting to miss a chance at more work, I said, 'Well, keep me in mind when the next Aerosmith tour comes around. I'd love to work with some really big acts.'"

When the Run-D.M.C. and Public Enemy tour of Europe ended, Andre and Krump exchanged telephone numbers, and Andre called Krump every couple of months to touch base. During one of those phone calls, Krump asked Andre if he would be in Phoenix anytime in the near future.

Andre, working with George Thorogood at the time, quickly reviewed the tour dates. He was, in fact, going to be in Phoenix in a month. Krump gave Andre the phone number of Bob Dowd, Aerosmith's tour manager.

Andre and Dowd met for lunch in Phoenix, and everything appeared to go well. Dowd, an intense ex-cop, also had an athletic background. A strict disciplinarian in the way he ran his crews and tours, Dowd liked Andre's personality, his attitude and the way he presented himself. Coupled with the fact that Andre came highly recommended by Krump, Dowd figured he had found Aerosmith's next venue security director.

Dowd began his rock 'n' roll career as a security guy, working with Billy Idol and other artists in the Eighties. But drinking problems soon interfered, Andre says.

When longtime Aerosmith manager Tim Collins pegged Dowd to helm the Pump Tour, he also brought him into the group's 12-step program and set him on the road to recovery.

"Bob Dowd would have gone to the ends of the earth for Tim Collins. Bob felt indebted to him for all that Tim did for Bob personally and professionally," Andre says.

Dowd soon became seduced by the rock 'n' roll lifestyle, Andre contends. The title of tour manager for Aerosmith and the power and money that goes with it sucked Dowd in, and Andre learned to never let himself get caught up in that whirl.

This was difficult to do at the time, considering that for Andre, Aerosmith's 1989-90 Pump Tour was a gigantic career leap. He wanted to work with some big names, and Aerosmith was as big as they come. Fresh off a tour with Guns N' Roses for an opening act, Aerosmith was hot again after spending roughly a decade in the ruts, due to a black hole of drugs and alcohol, infighting and record-label disputes. *Pump,* Aerosmith's 1989 major comeback record, stayed on the *Billboard* charts for 110 weeks, peaked at No. 5 and sold more than 7 million copies.

Andre was about to latch onto a rocket, and he owed it to Dowd, who Andre says gave him a renewed sense of discipline and dedication to his craft.

If Dowd had made up his mind about Andre's future that day in Phoenix, though, he forgot to tell Andre. Lunch went beyond Andre's expectations, but there was no confirmation of a position. The security man left excited, but nervous.

"I didn't know if I had the gig or not," Andre remembers. "A couple of months later, I got a call from Bob saying that Aerosmith was in Los Angeles, shooting a video. He invited me to come down, meet the guys and hang out for the day."

The video shoot Andre attended was for the second single from *Pump,* "Janie's Got a Gun," which was released in November 1989 and rose to No. 4 on the *Billboard* charts in early 1990. The video, directed by David Fincher (*Aliens*), quickly became one of the most requested clips in MTV's history.

As Andre entered the East Los Angeles production facility, he was in awe for the first time in his career. Everything was enormous. People occupied all corners, conducting business or just talking. Lighting equipment, camera crews and technicians scurried about. The set loomed large. Everything moved very quickly.

Andre made his way through security checkpoints and wandered out among tall scaffolding, past neatly aligned talent trailers and in front of the catering truck. This is the big time, Andre thought.

"I'm looking around, and everything is chaos, but controlled chaos," Andre says. "I remember thinking that this band is larger than life. This wasn't a couple of kids trying to put together a tour. This was big business."

Dowd noticed Andre, walked over to him, shook his hand and handed him an itinerary.

"Here's the schedule," he said sternly. "We'll need to head out at the end of the month. We are going to start in Charleston, West Virginia, work through the eastern corridor and take our first break in the Northeast. That way, we can get the guys home to Boston for a few days."

"Gotcha," Andre replied obediently, realizing that he apparently had the job.

No exchange of pleasantries, just quick and definitive words. Andre liked that.

Dowd ran down the rest of the tour, identifying starting points, breaks and other cities. Then Andre, who would be traveling with Aerosmith as venue security director, met the band.

20

DEMON A SCREAMIN'

Steven Tyler

"I CAN'T BELIEVE YOU'RE BRINGING THIS STUFF UP RIGHT NOW!"
Steven shouted.

Andre quickly recognized the thin, flamboyant figure with long hair coming towards him as Aerosmith's legendary vocalist Steven Tyler. Born Steven Victor Tallarico in Yonkers, New York, in 1948, the lanky lead singer walked quickly. His sinewy, 140-pound frame moved easily, his brown hair the perfect rock 'n' roll complement to his flamed "Ma Kin" tattoo on his left arm. Steven's brown eyes flashed wildly.

"Steven, you know we have to talk about this," Collins huffed in a nagging tone, puffing as he tried to keep pace with Steven's giant strides.

"Look, man, this is the biggest video of our careers, and you want to talk about this now? You are *unbelievable!*" Steven railed.

As the two approached, Dowd stepped forward. "Steven, I'd like you to meet Andre Augustine. He's going to be in charge of building security on the tour."

Steven and Collins momentarily stopped their walking and bickering. Steven shook Andre's hand. "Hey, how ya doin'?" Steven smiled for an instant and then, turning to Collins, said, "I can't talk to you right now." Steven stormed off and headed to the wardrobe trailer to check out clothes for the next take.

Collins, looking kind of dazed, shrugged his shoulders, turned and left Dowd and Andre without saying a word.

"So that's Steven?" Andre asked, turning to Dowd.

Dowd just smiled.

As Andre rose in the Aerosmith organization, he eventually became the band's personal security director, traveling with its members at all times. This closeness gave him a unique relationship with all the guys, which he shares to this day. But he spent (and still spends) the most time with Steven.

"Everything with Steven is an adventure." Andre says. "Just riding to the arena from the airport is an experience in 110 percent Tyler."

Andre remembers his first such trip. The private jet had just landed at Dallas/Fort Worth International Airport in Texas. Andre enjoyed the flight from Boston, and the guys were relaxed, joking and giving their egos a break.

The plane hit the tarmac and stopped in front of three waiting Lincoln Town Cars. The door opened and the steps folded out. Andre grabbed Steven's gig bag with all of the singer's personal belongings in it and was the first passenger to disembark.

As the other band members left the plane, Andre noticed them milling around, trying to look busy. "I felt something was going on," he says. "But, hey, I was the new guy. So I didn't want to say anything."

Steven, modestly decked out in an untucked tan henley and black jeans, was last off the plane. Andre pointed to the lead Town Car, and Steven nodded in approval, making his way quickly toward it. Andre opened the door for the singer and handed him his gig bag as Steven slid into the front passenger seat. Then he jogged around the front of the car and popped behind the wheel.

"Just riding to the arena from the airport is an experience in 110 percent Tyler."

"It was like a game of musical chairs, and the music had just stopped." Andre remembers. "The moment the other guys saw that Steven had chosen a car, they all scrambled to get in a car – any car that wasn't carrying Steven."

Immediately, Steven started digging frantically in his bag. Almost simultaneously, he turned on the air conditioning full blast and powered down all the windows. He found the cassette he was looking for, popped it in the tape player and cranked the volume. All this activity occurred before Andre had shifted the car into gear.

With the music blaring and the windows down, Steven sang, tapped his hands, moved to the beat and gabbed constantly.

Andre and Steven were rockin' 'n' rollin' at a stoplight when the second Town Car pulled up next to them. Andre felt this was a little strange, as typically the cars remain in a single-file caravan. Andre shot a look over his shoulder, and out of the corner of his eye he caught the rear window of the other Lincoln rolling down, revealing a hysterical Tom Hamilton and Joey Kramer, laughing and pointing. Andre could see them mouthing the words, "You got him now pal."

Andre knew he'd been had. "Its not that they don't like Steven, they do – very much," Andre says about the rest of Aerosmith. "But before a show, the others don't want too much activity going on. They just want to relax. When you are in a car with the other guys, there is no music. Just turn on the air. Nobody talks. It's completely the opposite of being with Steven. Steven is supercharged and outgoing. He is constantly trying to make you laugh, messing with your ears and tickling you. Steven is a fun person, but he's just out there."

Video director Michael Bay, who directed the 1998 film *Armageddon* and the "Falling in Love (Is Hard on the Knees)" clip from 1997's *Nine Lives* disc, told *Spin* magazine in May 1997, "With someone like Steven, you put the camera on him and you just say, 'Wow.'"

Andre remembers another classic pre-show Steven moment that made him say, "Wow."

"We were getting ready for a show on the East Coast and the group had a band meeting beforehand that, from all indications, did not go the way the group wanted it to go, and it *really* did not go the way Steven wanted it to go," Andre remembers. "He came into the hallway from the meeting room totally pissed off. He stormed past me and made his way to his private dressing room."

Steven always has a private dressing room because the rest of Aerosmith prefers not to be in the same room with him prior to curtain. The crew adds some personal touches to the area – wall coverings, tapestries, anything to lighten the usually drab cement block walls. They even lay an Oriental carpet. The best way to describe Steven's dressing room, Andre says, is "early-American hippie."

Before a show, Steven warms up his voice, blows a fan on himself and plays loud music. None of the others want to experience that scene, but Steven has to have chaos around him all the time, Andre claims. That's when Steven is most comfortable.

But this time, no music played as Andre approached Steven's private quarters.

"Steven, what's wrong?" Andre asked, following him into the dressing room. "What's going on?"

"Nothing. Nothing's goin' on, man!" Steven threw a towel across the dressing room and sat down in disgust on a banged-up metal folding chair.

Andre, not satisfied, continued to prod. "Was it something I did or something I said? Is there something extra that you need from me?"

Steven looked up and his eyes flashed wildly at Andre. "Yeah. As a matter of fact, there is something."

He stood up, turned his back to Andre and started rifling through his gig bag. Andre, rethinking his decision to enter Steven's dressing room, suddenly felt like disappearing.

Steven continued, "There's something about you that has really been pissing me off lately, that I don't like. I don't like it at all."

Andre felt the blood drain from his face.

Steven whipped around. His elastic face contorted into a menacing sneer, and he brought his right hand within inches of Andre's face.

"You don't smile enough, man!" Steven turned his hand to reveal a gag set of chattering teeth. "Smile, man!"

Steven then grabbed Andre by the shoulders, hugged him and said, "Thanks a lot for asking what was wrong. It's got nothin' to do with you. But I really appreciate you caring enough to come in here, seeing that I'm upset and asking me. And feeling that you *can* ask me." He kissed Andre on the cheek and said, "Thanks a lot." Then he sat down and went about getting ready for the show.

Steven can also be tough. *Walk this Way*, the 1997 Aerosmith autobiography written with Stephen Davis, documents his serious side. Megadeth opened several shows for Aerosmith on the 1993-94 Get A Grip Tour – until Tyler heard the band's lead singer and spokesman, Dave Mustaine, bad-mouthing the group during a radio interview.

"Yeah, we think we oughta be headlining, but we don't mind because everyone knows this is Aerosmith's last hurrah," Mustaine is quoted as saying. To which Steven replied, "Dave we'd like to help you out. Which way did you come in?" Megadeth was fired from the Get A Grip Tour on June 17, 1994, in Houston.

When not touring together, Steven and Andre chat regularly. Steven often calls during the holidays and checks in on the family.

For those reasons alone, Steven Tyler tops Andre's "Good People List." Steven is outgoing, personable, funny, entertaining and compassionate. "It may sound corny, Andre says, but the singer takes care of the people he loves. He has an amazing ability to lift your spirits at just the moment when you think you can't handle another day in the music business."

Perhaps Andre's wife, Heather, sums it up best when she says, "Thank God for Steven Tyler."

21
THE LESS INTERESTING 3

Joey Kramer, Tom Hamilton & Brad Whitford

"I THINK THOSE THREE FELT THAT IF THEY WERE REPLACED, NO one would really miss them," Andre says. "But that, of course, isn't the truth. They add a crucial dynamic to the band. It just wouldn't be Aerosmith without them."

"Those three" are drummer Joey Kramer, bassist Tom Hamilton and guitarist Brad Whitford. Together, according to *Walk This Way*, they comprise the self-titled "Less Interesting 3," or "LI3" for short.

Because much of the media's focus on Aerosmith is heaped on flamboyant Steven Tyler and brooding Joe Perry, the other band members don't get as much attention from the fans or the press.

"When we first met on the set, we spoke briefly, but he was very genuine." Andre says about Joey. "I found out that Joey is a little guy [5 foot, 6 inches tall] with a huge personality. But the public doesn't get a chance to see it much. I mean, he's not like Tommy Lee from Mötley Crüe. He's just not that kind of rock 'n' roll drummer. He's not really into all the fame and celebrity. He and I would hang out, eat lunch and talk about football and the old days – just like buddies. He was real easy to talk to and real easy to get along with. And he was always considerate. Joey would always check to make sure Steven didn't need me before he and I would ever do anything."

Andre describes Tom as "aristocratic, and one of the nicest guys you'd ever want to meet." Standing at slightly taller than 6 feet and sporting a tuft of blond hair, he is the tallest member of Aerosmith. A little-known fact is that Tom comes from a military family and his mother's side owns the gun manufacturer, Sturm-Ruger.

The third component of the LI3 is Brad Whitford. Checking in at about 5 feet, 7 inches tall and a slight 126 pounds, Brad goes his own way – literally. "Brad is a great guy who likes fast cars and cool leather jackets," Andre says. "The most challenging thing for me was to get him to the 'meet and greets.'"

Meet and greets gather special guests to meet the band, obtain autographs and take pictures. Typically, they are winners in a promotional contest sponsored by a radio station or music store, and they are usually limited to less than 100 people.

One of Andre's roles with Aerosmith included gathering and escorting Aerosmith to the pre-concert event and making sure it went according to plan from a security perspective.

"Come on, guys, it's time to go," Andre prompted during a routine meet–and–greet drill on the 1993-94 Get A Grip Tour.

It usually took Andre 15 or 20 minutes just to gather everyone, and tonight was no exception. Joe and Brad were warming up with their guitars, Joey was eating, Tom was flipping through a magazine, and Steven – well, he was just being Steven. Finally, after he rounded up the band, Andre moved the group towards the appointed room.

"Where is it?" bassist Tom Hamilton asked, inquiring about the meet and greet's location. Meet and greets are usually held in whatever room is available. Andre pointed past a catering area and led Aerosmith into the room.

As Aerosmith entered, the dynamic in the room shifted, as usual. Like air rushing in to fill a vacuum, fans moved immediately toward the group. Everyone smiled, shaking hands as the flashes from small 35mm cameras lit the room. Andre looked around. Everything was going according to plan.

Almost.

"Where's Brad?" Andre asked Tom in a voice loud enough to be heard over the noise in the room. Tom was about six feet away, signing a fan's *Get A Grip* CD. He looked up and shrugged his shoulders.

Andre rolled his eyes and wandered toward the door. This routine was all-too-familiar to him. He scanned the room, making sure the four present members would be OK. Then he exited quickly to find Brad.

"Brad! What are you doing?"

Standing at the side of the stage, talking equipment with his tech, Brad had gotten sidetracked on his 100-yard journey to the meet and greet. He shot an "I'm caught" glance at Andre and quickly ended the conversation with his tech.

Brad didn't intend to blow off the meet and greet, Andre says. He just sees something or someone and gets distracted. It could be his tech, the lighting director, the sound engineer, personal friends who are visiting or a phone in the production office that triggers a reminder to make a call.

Other than getting lost on the way to meet and greets, Brad is the consummate professional, Andre contends. "Subconsciously, he might have been thinking, 'I can go over here and do this for a bit, and they really won't miss me.'"

But Brad and the other members of the LI3 would most certainly be missed.

Joe Perry sums it up best in *Walk This Way*, by saying that when he left Aerosmith and formed the Joe Perry Project in the fall of 1980, "the only thing I really missed was Brad Whitford, my consummate string-bending comrade-in-arms. We had built up a certain chemistry that couldn't be replaced. I was shocked to realize that being the only guitar player onstage meant I couldn't afford to have any off nights. Brad had backed me up and made me look good all those years."

TOM HAMILTON'S HANDWRITTEN SPEECH FOR A RARE AEROSMITH APPEARANCE AT A POLITICAL EVENT.

Hi, I'm Tom Hamilton, I'm HERE ON BEHALF OF A GREAT MASSACHUSETTS Institution REPRESENTING GREAT WEALTH, POWER AND INFLUENCE DESPITE years of Personal Tragedy ... BUT Enough ABOUT Aerosmith.
- We HAVE A Song CALLED LIVIN on THE EDGE That's about Some of the crazy things going on in the world TODAY.
- A Lot of people who have heard it ask us If we're becoming a political band.
- We're not real political, but when we tour, we watch a lot of CNN and we see things that bother us a lot.
- we see a lot of crime and people trying to figure out How to deal with it.
- we see ignorance and not enough support for education.
- we see a lot of separation when what we need in this country is a Sense of Community.
- we see fear and Hatred being used by the far right to justify Censorship and that's something that affects us very deeply.
- In times like these, massachusetts needs a powerful representative in washington.
- we already have one - Let's keep it that way.
- Elections, like life, are about choices.
- we see only one choice
- LADIES AND Gentlemen, put your hands hands together for mr. TED Kennedy.

22
BOSTON'S BADDEST

Joe Perry

JOE PERRY AND BRAD WHITFORD, GUITARS STRAPPED OVER THEIR
shoulders, were working out a particularly challenging section of a song as Andre
approached with Bob Dowd that June 1989 day at the "Janie's Got a Gun" video shoot. As
soon as Joe saw them coming, he put down his guitar and came forward to exchange hellos.
"We've heard a lot about you," he told Andre. "It's nice to meet you."

Andre, a little taken aback by the fact that Joe Perry actually knew something about him,
remained cool as he introduced himself to Brad.

Joe Perry is the quintessential rock star. His long black hair, lean physique and brooding
stage presence adds to his image. When Steven Tyler introduces "Joe Motherfuckin' Perry" to
a concert crowd, he does so with the utmost respect and admiration. Joe is "cool"
personified – both on and off the stage.

"Joe is really into his family," Andre says. "He has several children whom he cares for
very much, and his wife, Billie, is terrific."

It didn't take long after his initial meeting with Joe on the set of "Janie's Got a Gun" for
Andre to learn a lot more about him.

Living outside of Boston, Joe has a great piece of property and a huge collection of
guitars. Free of past vices, he now spends a good portion of his downtime taking care of his
health by eating right and working out. He also insists on working out while on the road,
which occasionally poses some challenges.

Take one experience on the Get A Grip Tour.

"Do you know of a place where we can work out?" Andre asked the bellhop one
morning during a day off from the Eastern Bloc leg of the wildly successful tour. Not many

Czechs spoke English, and those who did weren't fluent. Andre tried to add a little nonverbal communication by moving his arms like he was doing dumbbell curls. "You know, exercise."

Finally, one bellman understood, nodded his head excitedly and ran outside to hail a taxi.

"Did you find a place?" Joe asked upon meeting up with Andre, his Boston accent still heavy after all these years.

"Yeah, a place called Coco's," Andre responded.

Joe had become very sophisticated with his workouts and required more equipment than can be found in the typical run-down hotel fitness center. Andre, an ex-professional athlete, understood and appreciated his needs.

The decrepit four-door sedan was just barely big enough for Joe and Andre. Because the cab driver appeared to know very little English, Andre showed him a slip of paper the bellman had given Andre with the name and location of Coco's on it, and the driver responded positively.

"OK. No problem."

Andre started to relax. He felt better knowing the cab driver had everything under control. When you're taking care of a guitar god like Joe Perry, you sweat the small stuff.

"It'll be about 10, 15 minutes, Joe," he said.

"Cool."

The desk clerk had approximated the time. Andre, who knows his way around just about any city in the United States, was out of his element and relying on someone else to get him around. It was an uncomfortable feeling.

Twenty minutes passed, and the landscape turned more and more remote.

"How much further?" he asked the driver.

"OK. No problem."

A sinking feeling came over Andre. The cab driver definitely knew a little English – apparently those three words.

"Yeah, that's fine, but how much longer?" Andre, relying once again on nonverbal communication, pointed to his watch.

"OK. NO PROBLEM!" The driver, obviously agitated, shouted at him.

"Maybe we should just go back," Joe suggested.

"It'll just be a little longer," Andre looked at Joe for a few seconds and then turned back to the driver. "Do you know how to get to Coco's?"

The driver threw up his hands and started driving faster. Apparently, Andre's tapping on his watch had an effect. Andre and Joe exchanged nervous glances. Now they were way out of town.

"Come on, Andre, let's just go back to the hotel," Joe urged.

"It's already 10 o'clock. If we go back now, we won't in get a workout." The trip had become more like a quest for Andre. "He's got the street and the name. We'll get there."

Finally the car came to a stop. The place looked like an old bombed-out building. Weeds grew around the front door and throughout the yard.

"Hmmm," Andre said, making his first impression known. Joe looked at him suspiciously.

Andre sat up and tapped the driver on the shoulder. Trying to overcome the communication gap, Andre smiled broadly. The driver, proud he had accomplished his task, smiled back.

"If you would please wait here, we are going to check things out and be right back. Please wait here."

"OK. No problem."

"Joe," Andre instructed. "You wait here with the car and I'll go take a look."

Entering the gym, Andre found the usual – some cardiovascular equipment, free weights and the cabled machines Joe required. He spun around and returned to the car.

"This'll do," Andre reported to Joe.

Joe snatched his bag and started toward the gym. Andre stuck his head in the rolled-down passenger-side window and settled up with the driver.

"Now please wait here. We will be done in an hour. We will pay you for your time to wait here for us." Andre once again referred to his watch and his wallet, hoping those two elements would help get across the message. Fearing they would never get another cab, Andre didn't want to lose this one.

"OK. No problem."

Andre quickly caught up with Joe in time to hold the door open for him. As Joe entered, Andre turned and saw the little car rev its engine, pull a 180-degree U-turn and head quickly back towards town.

OK, Andre thought. *No problem.*

As he and Joe entered the gym, they looked around to gather their bearings. Within seconds, Coco, the owner, recognized the famous rocker and gave Andre and Joe a tour of the facility. Coco spoke English fairly well.

The big, open room looked like any health club in the United States, just older. There they found weight machines, free weights, a couple of treadmills and a few rowing machines. The clientele, although small in numbers, were of all shapes and sizes.

Nothing out of the ordinary, Andre thought. *But much better than the hotel's facility.*

Then Coco revealed a devilish grin. "Now see real gym."

Andre and Joe looked at each other curiously. Coco moved quickly through a passageway, and the two Americans followed close behind. It was as if they entered Oz.

The three men entered what appeared to be an entirely different facility, and the customers were huge. "These guys made me look small," the 6-foot, 300-pound security guard recalls. "There were about 20 world-class bodybuilders and weight lifters going through their routines."

"Well Joe, you wanted a place to work out," Andre laughed.

As it turns out, the facility was the Olympic training center for Czechoslovakia's athletes, and Coco is a world-renowned trainer. Who would have thought? But working out alongside of these monsters didn't affect Joe. In fact, few things do.

Except, perhaps, a small boy in South America.

Moving through an open section of the airport in Argentina in January 1994, Aerosmith was smothered in a thick crowd of rabid fans clamoring to get the band's attention, Andre remembers. He kept careful watch, making sure nothing got out of hand.

A young boy, about 11 or 12, broke free from the throng and headed straight for Joe. Andre started to cut him off, but something stopped him. After all, Andre has sons of his own.

"Joe! Joe!" the boy shouted. He ran up to the guitar legend, threw his arms around him, and gave him a huge hug and a big kiss on the cheek.

"Joe isn't one to get flustered, but I think that shocked even him," Andre says.

Joe hugged the child back, perhaps a little uncomfortable with the public display of affection. Andre smiled. It was satisfying to see that kind of fan and artist interaction. After the incident, Andre quickly showed Joe the way to a waiting limo. That moment encapsulated just one of the things Andre likes about Joe: compassion.

Back on the set of the "Janie's Got a Gun" video shoot, Andre, not wanting to wear out his welcome, only hung around for a couple of hours. Later, he would go on to spend a lot of time on the sets of Aerosmith videos and can even be seen taking Joey Kramer out of a box in "The Other Side." Andre also clowns around on the production set for "Amazing" on the long-form home video *Big Ones (You Can Look At)*.

"I was pretty excited," he remembers about joining the Aerosmith camp. "It would be a huge career move, but I was cautious. Bob never said, 'You're hired,' so I didn't know if it was a done deal or not. But I never had someone share so much information with me like that and not ask me to go out on the road. So I felt pretty confident that I would working with Aerosmith."

And go on the road he did – on some of Aerosmith's biggest tours and biggest gigs. He even experienced the privilege of working with the band as they stormed the concert stage at Europe's most prestigious show. Twice.

32

AEROSMITH STORMS THE CASTLE

August 18, 1990: Donnington, England

"LOOK OUT!" ANDRE YELLED TO BOB DOWD VIA THE HEADSETS. "Here comes another one."

The plastic bottle landed on the left side of the stage, spinning, foaming and spilling its contents, before finally coming to rest by a mic stand. Another crew member ran out and kicked it off the stage.

"This is nuts," Dowd shouted back, as two more bottles hit the stage. "What's in those things?"

Andre and Dowd scrutinized the bottles and their contents from their pre-show perch on the side of the stage. Then they looked at each other, disgusted.

"Aw, man! We're going to have to dodge these all day," Andre complained.

The band:	Aerosmith
The place:	Donnington, England
The event:	Monsters of Rock
The date:	August 18, 1990
The bottles:	You don't want to know

More than 70,000 sweaty, smelly and drunk rock fans crowded into an area not much larger than an American football field turned on its side. With crowds that large, there are many security and logistical considerations – chiefly, rest room facilities.

"The kids bring plastic bottles and jugs filled with either water or some kind of booze," Andre explains. "They watch the show, drink their jugs, and the next thing they know, they have to take a leak."

He shrugs his shoulders. "What are they gonna do? Say to the person next to them, 'Excuse me, could you save my spot in this ocean of people while I go to the men's room?' No way! They drink their jug, and when it's empty – they fill it. And then they launch it toward the stage." Not one of Andre's most-treasured memories. And there were other much more painful memories of Donnington.

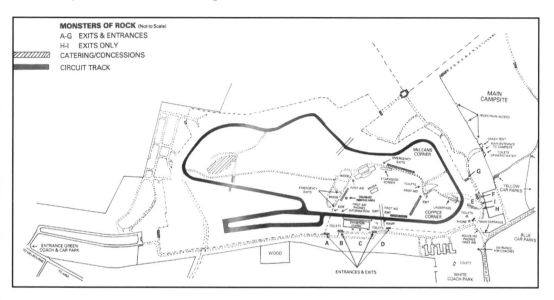

The annual festival suffered two fatalities in 1988 after two fans – Alan Dick, 18, and Landon Siggers, 20 – were crushed by the unusually large crowd of 107,000 during a set by Guns N' Roses.

Monsters of Rock took a year off in 1989 to ensure preventive measures against any more tragedies. Officials raised the height of the stage to 18 feet so more fans could see better, and they moved the stage back 42 feet from the audience.

The program for 1990's Monsters of Rock echoed the cautionary tone of the day:

> Welcome to the 10th Monsters of Rock. As you are possibly aware there was not a Monsters of Rock in 1989. Our thoughts must go back to the tragic accident in 1988, which resulted in the deaths of two young men, Alan Dick and Landon Peter Siggers and the serious injuries suffered by Gary Dobson. We have always considered Monsters of Rock to be a good day of music and fun. We want everyone to have a good day and go home safely. Please make a note of the

medical points around the arena. If you see someone who needs help please assist them. We have installed a large screen to the right of the stage and all of the bands will be shown on this screen. The stage is 7 feet higher than in previous years. There is plenty of space for everyone. If you are in front of the stage do not push the person in front of you. If you need help catch the attention of the security in front of the stage. They are there to help you.

Andre would be in a tough spot that day. Not only did he have to protect Aerosmith, he had to keep a close eye on the crowd and dodge flying jugs filled with urine.

And jugs weren't all that was flying.

The primitive backstage area at 1990's Monsters of Rock festival wound its way through a series of tents and trailers. The square compound had one side entrance. Equipped with running water and catering, the three trailers for Aerosmith were far from luxurious.

The sky, typical for an English summer day, looked a burnt shade of gray. A van dropped off Aerosmith at the compound's front gate, and Andre checked in the group and led the band members to their trailers. As usual, he walked with Steven.

The bill that day included Whitesnake as the headliners, preceded by Aerosmith, Poison, The Quireboys and Thunder. Steven wasn't too pleased with the lineup.

"Seven million records, and I feel like we're an opening band." Steven complained, commenting on sales of the band's latest album at the time, *Pump*, which would go on to sell more than 8 million copies.

"Hardly seems fair," Andre agreed.

Although Whitesnake enjoyed huge popularity in Europe, the band – since 1988, at least – couldn't even get arrested in the states. Whitesnake's stay on the U.S. charts with its breakthrough 1987 self-titled album was brief, and by the time the band released its next record, *Slip of the Tongue*, U.S. music consumers had moved on to more exciting music.

Aerosmith on the other hand was considered rock royalty in the United States — with more than 28 million album sales to the band's credit, a Grammy Award for "Janie's Got a Gun," and appearances on numerous awards shows and magazine covers.

Additionally, Aerosmith's years of non-stop touring built up a U.S. fan base that became the envy of almost every other band. But Europe is different – radio formats, the club scene, music videos, music marketing, and the music business in general is different.

For Aerosmith, not garnering the same status in England and the rest of Europe as the band did in the United States was bothersome. Frustrated, Steven and company reluctantly agreed to play Monsters of Rock as the semi-headlining act.

By contrast, David Coverdale, Whitesnake's lead singer, seemed thrilled to play the festival.

"Donnington? Well, what can I say? It's the big one, isn't it?" he is quoted in the event's program. "It's not that the other Monsters of Rock shows aren't as important to me as Donnington. Of course, they are, or I wouldn't be there doing them. But Donnington means Britain. And Britain still means home to me, believe it or not. And that makes playing there always just a little bit special."

Steven didn't share the same feelings, and as Coverdale approached Andre and Steven to pass them on their way to Aerosmith's trailers, the animosity took root immediately.

Coverdale glanced over at Steven and nodded warily.

"Hey, how ya doin'?" Steven said without breaking his stride and in an uncharacteristic monotone.

With Coverdale out of earshot, Steven muttered to himself, "Fuckin' joke."

Andre kept quiet. The lead singer shook his head.

Steven's desire to prove to England that Aerosmith was a force to be reckoned with showed through on the stage that night. The band played a pulverizing set that some critics claimed upstaged Whitesnake. Local boy and former Led Zeppelin guitarist Jimmy Page even hopped onstage to join the band for a memorable rendition of "Train Kept A Rollin."

Steven reportedly rated the show FG: Fuckin' Great.

Just four short years later, on a chilly and rainy April day, Aerosmith returned to Europe with another best-selling album, *Get A Grip*, and a headlining slot at the Monsters of Rock. The band's popularity was finally catching on throughout Europe – after 20 years of playing.

It's not unusual for artists to harbor feelings of animosity or resentment towards each other. After all, they are all looking for the same thing: adoration from their fans. But sometimes employees become frustrated with their artists, too. Andre has felt that frustration.

24

BABES IN TOYLAND

Nelson

Summer 1991

"DON'T YOU EVER DO THAT AGAIN!" ANDRE PACED BACK AND
forth in front of the two blonde brothers, their heads down and their eyes toward the ground.
"Do you have any idea what sort of trouble you could have gotten into? Well? Do you?"

The room fell painfully quiet.

"We won't do it again," the one on the left offered sheepishly.

Andre replied, "You better not. Fans can hurt you."

He was talking to the Nelson twins.

Andre recalls the situation, which came between Aerosmith and Kiss tours. "It was one of
our early shows. These guys were really selling tickets. Everywhere we went, it was bedlam.
This particular gig wasn't far from the hotel. But with all the fans hanging around, I wanted to
make sure we had a safe route and that there wouldn't be any problems. I put the guys in the
hotel about an hour before we needed to be at the venue, and I told them to stay put."

This precaution became standard operating procedure for Andre working with artists
undergoing intense periods of popularity. Especially when adored by hordes of young girls.

"I told the guys to wait in their hotel rooms and I would be back to get them at 5:15,"
Andre continues. " I checked the route to the venue, and returned to the hotel exactly at
5:15, and they were gone! I couldn't find them anywhere."

The twins decided to take themselves to the show. They grabbed their gig bags, took the
nearest elevator out of the building and walked to the theater. Incredulous, Andre dealt with
them sternly.

The Nelson twins – Matthew and Gunnar – were stereotypical teen idols who blasted into pop's mainstream in 1990 with a famous name (the boys' father was the late Ricky Nelson, another former teen idol) and a slick album of pure power pop called *After the Rain*. Matthew, Gunnar, and the rest of the Nelson band were selling out concerts, thanks in large part to the success of the single "(Can't Live Without Your) Love and Affection." The two singers wore pink and powder-blue outfits, which, coupled with their long blond hair, made them irresistible to teenage girls.

"In retrospect, it's funny," Andre remembers about the image-conscious siblings. "They couldn't understand why they weren't being taken seriously by the rock community. They were on the cover of every teen magazine, but they wanted to be on the cover of *Rolling Stone*. Those were tough tours. We had to explain and rationalize every move. Instead of them looking at the tour itinerary every day, we had to keep them informed of the travel plans."

For example, one Las Vegas gig went exceptionally well during the brothers' initial sold-out U.S. tour in 1990. The show ended and the usual backstage wrap-up ensued – including the hand-holding.

"But why can't we stay?" Gunnar asked insistently.

"Gunnar," Andre replied, "we can't."

"Why?" he whined. "We're in Vegas."

"That's exactly why."

The young singer didn't understand.

Andre continued. "Look, Gunnar. Do the math. The next show is in Albuquerque. That's 485 miles away. If the bus travels at 50 mph, it will take us 10 hours to get there. If we leave at 1 a.m., which it doesn't look like we'll do, we will arrive at 11 a.m. That gives the guys four or five hours to set up before sound check. Now do you understand why we can't spend the night in Vegas?"

"Yeah, but we're in *Vegas!*"

Andre rolled his eyes. "We are leaving at 1 a.m."

"And the most incredible aspect," Andre shakes his head, thinking back, "was that we used to have those conversations on a daily basis. They are talented guys, but I think this twisted self-perception, coupled with the fact that they were constantly badgering the record company to release another single, gave them a huge ego trip. Trust me, the people at Geffen got as much as they could out of *After the Rain*."

Apparently, so did critics. Subsequent albums bombed in the United States but survived in Japan. In spring 1998, Nelson released *Imaginator*, which moved *Entertainment Weekly* to grade the album with a seldom-issued "F+."

25
'I DIDN'T DO IT ... HONEST'

Nelson

Summer 1991: Atlanta, Georgia

"SHE SAID I DID WHAT?" ANDRE'S VOICE ROSE. "I CAN'T BELIEVE IT."
Then the voice on the other end delivered the kicker.

"She's suing?" Andre repeated the message.

The music industry can be dangerous and litigious. The one and only time Andre ever had a lawsuit filed against him happened while on tour with Nelson.

Gunnar, Matthew and the rest of Nelson played Atlanta's Star Circle Theater in 1991. Andre walked the stage as he did during every night's performance, assessing the situation. It was an older theater with a permanent stage that appeared to be constructed after the theater was built. Because of this, the stage was built much higher than usual. It measured approximately eight feet from the stage to where the audience was seated. Andre figured there wouldn't be any problem with jumpers that night; they would have to be catapulted to get up there.

There were sets of stairs on either side, leading from the floor to the top of the stage. The whole center of the stage was open. Andre couldn't believe that there weren't any railings or supports, just an eight-foot drop off!

"It was a dangerous setup." Andre recalls. "I remember thinking to myself during my pre-show inspection of the area that we would have to tell Matt and Gunnar to be extremely careful."

The audience, typical for a Nelson show, consisted mostly of pre-teen girls. The pitch of the crowd was not the same as the roar that can be heard at Public Enemy or Aerosmith shows; rather, it was a deafening squeal. Andre didn't think he would have much to worry about that night. After working with some of his other artists, he expected the crowd to be a piece of cake.

And then the impossible happened. About three songs into the show, a blond girl –
probably fifteen years old and 105 pounds – appeared on the stage, running toward Gunnar.
Andre shot out from his position.

He recalls the moment: "She gets up there, throws a big hug around the guy and then
turns to give the thumbs–up sign to her friends in the audience. By this time, I am well on
my way, but trying not to charge full–speed because I don't want to knock her out."

"Hey, let me go!" the girl protested, trying to struggle free after Andre rushed over and
scooped her up. He grabbed her by her belt at the small of her back. This is the least violent
and most effective way to remove someone from a stage. It immobilizes them, and because
most concertgoers wear jeans, it makes for a reliable and strong hold.

"Young lady," Andre said sternly over the din, "this is a dangerous place to be."

"Let go of me!"

The girl started struggling frantically. Slapping Andre and pulling to get away, she
unleashed a string of profanity that would have made a sailor proud.

"You are coming with me. NOW!" Andre ordered.

She was definitely not his usual opponent. Andre started to walk her toward the side of
the stage as gently as possible.

"I remember intentionally putting up with more crap from her than I would from anyone
else because she was just so young. I really made sure I used kid gloves," Andre stresses.

As Andre walked her off the stage, the lights went down and the band prepared to do
another song. With the stage drenched in darkness, Andre stopped, instantly remembering
the eight-foot drop.

At the bottom of the stage-left stairs were the mixing board, the sound guy and several
other technicians. There were sure to be anvil cases and cables; Andre just couldn't
remember where they were. As he slowly started to move, the lights came up again, and
Andre and his newfound "friend" made their way off the stage.

"What are you doing? Where are you taking me?" the feisty teenager persisted. Andre
marched the girl straight toward the exit door. A yellow-jacketed guard watching the door
suddenly stood at attention when he saw Andre with the girl in tow. Andre transferred her
into the man's control.

"She's out of here." Andre said with a jerking motion of his thumb. The yellow-jacketed guard nodded, and Andre watched as he escorted her out the door. He could see the expression on the girl's face, as if she had no idea what she'd just done. Andre returned to his post, and the show ended without further incident.

One week later, Andre and the Nelsons returned from a visit to the Mars Cheese Castle in Racine, Wisconsin. The twins were in a silly mood, buying all kinds of cheesehead hats and key chains. Andre entered his hotel room just in time to receive a phone call from the management office.

"What happened in Atlanta?" came the nervous voice on the other end. "We've been told you beat up a girl."

"What?" Andre asked incredulously. "Why in the world would I do that?"

Apparently the girl's mother was an attorney. Her daughter, embarrassed she had been kicked out of the show, decided to seek revenge by suing Andre.

The girl's mother had driven the group of girls to the show that night. Upon being removed from the theater, she called her mom to pick her up. When the woman inquired about the whereabouts of her daughter's friends, the embarrassed girl made up a story, telling how the crowd pushed her onto the stage and a security person beat her.

The claim alleged that she was thrown to the floor, jostled about and that her head was bashed into a wall.

When asked if perhaps the girl did get roughed up a bit, Andre becomes annoyed. "First of all, there is no way the crowd would push her onto the stage," he says. "For her to reach that height, she would have to have been shot out of a cannon. She obviously tried to get up there, and had help from her friends. Second of all, there is no way in the world I would ever manhandle some kid, especially a fourteen-year-old girl."

The case was eventually dropped because the girl was never able to describe her "attacker."

In between Andre's high-profile gigs with rock's biggest stars, he needed to keep working. He took positions with such second-tier acts as Nelson, Cinderella and Arcade. But when one of rock 'n' roll's greatest group of bad boys came calling, the choice between Gunnar Nelson and Gene Simmons was a no-brainer.

26

YOU NEVER FORGET
YOUR FIRST ...

Kiss

San Fernando Valley, California

ANDRE AUGUSTINE, NOW SPORTING A PONYTAIL, WALKED INTO THE Third Encore recording studio in the San Fernando Valley at 1 p.m. for his introduction to one of rock's most influential acts of all time, Kiss.

"Steve Wood, Kiss' tour manager at the time, hired me," Andre remembers. "I had Aerosmith and the Pump Tour under my belt, and that was my big calling card."

Andre walked into the main room and immediately noticed Wood. He came over with a big smile and said, "Hey, what's goin' on? Glad you came down. Let me introduce you to the guys."

On the couch sat Gene Simmons and Paul Stanley, the bass–and–guitar duo who founded Kiss in 1973 in New York. Also present were the two newer members of the band's most recent incarnation: lead guitarist Bruce Kulick and drummer Eric Singer – the one player in the band back then who Andre says made touring with Kiss fun.

"Eric was a real bright spot," Andre says. "His personality is just fun." Andre's sentiments are backed up in the *Kiss Exposed* video, in which Eric chides Andre backstage calling him "Andre the Giant."

Back at Third Encore, Gene stood up immediately and walked over to Wood and Andre.

"You must be Andre. I'm Gene Simmons."

"Hi, Gene. Great to meet you."

To Andre all four band members appeared to be low-key guys; he couldn't have been more wrong.

When Andre signed on for 1992's Revenge Tour, Kiss was about the last band most music fans wanted to see. The group had gone through several lineup changes since the dissolution of the original four – Gene, Paul, drummer Peter Criss and guitarist Ace Frehley – and the music industry was high on the alternative grunge craze fueled by bands like Pearl Jam, Nirvana and Stone Temple Pilots.

"The guys' mental attitude was different [than it was five years later on the reunion Alive/Worldwide Tour]," Andre says. "Pretty much the same Kiss fans, but different band mentality. During the Revenge Tour, Kiss was down in the dumps. They weren't selling out. Nobody cared. That whole genre of music was on its way out the door. Concert attendance would fluctuate from 10,000 to 3,000 or 4,000 in a house that seated 15,000. It was pretty bad. Sometimes it would have been better to cancel the date. But Kiss refused to cancel any dates, and instead of taking a hit, they kept getting their full amount. Guaranteed payment, regardless of attendance." This may be one of the key reasons Kiss has stayed in business when other bands haven't.

"There were a couple of times when promoters tried to have a conversation to plead with them to take a reduction on the guarantee," Andre continues. "I would be backstage, and a promoter would come up and say, 'Look, come on, man. I gotta talk to Gene.' And I'd have to say, 'I'm sorry. He's getting ready for the show.' Then I'd go in and tell the guys what was happening. And they would hover and hang around until a few minutes before the show. They would put it off a bunch of different ways. They put a lot of promoters out of business because they wouldn't give money back. But business is business."

To liven up the dismal shows, tour/production manager Tim Rozner hired strippers in various cities to join Kiss onstage during the performance of "Take It Off" from the *Revenge* album.

Despite Kiss' attempt to spice up the Revenge Tour, it was not considered one of the band's best efforts. By now, even the Kiss Army fan base was questioning whether their favorite band would ever again come near the superstar status it achieved in the 1970s with hit albums and monster tours.

A few years later, in January 1995, the stock market was up, President Bill Clinton was down, Iraq was threatening and grunge was slowly dying. The time was ripe for another rock 'n' roll phenomenon: The Kiss Convention.

Gene and Paul were planning the first "official" Kiss Convention Tour. Fans had been holding unofficial Kiss conventions for years, and the movement could no longer be ignored by the band.

In cities throughout the world and at almost any time of year, you can find a Kiss convention. Primarily organized by an entrepreneurial fan or fan club, the events are usually held in hotels with dozens of exhibitors hawking Kiss memorabilia. This isn't surprising, given that at one point in history Kiss was the most merchandised band in the world. Lunch boxes, trading cards, pinball machines, bikes, toy guitars, real guitars, motorcycles and frozen food were all part of Kiss' product machine. Name the product, and it more than likely had a Kiss logo on it at one time or another. Many of these items – in addition to the usual rock 'n' roll collectibles like backstage passes, stickers, pins, posters, picks and bootleg recordings – can be found at Kiss conventions.

Another phenomenon at these events is the ever-popular Kiss tribute band, which imitates as closely as possible its members' musical idols – in this case, the group's original lineup.

Hundreds, sometimes thousands, of Kiss fans attend, wearing Kiss T-shirts or denim jackets with dozens of Kiss pins, patches and other logos. Some attendees dress up in Kiss regalia in honor of their favorite character.

Gene and Paul finally decided it was time to get involved.

"After the Revenge Tour, what was there for them to do?" Andre asks. "Enough time had passed between the original Kiss and the current Kiss. They were looking to do something now or forever hold their peace. The conventions were a way for Kiss to put a minimal amount of money on the table, produce the tour themselves and make a lot of cash. If the Convention Tour and the reunion hadn't happened, the end would have been near for Kiss."

The band endeavored to host official Kiss-sponsored conventions, and they needed to put together their own crew to help make it happen. Gene called Andre.

"We have no idea how these things are going to go over," Gene told Andre glumly one January 1995 afternoon, engaged in negotiations in the basement office of his Beverly Hills guesthouse. "We want you to be involved and help with the security and on-site execution of these events, but we have to be careful about compensation."

Andre chewed on his tongue for a few seconds, gazing up at the Kiss memorabilia and posters adorning the office walls. His eyes came to rest on an oversized portrait of Gene's longtime companion, actress and *Playboy* Playmate Shannon Tweed.

Andre knew full well that this upcoming convention tour was the talk of Kiss fandom.

Finally, he retaliated. "Well, Gene, let's look at the work. On the Revenge Tour, I really just performed a security function. Now you're adding an organizational function. That's two jobs."

"Hold it right there," Gene snapped back, as if Andre had just insulted his mother. "We're all doing two jobs. I'm setting this thing up, making the calls and performing."

Yeah, Andre thought. *You also get to keep the profits.*

Granted, it was Gene's gig, but it wasn't as if Andre was asking to participate in a profit-sharing program. Nevertheless, Andre's resolve was weakening.

Gene sensed it and went in for the kill. "Oh, yeah. We aren't paying per diems anymore, either."

Per diems are meal and living expenses that the band pays while on the road. Many bands pay $35 to $100 a day, depending on variables like group and location of the tour. Cutting per diems was the ultimate in stinginess, but Andre knew what inevitably drove the decision.

"On the Revenge Tour, Bruce and Eric saved their per diems by eating at the crew catering tables at the show. They made their own sandwiches and grabbed bags of chips, some fruit or a couple of sodas, and then stuck them in their gig bags for later," Andre says. "They'd do whatever they could to save money because they basically were paid as hired hands, not as official members of Kiss."

The practice of paying other players as sidemen would continue on the Alive/Worldwide Tour, with reports in several publications stating that Ace and Peter received merely chump change compared to Gene's and Paul's take.

Gene and Paul, although thrifty in other ways, didn't approve of Bruce's and Eric's "doggie bag" program. Andre pinpoints the issue. "Eric Singer had a tendency to brag at the end of a tour leg, 'Hey, I saved $2,000! I haven't spent a dime of my per diems.' Gene and Paul started asking themselves, 'Why are we paying per diems when nobody's using them as intended?' They looked at the bottom line and found per diems to be a significant expense item."

That afternoon at the guesthouse, Gene spent a great deal of time going over financial points with Andre. Per diems wouldn't affect Andre personally, Gene assured him. If there wasn't any catering at the venue, Andre could always get something at the hotel. But it would make managing the production crew a nightmare.

Imagine dozens of workers breaking for lunch in Detroit, having them all go their separate ways for lunch, and then trying to stick to a set-up schedule.

During the entire conversation with Andre, Gene shuffled papers and looked at items on his desk. Andre couldn't tell whether this was a negotiating tactic or if Gene just wasn't interested in the conversation.

Pulling out a piece of paper from his notebook, Andre uncapped his pen and started writing.

"You paid me this much for the Revenge Tour," he said, sliding the paper across the desk under Gene's gaze.

Gene read it, looked up and asked quickly, "What do you need this time?"

Andre did some quick calculations and wrote down another figure – one higher than what he earned on the Revenge Tour, but also a fair one, given the newly developing assignments and responsibilities.

Gene looked at the number and in a split second replied, "OK."

The whole exchange puzzles Andre to this day. "I can't figure out whether he is so savvy that I don't get it, whether he really didn't care about the numbers and just liked to go through the gyrations, or whether he really wanted me to come along and didn't care what it cost. I don't know."

The Convention Tour accomplished what Gene and Paul set out to do: re-establish the Kiss name and bring Ace Frehley and Peter Criss back into the fold. That strategy led to the MTV *Unplugged* special in October 1995 and ultimately to the big announcement of the long-awaited reunion tour.

By the summer of 1997, a mere two years after Gene played hardball with Andre over his Convention Tour paycheck, Kiss had earned more money than any industry insider could have imagined – $47.1 million during six months in 1996 alone. The demand for a reunited Kiss went beyond all expectations – except maybe those of Gene Simmons and Paul Stanley.

"That whole reunion tour was part of the master plan," Andre contends. "Gene is very strategic. He was cooking that up for a couple of years. But it had to be the right time. And he timed it perfectly."

Not only was the timing perfect, but Andre soon would meet the one man who could bring the Kiss brand of rock 'n' roll circus back to the masses and figure prominently in Andre's life.

27

THE MAN BEHIND THE BAND

Doc McGhee

DOC MCGHEE HAS BROUGHT MANY A ROCK 'N' ROLL CIRCUS TO town. Bon Jovi, Skid Row, Mötley Crüe and Kiss were all, at one time or another, under his management. Doc also contributed a great deal to Andre's career.

"A person can learn more about business just listening to Doc on the phone than through any business course," Andre praises. "We have only worked together for one tour, but Doc made a huge impression on me. He was a friend, a confidant, a teacher and a father figure – all rolled into one."

McGhee's personality enabled him to share his knowledge of the music industry with Andre, never hiding information and always encouraging Andre to improve. "Doc (reportedly "Doc" is McGhee's given name and not a nickname) wants to improve everyone's skills and abilities," Andre says. "That way, all things related to projects and tours go more smoothly." And in the music business, that's sometimes all that matters.

Andre met McGhee at the House of Blues during a George Thorogood show in the mid-Nineties. By that time, the security chief had moved on to other high-profile projects, but he still kept in touch with the Thorogood family.

For Andre, a night like this was as much about networking for new business as it was about seeing a great musician. He scanned the crowd to see if there was anyone he knew or wanted to know. That's when he noticed Doc McGhee – easily recognizable with his stocky figure and shiny forehead – networking with a small group of people, telling stories and having a good chuckle. His infectious laughter could be heard over the din.

Andre looked for an opportunity to introduce himself, drop some names, establish a relationship and see if he could get a gig or two. Unfortunately, he got too close to McGhee, turned quickly and almost knocked the man over before he could even develop a strategy. "That was not how I wanted to start," Andre says. "I didn't want to say, 'Sorry about knocking you out, Mr. McGhee. By the way, hi. My name is Andre.'"

Instead, Andre stuck out his hand and said, "Doc McGhee. Hi. My name is Andre Augustine. It's great to meet you."

"Really?" McGhee said. He got this approach a lot.

"I've worked with Aerosmith, Kiss and a couple of other groups."

"Really." This time McGhee was impressed.

Andre had gotten to know the guys in Skid Row while working with Aerosmith on the Pump Tour. He knew McGhee managed the late-Eighties rockers, so he inquired about them.

"How are Sebastian and the boys doing?" Andre asked, referring to Skid Row's colorful lead singer, Sebastian Bach, who still tours as a solo act.

"Great. They're really doing well," McGhee responded, typically upbeat. He and Andre exchanged small talk for a few more minutes, and then Andre, not wanting to monopolize McGhee's time, ended the conversation.

"If you ever need anyone who does what I do, here's how you can get in touch," he said, handing a card to McGhee, who took it and slipped it into his pocket. The two shook hands, and Andre turned around and headed to another part of the club.

Although Andre was unaware of it at the time, McGhee, not enjoying semi-retirement, was trying to get back into the music business. In a matter of months, McGhee and Andre would help make Kiss' Alive/Worldwide reunion tour a success with the help of another road warrior Andre met on Aerosmith's Get A Grip Tour.

28
GETTING A GRIP ... ON LIFE

Tony Morehead

THE COLD, STEEL BARREL OF THE PISTOL HAD NO TASTE, AND THE
walnut grip of the handle had no texture. He thumbed the safety off. It seemed way too easy
to stick this pistol in his mouth. Now all he had to do was pull the trigger.

With an ex-Army Special Forces background, the man's military training gave him lots of
experience with weapons. M16s, small arms and explosives were all familiar to him.
Vietnam gave him lots of experience at trying to take human lives. In rice paddies, jungles
and mountains, he fired his weapon dozens of times – always shooting to kill. But nothing
prepared him for this moment. He was about to commit what some would call the ultimate
sin. Tony Morehead was about to take his own life.

It began during the war. As it does for millions, it started innocently enough, blowing
off steam with guys in the unit. Then it became a way of coping. And then it got out of
hand. Cocaine.

After returning from 'Nam, Tony fought his addiction fiercely. He was successful at first,
but then the lure proved too much for him. He finally hit bottom in Los Angeles in spring of
1980, when he lost his wife, his home and his thirst for life.

Now Tony Morehead sat in the darkness of his bedroom closet, the entire world
crashing down on him. He wanted relief; he wanted the pain to end.

Morehead heard the closet door creak and saw a stream of light pour through the crack.

"Tony, are you in here, man?"

It was Morehead's next-door neighbor. Walking by, he noticed Morehead's front door
ajar and came in to make sure things were all right. The neighbor, also a member of

Alcoholics Anonymous with a history of drug abuse, had noticed telltale signs of relapse in Tony's personality recently. He had been especially watchful of late.

"Tony?"

As the neighbor pushed open the door, he found Morehead – dark circles under his eyes, sweating profusely and holding a handgun.

"Come on, man. We can work this thing out."

After much consoling, the neighbor talked Morehead out of taking his own life and convinced him that suicide was a permanent solution to a short-term problem.

Tony Morehead embraced his second chance at life. He thanked his neighbor and his creator and never again looked back at the world of drugs and alcohol.

March 1993 - 13 Years Later

Andre strolled out of the terminal of the Kansas City International Airport and saw his ride, standing next to a Jeep Grand Cherokee outside of baggage claim.

Immediately, Andre got good vibes from this guy. *Curbside service, not too shabby.*

"Hey, I'm Tony Morehead," said the man, about Andre's size, dressed in black jeans and a black T-shirt.

"Andre Augustine."

Andre and Morehead shook hands. It felt very comfortable. Morehead, acting as assistant road manager on this outing, had heard of Andre. Everyone in the Aerosmith camp talked positively about him.

Morehead grinned. "We're gonna have a great time on this tour."

Andre nodded in agreement.

"Everybody's anxious to see you again."

Andre received the call four weeks earlier. Aerosmith, planning a huge U.S. tour, wanted him to join them. The band was riding a wave of post-*Pump* popularity with the release of 1993's *Get A Grip.* Although the album's sales numbers were similar to those for *Pump, Get A Grip* was not as well-received by critics. Nevertheless newer fans ate up radio-friendly power ballads like "Amazing," "Cryin'" and "Crazy." It was a big tour, and the group needed Andre's help.

The band was holding production rehearsals in Topeka. Using out-of-the-way cities like Topeka allows bands to rent halls for long, uninterrupted periods of time. It also enables them to kick off the first few shows, working out bugs far from the bright lights, large crowds and critics. Plus, "secondary market" fans are less jaded than those in New York or L.A., often more willing to give band members a much-needed ego boost.

Andre threw his gear into the back of the Jeep, and the two men took off. The ride that day from Kansas City to Topeka would last about ninety minutes, so the men immediately started getting to know each other, exploring backgrounds and key issues on the tour. The most important topic proved to be the policy prohibiting drugs and alcohol.

This wasn't news to Andre. The same policy was in effect for the Pump Tour. But recovery from drugs and alcohol is something you can never say is over, and the clean-and-dry policy remained a major tour priority. And by all accounts, everyone stuck to the policy.

Andre remembers his conversation with Morehead. "It seemed as if everyone around the group was in recovery. Tim Collins, the band's manager at the time. Bob Dowd, the tour manager. And I found out later that Tony was in recovery, too."

After almost an hour of getting to know one another, Morehead asked the question.

"Were you ever addicted to anything?" He locked eyes with Andre for a second before turning back to the road.

There was an uncomfortable moment during which the only sound that could be heard was the rubber of the tires meshing with the pavement. Andre stared at the dashboard.

Morehead is a very active member of Alcoholics Anonymous, and he was prepared to hear yet another story of how drugs and alcohol took over a life.

"Well, let's have it," he pressured. "What was it, man? Alcohol? Cocaine? Heroin?"

Andre sat stone-faced, not responding to any of the questions. The silence seemed to last forever. Finally, Andre answered.

"Worse."

"Worse than smack?" Morehead asked, amazed. "Man, what was it?"

There was a pause.

"Ribs."

"Ribs?"

"Yeah! Ribs, man" Andre rubbed his stomach. " I couldn't stop eating ribs."

Both men looked at each other before busting their guts. They were going to get along just fine.

The 225–city Get A Grip Tour opened in Topeka, Kansas, on June 2, 1993. And as it turned out, Andre was perhaps the only person on the tour not in recovery. He had the occasional social drink or cigar, but drug and alcohol addiction isn't in his repertoire. Andre doesn't even drink coffee.

Life on the road hasn't been easy for Steven Tyler or Joe Perry, who are still tempted by chemicals. "I'm a drug addict today, I'm just not using them – as well as everybody else in the band," Joe told *Metal Edge* in February 1997. "The day is young, but I think I'll be OK today. We're all well. We're as crazy as ever, and a lot of people interpret the insanity around the band as potential drug use."

But the Aerosmith wives know the truth. They contribute greatly to the band's success and sobriety. They travel with the guys and play an enormous and influential role in the group's decision-making processes. Andre and the crew refer to the musicians and their wives as the "Band of Ten."

"It was great to have them around," Andre remembers. "Especially when it came to touring. Having them and the kids there seemed to take some of the harshness out of being on the road. I believe they have contributed a great deal to the success of Aerosmith. They are very supportive and dedicated to the band's recovery and sobriety."

Andre recalls one incident in particular, that sums up the power the Aerosmith wives wield. The band was preparing to go to Los Angeles for a few weeks, and the wives were especially psyched. The road had become tiresome, and the cutting-edge designer fashions of L.A. beckoned. Everyone looked forward to a little shopping.

Tony Morehead walked into the hospitality room backstage one night shortly before a concert and started what he considered to be a friendly conversation with Joe's wife.

"Hey, Billie," he called. "Are you excited to go to L.A. and spend some of Joe's money?"

Billie Perry turned and looked directly at Morehead. She was angry, and he knew he was in trouble.

"Obviously, there is something you don't understand, Tony," Billie began. "Joe's money is my money. And I will spend *my* money any way I see fit."

Morehead wasn't intentionally condescending. Offending Billie had been the farthest thing from his mind. But Billie made it clear that even though the wives do not play an instrument, they contribute significantly to the band's success and attitude.

It took four months for Morehead to get out of the doghouse with Billie Perry.

Andre also likes to tell another Morehead story: One day near the end of the Get A Grip Tour, Morehead volunteered to hang with Steven for the day, a task that usually fell to Andre. Morehead phoned Andre in his hotel room late that day, reaming out the security director for sticking him with Steven.

"I can't believe you did that to me!" Morehead screamed into the receiver at Andre.

"What are you talking about?"

"I can't believe you did that to me! You know what we did, don't you?"

"Yeah. You probably went shopping."

"That's exactly what we did! We spent four fuckin' hours in the mall! We must have been in and out of every single store three or four times!"

"That's what Steven does," Andre says. "He'll go to a store and then he'll walk a little more, go to a different store and then a different store and then say 'You know what? I think I want to get that whatever.' And he'll go back to the store he was in three stores ago!"

Today, Morehead still brings Andre along on a gig. If he gets a job and needs help, he calls Andre and asks if he's interested. And Andre reciprocates.

Two years later, Andre phoned Morehead the moment he realized he needed another person on Kiss' Alive/Worldwide Tour for venue security. Morehead was terribly overqualified for the position, but he never made a big deal about it and performed his job as a consummate professional.

29
COME TOGETHER
Steven Tyler & The Artist Formerly Known As Prince

European MTV Music Awards

October 26, 1993: Berlin, Germany

AS A SECURITY DIRECTOR, ANDRE TYPICALLY KEEPS PEOPLE AWAY from performers. But occasionally he gets an opportunity to bring artists together.

Andre played an important role in developing the relationships between some of the greatest performers of our time, including Steven Tyler and Prince (now referred to by the media as "The Artist Formerly Known as Prince" or simply "The Artist").

In late 1993, while on the Get A Grip Tour, Aerosmith accepted an invitation to perform at the European MTV Music Awards in Berlin, Germany. The airplay Aerosmith received on MTV back then was crucial to their staying power on the charts and their drawing power at arenas.

At the time, rumors circulated that a rift had developed between Steven and The Artist. Unsubstantiated reports claimed Steven was comparing Aerosmith to The Artist's band, New Power Generation, and was less than flattering towards NPG. The story made it seem like Steven was putting down The Artist's supporting musicians.

The media took Steven's comments out of context, he claimed. He wasn't talking about musicianship or technical ability; rather, he was saying that Aerosmith was an entity and The Artist was a standout single artist and performer. A magazine quoted him and made it sound as if Steven boasted that Aerosmith played better than The Artist's band. Word on the grapevine also had it that The Artist had read the comments and was ticked. Andre knew it bothered Steven, as he talked about it several times during the tour.

Aerosmith had just wrapped up their sound check prior to that evening's performance, and the hall still reverberated from Steven's last scream as Andre led him back to the hotel.

In the creeping darkness, Germany's history seemed to come alive. Dim, narrow streets and large, stone buildings lent a medieval mood. Andre imagined what it must have been like to live in Berlin during World War II. The streetlights seemed the only indicator of modern times. Andre and Steven walked alone on the damp street, approaching their dignified hotel located in the old East German part of the city. The Kempinski featured a gothic exterior that Andre describes as "very Eastern Bloc." Although older, it had been refurbished. A very sobering brown–and–beige color scheme could be found throughout the hotel, and the rooms were spartan – consisting of little more than a bed and a bathroom.

The elevator doors opened, and Steven and Andre stepped onto the antiquated lift. Steven, drenched in perspiration, dabbed himself with the towel wrapped around his neck. His breathing had just started to slow.

"So you think it went alright?" Steven asked.

Andre was used to Steven asking for input. "Yeah, it was great. It's going to go over really well."

"I just hope the sound is alright. You know how these TV gigs go."

Andre nodded. Aerosmith played a lot of televised performances and always worried about the sound – a valid concern. Satellite transmissions and television speakers can do terrible things to an otherwise great performance.

A bell rang, and the elevator slowed and stopped on their floor. The doors opened; Andre held them for Steven to exit. The two started to make their way down the hall when Andre felt something.

"It was strange," he recalls. "All I can tell you is the vibe immediately turned heavy. The energy in the air changed."

And then they saw him. Moving very quickly, dressed in a white cape with a hood and flanked by two security men, the figure headed towards the elevators. Andre knew it was The Artist.

Andre nudged Steven. "Look, here he comes."

Before Steven and Andre had a chance to say another word, they were upon him. Steven, without hesitating, stepped right in front of the small group, stopping all three men. The security guards, recognizing Steven, parted their protective curtain and gave him access to The Artist.

Steven stuck out his hand. "Hey, man, I really dig your stuff. I think you're a great performer."

Silence. To Andre it seemed like forever. He wondered how the usually shy Artist would respond to Steven's extroverted personality. Andre held his breath.

The Artist slowly raised his eyes to meet Steven's and smiled shyly. He shook Steven's hand and in a child-like voice said, "Thanks a lot, man. Thanks a lot."

Andre found himself in a trance-like state, witnessing the dynamics between these two legends. He looked up to see one of The Aritist's security guys looking him straight in the eye. It was his old touring–circuit pal, Coco!

Coco and Andre nodded in silent acknowledgement of each other. Although old friends, this was neither the time nor the place to catch up on each other's career paths.

"You're going to sound check, right?" Steven asked The Artist.

"Yeah," The Artist replied.

"Well, have a great one."

The two groups nodded to each other as Steven stepped aside, and The Artist and his entourage went on their way.

"Wow, what are the chances of that?" Andre asked.

"Yeah," Steven responded, smiling. "Go figure."

Steven had just taken the first step toward setting the record straight with The Artist. Andre kept the fact that he knew one of the security guys to himself.

The Aerosmith performance went off smoothly. Because the band was already in Europe, there wasn't any jet lag, and there were no indications of sound problems.

Afterwards, Steven and the band returned to their seats in the audience to watch the rest of the show. Andre stayed backstage to try to catch up with Coco.

Coco, a 280-pound stocky guy built like a bulldog, came from the streets of L.A. and had worked for The Artist only a brief while. "He and I had a few minutes to hang out," Andre remembers, "but he didn't have much time to talk. The Artist and his band were moving towards the stage and taking their ready positions. Once you get your artist in the ready mode, everything else shuts off. You just concentrate on what you need to do.

"Coco had shut me out," Andre continues. "I just tried to be still. I didn't want to draw too much attention to myself or disturb the 'presence of the area.' The Artist had his guitar on and acted kind of fidgety. But I was looking at him, looking at his eyes. He glanced at me and then looked away. You could tell he didn't want to invite conversation or interaction."

"I can't remember anyone spending so much time alone with The Artist after a performance."

The Artist turned his back, and Andre slipped away.

The Artist closed the awards ceremony that night.

"This guy was phenomenal," Andre says. "Not only did the crowd go wild, but so did Steven."

The outstanding performance intensified Steven's need to clear his name with The Artist. Steven met Andre backstage and announced, "I want to see him. I want to go talk to him."

Backstage, the dressing rooms were in very close proximity to each other. Andre could see The Artist's dressing-room door from Steven's. Steven paced in his doorway and watched Andre as he approached The Artist's quarters.

Getting an audience with The Artist right after a performance is usually impossible. But with Coco, there was a chance.

"Steven wants to come in and hang out. Think that'd be cool?" Andre asked Coco, gesturing toward the dressing-room door.

"Hmm, I don't know. Boss doesn't usually see anyone after a show."

"Come on, Coco. Just go see."

Coco mulled the idea for a second, then disappeared into the dressing room. After a few minutes, he returned and nodded "yes." Andre turned and nodded to Steven.

Steven hurried over, as anxious as a star-struck fan meeting his idol. Andre extended his arm, inviting Steven to enter The Artist's dressing room. Steven looked at Andre, winked and moved quickly through the door. He was in there for almost 30 minutes.

Andre, who has seen The Artist in several backstage situations throughout the years, now recalls the event. "I can't remember anyone spending so much time alone with The Artist after a performance."

When he exited The Artist's dressing room, Steven quickly looked left and right, trying to spot Andre. Andre rushed to Steven's side and couldn't contain himself.

"What'd you say? What'd you guys talk about? What were you guys doing in there for so long? What'd you say?"

Steven smiled broadly, white teeth everywhere. It wasn't typical client protocol to ask such questions, but The Artist was an enigma – even to industry insiders.

"I told him I heard he was upset. I explained to him what I had said and how it was taken out of context. Then we spent the rest of the time talking about music."

Since then, Steven makes an effort to show up at The Artist's concerts, feeling the show's electric buzz for days. In fact, when *Spin* magazine writer Chris Norris interviewed Steven for a May 1997 cover story, Steven had just seen The Artist perform at Boston's Roxy the night before.

When Norris and Aerosmith guitarist Joe Perry entered Steven's South Shore Boston pad, the phone rang, and Steven picked it up. Wrote Norris: 'Oh, that's him,' [Steven] jokes. 'Yo, Formerly Known As!'"

"It had to be fate," Andre remembers now. "Not only were we in the same hotel as The Artist but our sound checks were back to back. Steven wanted to set the record straight and he did."

And Andre helped.

30
ROAD WARRIOR
Andy Gilman

ANDY GILMAN, JOEY KRAMER'S DRUM TECHNICIAN FOR MORE THAN a decade, worked with Andre from 1988 to 1994. While touring with Aerosmith, Andre and Gilman shared good times, long hours and a ton of dry, catered chicken.

"Andre Augustine is like my big brother!" he exclaims. The statement sounds funny coming from Gilman, a white guy who stands about 5 feet, 7 inches tall and might weigh 140 pounds.

Gilman, himself a drummer, grew up in New England and spent two years at the University of Bridgeport in Connecticut. He left to follow his rock 'n' roll dreams when he was twenty and snagged a job working for Sun Sound Audio in North Hampton, Massachusetts.

"I started doing shows for them – local Boston club dates, just hauling cabinets and wrapping cables," Gilman remembers. "Sometimes we carried equipment up three floors, and the pay wasn't great – $50 a night, and we worked from noon until 4 the next morning."

After paying his dues, Gilman soon found himself with bands of note, including Boston-based Jon Butcher Axis, described by Gilman as "always the bridesmaid, never the bride." Jon Butcher Axis opened for some of the biggest bands on their biggest tours: Def Leppard on the Pyromania Tour, Scorpions on the Love at First Sting Tour, Rush on the Moving Pictures Tour. But Jon Butcher Axis never reached headliner status.

"After Axis, I took a gig with Foghat on a reunion tour in 1986," Gilman says. "It was a torturous club tour. But, hey, a gig's a gig." After the tour, Gilman was home for three months when he received a call from Danny Murphy, a friend of Aerosmith sound man Toby Francis.

He asked if Gilman would be interested in working with Aerosmith, who – fresh from rehab – was gearing up for the 1987 Permanent Vacation Tour.

To a drummer growing up just outside of Boston, Aerosmith was a legend.

"I went down to meet everyone at Aerosmith's rehearsal space in Somerville, Massachusetts," Gilman recalls. "The building was shared with a carpet-installation company on one side, and a lighting company on the other. It was just a big warehouse, a bunch of square footage, a cement floor, metal walls, 25-foot ceilings and gear everywhere."

Gilman laughs, "Aerosmith doesn't throw anything away. They had equipment there from 1975. Foam disintegrating from cases ... the whole deal. I think they even had the original keyboard Steven used to perform 'Dream On.'

"As kids, we loved Aerosmith," Gilman continues, "even if they didn't always make it through the whole show." It seems incomprehensible to him now that the band would just stop playing in the middle of a performance. "My friends and I would go to shows and bet on how many songs they would make it through before Steven would fall down, the house lights would go up and the show would be over."

Gilman shakes his head, "It got to the point where we didn't want to spend money for tickets because we knew we weren't going to see the whole show." His voice becomes mischievous and his eyes sparkle. "That's when my friends and I learned how to sneak into the Boston Garden."

Those skills would come in handy when he met Aerosmith at the warehouse in 1987.

Gilman felt good that day. Up for the position of drum tech, he felt at ease with all of the guys, especially Joey. "We shook hands and talked," he remembers. "Joey cracked jokes, we were all laughing, having a ball." Gilman made a great impression, and after spending several hours with the band, he thought his chances were good. But they were about to get better.

As rehearsal wrapped up, the band's wives arrived, ready to go out and relax with the guys after a long day of jamming. They probably headed to Redbones, reportedly Joe Perry's favorite restaurant in Somerville.

Joey introduced Gilman to his wife, April, as "the possible new guy." Everyone said their good-byes and Joey said he would make a decision and call soon. The wives and the crew started moving toward the exits. The band members lingered to talk about a few things amongst themselves.

Once in the parking lot, April discovered she had inadvertently locked her keys inside her Jeep. Frustrated, she explained what happened to Gilman. "I can fix that," he said. Certainly someone who could sneak into the Boston Garden could get keys out of a Jeep.

He went to work with a coat hanger. After about 10 minutes, Gilman popped the lock just as Joey approached the car. April turned to her husband and said, "Joey, you *will* hire this guy!"

One week later, Gilman received the call confirming his place on the Permanent Vacation Tour. One year later, he would meet Andre during preparations for the Pump Tour. The friendship would be a lasting one.

"We held pre-production rehearsals in Charleston, West Virginia. Everything was kind of crazy and there really were no formal introductions. I remember seeing Andre around and thinking, *this guy is huge.* We met shortly thereafter," Gilman recalls. "That's when I found out Andre isn't your ordinary security guy. He's intelligent, articulate and intimidating. A perfect combination for a rock 'n' roll security director.

"It's that combination that enabled him to grow in responsibility with Aerosmith," Gilman continues. "One of Andre's responsibilities included getting the guys to take the stage on time."

That was a very important assignment. A fifteen-minute delay can mean thousands of dollars in union labor, hall charges or schedule changes. Overtime charges are often clocked by the minute. Andre took Aerosmith's success personally and did his share to make sure they didn't incur unnecessary financial penalties.

"It takes a while before a band will allow you to walk right into their dressing area," Gilman says, "let alone, come in and tell you to quit talking, stop eating and get dressed. 'You're going onstage in five minutes.' But Andre gained acceptance and respect quickly. I witnessed his struggle to get those guys onstage everyday. I knew what he went through because I had to get the set list together everyday, which wasn't always the easiest thing to do, either."

Take one long December day in 1993 during the Get A Grip Tour. The band wrapped up an autograph session at Tower Records in London's Piccadilly Circus, then moved quickly back to the Le Meridien Hotel to clean up. A fifteen-mile ride to Wembley Arena meant tight timing. Aerosmith arrived at the venue and headed toward the dressing rooms.

Andre circled the communal dressing room. "Let's go, gentleman. We're onstage in five minutes. Let's go!" Tonight's show had to be on schedule. The band, slated to do an after-show performance at London's Hard Rock Café for a TV simulcast for *Billboard* magazine's music awards show in Los Angeles, would go on again at 2 a.m.

He didn't need to worry. Joe Perry, Joey Kramer, Brad Whitford and Tom Hamilton defined consistency. They were always ready. Andre quickly departed for Steven's dressing room, while Gilman continued talking to Joe Perry.

"What do you think we should do?" Joe asked Gilman, fishing for set-list suggestions. "And something other than 'Kings and Queens' or 'Lord of the Thighs.' You always suggest those."

The roar of the London crowd – 11,000 strong – beckoned as show time neared. Gilman knew just what to say. "Let's add 'Milk Cow Blues,' and that'll do it." The savvy set-list maker knew Joe liked the old songs, and "Milk Cow Blues" proved one of his favorites.

"Go see what Steven says," Joe suggested.

Meanwhile, Steven wasn't dressed. The backstage area bustled with activity, but that paled in comparison to the mood in Steven's dressing room.

"What do you want to wear for the encore?" a wardrobe person asked the singer, who stood in the middle of his private dressing room wearing nothing but a G-string. Blowing fans, blaring music and Steven's occasional diversion to the keyboard to warm up his voice added to the chaos.

"Encore?" An incredulous Andre entered the room. "What are you gonna wear for the encore? Steven, I want to know what you're gonna be wearing when the curtain falls, because you will be onstage in five minutes."

"Don't rush me, man!" Steven shot back. "This is an important gig."

"I know it's important. That's why we're not going to be late."

"This one ain't gonna be no MFO show." Steven rapped to no one in particular. MFO, one of three categories Steven uses to rate Aerosmith performances, reportedly stands for "Medi-Fuckin'-Ocre."

Andre, familiar with the constant struggle between performer and the regimen of the show, didn't react. He remained calm, as always.

Gilman entered, carrying the well-worked set list on a clipboard in his left hand, a Sharpie marker in his right. Without taking his eyes off the list, he walked into the dressing area and said, "Joe wants to add 'Milk Cow Blues' and that'll be it. OK?"

"Joe always wants to do 'Milk Cow Blues.'" The singer pulled on form-fitting pants and a colorful shirt. "Why not 'Lightning Strikes'? I love that song, and the lighting guys can do their thing."

"It's a great song, Steven," Gilman agreed. Then added hopefully, "I suggested 'Lord of the Thighs.'"

Steven rolled his eyes as he primped in the mirror. "You always suggest that."

"I don't care what you play. We gotta get onstage, or this is gonna cost us a fortune," Andre interjected. "Now pick."

Gilman smiled. "Should I see if Joe wants to do 'Lightning'?"

"No," Steven replied. "Fuckin' guys, gotta get onstage, don't wanna do ... " His voice trailed off as he muttered under his breath.

Andre and Gilman looked at each other and laughed. They had been here before. The nightly ritual to bring the band to the fans sometimes felt like a struggle. But these two wouldn't trade it for the world.

The crowd roared. The curtain fell. And Aerosmith tore into the first verse of 'Eat the Rich.' Andre surveyed the crowd, then checked the positioning of the building guys. He looked at his watch. It read 8:41 p.m. – eleven minutes past the posted start time. *Perfect*, he thought. *Just perfect.*

Touring frustration can get the best of anyone. *Get A Grip* was selling by the thousands. Promoters scrambled to add dates, media types wanted interviews, and TV shows demanded appearances and video productions to support new singles. "When a band's hot, they get worked," Gilman says.

"At the beginning of the tour, management introduces themselves to the crew by gathering everyone together and giving an overview of the tour route and schedule," Gilman says. "The plan for the Get A Grip Tour included six weeks on, two weeks off. That didn't last long.

"At one point, we had just done ten straight weeks on the road and, mercifully, we received ten days off. Everyone quickly scheduled family time, personal stuff and some time to get their heads together." Gilman shakes his own head. "Three days into the break, we got a call telling us we had to go back to Europe. It seemed like we had barely enough time to do our laundry and take a shower. Then we packed everything back up and hauled our asses back to the airport, knowing it would be another ten weeks until we'd be home again."

Not long after the abbreviated break, tempers flared among the crew.

"I don't even remember how or why we were getting into it." Gilman says. "But after two days of not talking to one another, Andre and I stood face to face on the tour bus, like we were in some sort of gunfight."

The two worked things out, but not before some shouting, finger pointing and heated debate.

"We sort of looked at each other and said 'What are we doing?'" Gilman says. "We actually ended up laughing."

Andre and Gilman quickly rekindled their friendship and went back to acting like high schools kids – as they did when Andre found out that Gilman and Joey Kramer were headed to legendary Led Zeppelin drummer John Bonham's grave site one afternoon while touring in England.

"Really!" exclaimed Andre, who grew up idolizing Led Zeppelin.

"Yeah. Joey told me last night he got directions from Robert Plant."

Aerosmith had played the Hammersmith Odeon, and Robert attended the show. Robert made Joey promise he wouldn't tell anyone else. And neither he nor Gilman would break that promise. Joey even swore the cab driver to secrecy.

The morning before Gilman and Joey headed out in search of the famous drummer's resting place, Andre made certain that Gilman planned on reporting back to him immediately upon their return.

Gilman describes the trip. "We drove outside of London. I won't tell you where, but let's just say it was some distance." Rolling hills colored with bright, brilliant green grass, flocks of sheep and winding roads lent a picturesque view of England.

They pulled up to a rusted wrought-iron gate in front of a very old church. The cab driver looked down at the written directions, then turned and said quietly, "I think we're here."

It had been a quiet ride, both men keeping to themselves. Now they looked solemnly at each other, unsure if they had truly found the final resting place of one of the world's greatest rock 'n' roll drummers. Joey asked the driver to wait.

Then he and Gilman walked through the gate, past the small church and toward the adjacent cemetery. Some of its residents had been there for centuries. The weather-beaten markers chipped and sloped from the weight of the years and the shift of the earth. Grass grew tall over most of the area.

Finally, the two stopped and gasped.

The neatness of the perfectly manicured grave contrasted with the rest of its environment. The headstone stood about three feet high, the arch of brilliant white stone supported by two small pillars on each side.

The gold leaf letters read:

CHERISHED MEMORIES OF

A LOVING HUSBAND AND FATHER

JOHN HENRY

BONHAM

WHO DIED SEPT. 25th 1980

AGED 32 YEARS

He will always be Remembered

in our hearts

Goodnight my Love. God Bless.

Joey moved silently and stood at the foot of the grave, his mood heavy and somber. The sun shone brilliantly, and an occasional bird sang. But neither drummer nor technician spoke. Gilman then gave Joey some time alone with his fallen hero. After about an hour, the two headed back to London.

"Well, what was it like?" Andre asked excitedly as he opened his hotel room door for Gilman upon his return.

"Awesome ... " Gilman surmised. " ... And sad. For him to die so young and so senselessly was tragic."

Andre grew concerned. "How's Joey?"

"He'll be OK."

Andre and Gilman spent the next hour talking about the trip to Bonham's grave and the way that entertainers, especially musicians, impact people's lives. They were even more thankful than usual that their bosses, the Aerosmith guys, had given up drugs. For the most part, they're now family men, as is Andre.

"The one thing you need to know about Andre Augustine," Gilman sums up, "is how much he loves his family. For some people, life on the road is great. They carouse, chase women, do whatever. That's what made the road tough for Andre. He cares so much for his wife and family. He's proud of his kids, and he's very, very proud of his wife and the relationship they share. I definitely admire him for that. There's a lot of bullshit out there on the road, and Andre is never a part of it."

And Andre feels the same about Gilman. "He is a professional, through and through."

Andre and Gilman's shared admiration for each other is just one of the things that keeps them close friends to this day.

31
AERO-PORT ANXIETY

Aerosmith

Winter 1993: San Juan, Puerto Rico

THE KIDS WAITED FOR HOURS. THEY CLAMORED AROUND THE empty vans and white Town Cars that were waiting to take Aerosmith from the airport to the band's hotel. Whether chanting "Air-o-smith," singing the chorus to "Love in an Elevator" at the top of their lungs or scrambling to find the terminal at which the group would arrive, they all hoped to catch just a glimpse of their rock 'n' roll heroes.

For some reason, the vehicles were parked at the curb outside of the airport instead of on the tarmac, as Andre would have preferred.

"There's about 2,000 kids out there, running all over the airport," announced an airline employee who boarded the commercial plane after it landed in San Juan. "I don't know what we're going to do or how you gentlemen are going to get out of here."

Andre glanced at the airline employee and then turned around to face the five musicians and the touring entourage for which he was responsible. "Everybody just stay put," he said. "Let me go out there and see what's going on. I'll be back in a minute."

Andre stepped off the plane with the official and was taken aback by the magnitude of the crowd. *It's never like this back in the states,* he thought. *This could be trouble.*

Sometimes, local radio stations or fan clubs leak information about which airports and gates artists will arrive at. Usually Andre, the promoter and local authorities are able to divert the majority of fans – or at least have a strategic plan to move the artist through a crowd ... but not in San Juan.

"I was depending on the promoter to have the airport scoped out so we could avoid a fan frenzy," Andre says. "Fans outside of the continental United States can be crazy when it comes to rock stars. I came out of the terminal, and these kids started holding up signs, thrusting pens and paper in front of me and cheering like I was Steven Tyler. There was nowhere to go."

Unfortunately, local authorities would not allow the cars on the tarmac.

"We have to go to where the cars are," Andre told the band when he returned to the plane. "I'm going to need a few minutes to set this up, but once I do, we'll be able to get out of here safely."

Andre went to work, directing the promoter to leave one vehicle parked by the curb and to move the others down to a lower level near the baggage-claim exit. He sent band manager Tim Collins, tour manager Jimmy Eyers and two or three other members of the touring team – dressed in full Aerosmith regalia with tour jackets, hats and shirts – to the car at the curb. They were escorted by one of the local promoter's staff people.

Upon seeing official-looking people obviously affiliated with the band, the kids figured Steven Tyler and company wouldn't be far behind. They were right.

However, the band was hustled through a different part of the airport and down to the baggage-claim area.

"Tim and Jimmy and the others were surrounded by these kids yelling and screaming and holding up signs," Andre laughs. "It was hard for them to even walk. And there I was on the other side, walking the band with magazines and newspapers folded up over their heads."

As Andre led the guys onto the down escalator, a small group of fans realized what was happening and made a dash for the relocated vans. The group signed a few autographs, posed for a couple of pictures, hopped in the vans and went on their way. Clean getaway.

"We tricked almost everybody with that one," Andre says. "But it had to be done. There was no other safe way to do it. We would have been trampled."

Fighting fans at airports can be a dangerous game, especially with large crowds. Typically, local or airport police officers are not skilled at crowd management, and the whole scene becomes a "them against me" mentality, Andre says.

"Unless some sort of crowd control is initiated by me, the police usually just stand there floundering. They don't know what to do. And it's real hard for me because these guys don't like to take direction from or listen to anybody outside of their organization. I may have been in this particular situation 100 times, and I know exactly what will work and what won't work, but they won't listen to me because I'm just some guy working with a band."

That day in a Puerto Rican airport, surrounded by frantic fans, "some guy working with a band" pulled off a great maneuver.

32

GETTIN' GOBBED

Aerosmith

January 1994: South America

OF THE THOUSANDS OF SHOWS ANDRE HAS WORKED, SOME
really stick in his head. And often the most memorable gigs have been in countries other
than the United States. Different markets mean different fans. And in South America, fans are
the spitting image of ... well, themselves.

Aerosmith, huge in the states, hadn't toured much in South America until the Get A Grip
Tour. When the band first traveled there in January 1994, group members immediately
noticed the increased audience intensity.

"Kids everywhere, crowds everywhere," Andre says. "The guys loved it. The fans are just
so passionate. But the Aerosmith guys really had no idea what they were in for. Especially
when it comes to South American fans showing their appreciation."

That first show featured general admission seating. A 20-foot-high stage and a couple of
ramping levels meant that the band came within 15 feet of the crowd, which was the perfect
distance for audience interaction.

The curtain fell, and like a fighter jet, Aerosmith took off. The first song, "Eat the Rich," a
strategic fire 'em up selection, really did the trick and worked the thousands of fans into an
early frenzy. Steven planted the mic and screamed into it. Then he picked it up and twirled it
around, swirling the long and colorful silk scarves tied to the mic stand. Again, he planted
the mic and continued the scorching lyrics.

Finally, he and Joe made their move.

As always, when the dynamic duo moved out front, the crowd roared. And then it
started. The former Toxic Twins were shocked.

"Joe and Steven went to the front of the stage for the first time, and it was like a missile attack," Andre laughs. "Joe was out of there in an instant. But Steven stayed. Hey, if it's fan adulation, he loves it."

The fans were spitting at Aerosmith. Not spitballs, but big and vigorous gobs of saliva. "They were trying as hard as possible to hit the band," Andre says. "In South America, when the fans really, really like an artist, they spit on them. It's a cultural thing."

Andre spied Brad Whitford and Tom Hamilton exchanging horrified looks. Their faces twisted with disgust as they kept to the rear of the stage and kept playing. Being a member of the LI3 has its privileges.

As that first show wore on, Joe made certain he was out of harm's way. So did the rest of the band. Steven, drenched by the end of the night, loved it.

"You should have seen them exchanging looks during the show. It was as if they were asking each other, 'What in the world is going on here?'"

Andre continues, "We had been warned about this and, of course, I told the guys beforehand, but I'm not sure they really believed me," Andre speculates. "You should have seen them exchanging looks during the show. It was as if they were asking each other, 'What in the world is going on here?'"

While Aerosmith could play away from the front of the stage and avoid getting wet, its security guys had no choice but to weather the storm. Andy Gilman, Joey Kramer's drum tech, recalls Andre's dilemma. "The band could move around. But Andre had to stand there and take it. He and Venue Security Manager Mike Henry had nowhere to go. They had to stay and protect the band, Gilman says." Henry reportedly wore a raincoat for protection.

Not only were the fans spitting, but they were jumping on stage like crazy. "I've never seen so many kids try to take the stage," Gilman recalls.

At first, Andre treated the gig like any show in the states. A kid would somehow get launched up on one of the ramps, and Andre would go out and help him back into the crowd (all very gingerly, of course). But after seven or eight times of running out and sending kids back into the crowd, he stayed positioned on the ramp. This show, for Andre, meant an endless cycle of stage jumpers.

"I felt like I was in training camp for the Jets all over again." Andre remembers. "I was sore for weeks. Because of the positioning of the stage and the number of people, the kids just kept coming and coming."

"I've probably seen Andre take out about a hundred stage jumpers throughout our time together," Gilman estimates. "In that one night, he handled more than two dozen."

Finally, the crew got strategic. After that first night, when the crowd started to gob the band, crew members turned 40-inch oscillating fans toward the audience, sending the saliva wads right back from where they came.

33
DOWN ON THE FARM
Aerosmith

1:15a.m., August 14, 1994 - Saugerties, N.Y.

Wake up, kids, it's half-past your youth

Ain't nothing really changin' but the date.

You're a grand slammer but you're no Babe Ruth.

You gotta learn how to relate

Or you'll be swingin' from the pearly gate

Got all of the answers, low and behold

You got the right key, baby, but the wrong key hole. Yo!

STEVEN TYLER RIPPED INTO THE OPENING RAP OF "EAT THE RICH" as God dumped oceans of rain on the 350,000 mud-soaked residents of 1994's Woodstock Nation. Many of them weren't even born when Steven and Joe Perry attended the original 1969 Woodstock festival 25 years ago – which this three-day concert, featuring modern-day performers, deemed to commemorate.

It was 1:15 a.m. on Sunday, Aug. 14, 1994 – 75 minutes after Aerosmith originally was scheduled to take the stage. Steven pranced through raindrops as big as dimes, and the band played through two hours and fifteen minutes of high winds and lightning to close the second day of Woodstock '94.

"It was just amazing. It was an incredible event," Joe later told MTV. "Whatever anybody says about it not being the same as the other one, on its own, it was an incredible event."

One of the set's highlights came when a soggy Tyler paused after he told the crowd, "For those people out there that had the slightest shadow of a doubt that this gig wouldn't get pulled off ... " and then capped the statement with a giant belch.

The rains hadn't yet begun when the Aerosmith entourage – including the band's wives – made their way to Saugerties, N.Y., earlier that Saturday via jet, boat and van. The day was cold and damp. The band flew to Poughkeepsie, N.Y., then traveled upriver to Saugerties. A van with tinted windows took them to the backstage compound, where they arrived in time to hear part of the Crosby, Stills & Nash set.

"Steven and Joe were tripping a little bit, because there they were, 25 years after being in the audience at the original Woodstock and experiencing the music that really shaped their lives," Andre remembers. "Everything had come full circle, because now they were doing that same thing for people at Woodstock '94. They were one of the concert's more veteran bands."

Other acts during the three-day festival included younger rockers such as Green Day, Nine Inch Nails and Sheryl Crow, alongside veterans like Metallica, Traffic and Melissa Etheridge.

"There was a roof over the stage, and everybody pretty much stayed in back except for Steven and Joe," Andre says. "They all thought Steven was loving it. It was perfect for him, and the weather didn't really affect the band's performance."

The gig didn't pose many security threats, Andre says, because of the high stage.

Rather, the main problems occurred backstage, where corporate greed, MTV's choreography-on-demand and inflated egos added to the tension among the bands performing at Woodstock '94. According to Andre, longtime Aerosmith manager Tim Collins made a stressful situation worse by confronting John Scher, the concert's co-producer, about shared dressing rooms and the fact that Metallica was allowed to sell its own merchandise and use pyrotechnics when Aerosmith could not.

In fact, things got so tense during the scuffle that Scher reportedly sucker-punched Aerosmith tour manager Jimmy Eyers during the dispute and was escorted out of a backstage compound trailer.

The relationship between Collins and the rest of the band was already on rocky ground, and his performance at Woodstock '94 did nothing to strengthen it.

"Here is one of the biggest events of the Nineties, and he's still trying to impose how he thinks Aerosmith ranks compared to the rest of the world," Andre says. "He should have been getting in tune with the event. He should have been relaxing and allowing some of the other things to go on that wouldn't have compromised anybody's position."

Consequently, Aerosmith hardly interacted with the other performers.

None of this mattered to Andre. "I can't even remember who all was there," he says. "It wasn't a big, fun, party atmosphere. Tim Collins wouldn't dare allow any of those other type of bands to be around his Aerosmith. The guys in the band may have enjoyed the gig, but I just wanted to get the hell out of there. It was a terrible, horrible experience."

Two years later, Collins was fired by the band and launched a very public battle in which he went to the press with allegations that Aerosmith had relapsed into drugs and alcohol, which had nearly destroyed the group in the Eighties.

"I was blown out of the water for, like, eight weeks," Steven told *Entertainment Weekly* in March 1997 about the Collins fiasco. "It was the lowest point in my life. I was devastated ... I cried for weeks."

Collins still thinks highly of Aerosmith as a unit, a point he made clear to *Spin* magazine in May 1997. "I believe that Aerosmith is a national treasure," he said. "There's a depth to Aerosmith, there's a meaning to Aerosmith. From their first hit, 'Dream On' – 'dream until your dreams come true' – there's a message of hope. From the first time I met them, and before, growing up in Boston ... they were gods. I mean, there's great music, but the message also has so much depth. They cared, you know?"

Andre cared, too. But not just about the deep meaning of Aerosmith's lyrics. Like many of the other performers he's worked with, Andre came to care for the band as individuals and friends. That's why, when he received news of an old friend's illness, he returned to his rap roots to say good-bye to someone who left an indelible mark on Andre's life.

34

FINAL DAYS OF FRIENDSHIP

Eric Wright/Eazy-E

Cedars-Sinai Medical Center

March 1995: Los Angeles, California

JUST AS THINGS WERE GOING SO WELL FOR ANDRE'S CAREER ON
the rock side of the music business, he was called once again back to his beginnings – back
to the world of rap and his friend Eazy-E.

The nurse came into the room to check vital signs at 6 a.m. She fluffed his pillow and
then checked his chart, shaking her head sadly.

So young and cared for by so many, she thought. The room was filled with cards,
flowers and balloons. It had been thirty days since controversial rapper Eazy-E had been
admitted to famous Cedars-Sinai Medical Center under the alias "Eric Lollis" on February 24,
1995. Hospital spokeswoman Paula Correia later told the *Los Angeles Times* that the hospital
was flooded with calls from concerned fans, "more calls than were received from fans of
Lucille Ball when she was dying." At one point, Reuters News Service reported that the
hospital received more than 2,500 calls per day for Eazy.

The chart slid easily back in place at the foot of the bed with a quiet metallic click, and
the attending nurse quickly exited the room.

She moved past four Fruit of Islam members standing watch. They were the security arm
of the Nation of Islam and part of the new security crew brought in by N.W.A. manager Jerry
Heller after Andre left the entourage and the situation got tense with record-label giant Suge
Knight over Dr. Dre leaving N.W.A. The nurse didn't care much for those guards.

She walked quickly past them and Eazy-E's small group of friends and family.

Andre slept, slumped over in a guest chair, since late the previous night. He had been coming to the hospital for three weeks but was unable to see Eazy.

Tomica Woods-Wright, Eazy's bride of approximately twelve days (reportedly the marriage certificate filled out in the hospital wasn't even signed by the rapper) tightly screened all of his visitors.

Vibe magazine reported that Eazy and Tomica recited their vows at approximately 9:30 p.m. on March 14, 1995. Eazy's parents, Katie and Richard Wright, attended, as did his brother and sister, Kenneth and Patricia. Eazy was too weak to stand. That same night, it was reported by the media that Eazy signed a will naming his attorney and Tomica co-trustees of his estate. He had been diagnosed with AIDS. Two days later, he released this statement:

A STATEMENT FROM ERIC WRIGHT, AKA EAZY-E,
WHEN DIAGNOSED WITH AIDS
As Read by His Friend and Attorney, Mr. Ron Sweeney:

"I may not seem like a guy that you'd pick to preach a sermon, but I feel it's now time to 'testify' because I do have folks, that care about me, hearing all kinds of stories about what's up.

"Yeah, I was a brother on the streets of Compton, doing a lot of things most people look down on, but it did pay off. Then, we started rapping about real stuff that shook up the L.A.P.D. and the F.B.I., but we got our message across big-time and everyone in America started paying attention to the Boyz in the Hood. Soon our anger and hopes got everyone riled up.

"There were great rewards for me personally, like fancy cars, gorgeous women and good livin'. Like, real non-stop excitement. I'm not religious but, wrong or right, that's just me. I'm not saying this because I'm looking for a soft cushion wherever I'm heading. I just feel that I've got thousands and thousands of young fans that have to learn about what's real when it comes to AIDS. Like the others before me, I would like to turn my own problem into something good that will reach out to all my homeboys and their kin because I want to save their asses before it's too late. I'm not looking to blame anyone but myself. I've learned in the last week that this thing is real and it doesn't discriminate. It affects everyone.

"My girl, Tomica, and I have been together for four years, and we recently got married. She's good, she's kind, and a wonderful mother.

We have a little boy who's a year old. Before Tomica, I had other women. I have seven children by six different mothers. Maybe success was too good to me. I love all my kids. And I always took care of them.

"Now I'm in the biggest fight of my life and it ain't easy. But I want to say 'Much love' to those who have been down with me, and thanks for all your support."

Andre had left the rap world behind and toured the globe with some of the biggest names in rock. And now he wasn't even allowed access to an old friend who lay dying only a few feet away.

"How is he?" Andre asked the nurse. She stopped and looked down. By this time, the staff at Cedars-Sinai knew Andre by name.

"He's not improving, Andre" the nurse replied. "It's good that his friends are here."

Andre felt a wave of sadness wash over him. It was hard to believe the street-tough, scrappy little guy from Compton, the one who brought thousands of people to their feet with the hardcore music and imagery of N.W.A., was now so weak from the AIDS virus that he could not stand.

"Come on, let's go get some juice," came the voice of Andre's old friend and former security partner, Ron Scoggins. Scoggins, who also worked with N.W.A., kept vigil with Andre.

After Andre left the rap group, Scoggins worked with Eazy-E for years. At one point, Scoggins and the rapper even lived together. Scoggins was one of the few members of the old crew who still had access to Eazy.

For the past twelve months, Eazy had avoided the reality of his illness. He lost weight and wore layers of clothes to hide his condition. He also exhausted easily and would often excuse himself, close the door to his office and rest. But through all of this, he continued his business – until it all became too much for him.

"As a man of the street, you can't show weakness," Andre reflects. "You can't cry. You can't show emotions."

Around 4 p.m. that day, Scoggins looked at Andre and said, "Come on, let's get you some food, a shower and a change of clothes. You look like you need it."

The two men drove to Andre's home a few minutes away. The kids were just coming home from school, and his wife sat at the kitchen table, catching up on some paperwork for her catering business.

"How is he?" Heather asked, as the two men walked in and plopped wearily on the couch.

"Not good," Andre said.

"He can barely talk," Scoggins added.

"You get cleaned up, and I'll get you two something to eat."

Andre showered and changed into a fresh set of clothes. He and Scoggins quickly ate the sandwiches Heather made, jumped in the car and headed back to the hospital.

When they arrived, the smell of disinfectant, food service and disease became even more sickening than usual. The two men made their way quickly to Eazy's room.

As they approached, they could tell something was wrong. People milled about, crying. Andre and Scoggins reached Eazy's room, where the door was propped open – which was unusual.

The dozens of flowers sent by friends, family and fans were gone, as were the piles of magazines near the bed. As Andre's eyes fell to the perfectly made bed, his mind spun, and fear of the worst began creeping in.

Andre shot down the hall and looked left and right. He saw the nurse who checked Eazy's vital signs earlier that day.

"Ma'am?" Andre asked anxiously. "Where did you move Eric?"

The nurse turned. Her eyes filled with sadness as she looked at Andre. "Eric's passed."

"What?" Andre said in disbelief. "We just left to change clothes. He couldn't have ... "

The nurse reached up and slowly rubbed Andre's broad left shoulder, nodding slowly. Andre sat on a nearby bench and tears filled the big man's eyes.

Eric Wright, who will always be known to his fans as Eazy-E, died on March 26, 1995, at 6:35 p.m. from complications of the AIDS virus.

His funeral was held Friday, April 7, 1995, at the First African Methodist Episcopal Church in Los Angeles. Scoggins was an honorary pallbearer; Andre and Heather attended.

Here is Eazy-E's obituary (reprinted from the Order of Worship):

Eric Wright was born on September 7, 1964, in Compton, California, to the proud parents, Richard and Katie Wright. He received his education in the Compton Unified School District.

Deciding on a career in Music, he became a well-known Rap Artist, "Eazy-E," and built his own recording company, Ruthless/Comptown.

Eric was a gentle, kind and warm-hearted person who was always willing to help others. On Sunday, March 26, 1995, at Cedars-Sinai Medical Center, Eric Wright was called home to his final resting place. His charming smile and wonderful personality will always be remembered.

Eric leaves fond memories in the heart of his wife, Tomica; parents, Richard and Katie Wright; his children, Eric Darnell, Sharan Marie, Erica Shanel, Derrek Deon, Marquise, Christopher, Erin Bria, Raven and Dominick; one sister, Patricia Wright; brothers, Kenneth Wright and Donald Brown; sisters-in-law, Lorrian and Pam; grandmother Estella Wright; and a host of nephews, nieces, aunts, uncles, cousins, friends and fans.

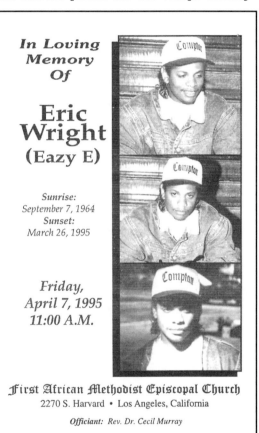

In Loving
Memory
Of

Eric Wright
(Eazy E)

Sunrise:
September 7, 1964
Sunset:
March 26, 1995

Friday,
April 7, 1995
11:00 A.M.

𝔉irst 𝔄frican 𝔐ethodist 𝔈piscopal 𝔆hurch
2270 S. Harvard • Los Angeles, California

Officiant: Rev. Dr. Cecil Murray

[Editorial note: There is a discrepancy between the number of children Eric is quoted as having in his final message to his fans (7) and the listing of children in the Order of Worship from the funeral service (9).]

Three years later, in March 1998, Eazy-E's Ruthless Records released a two-disc anthology called *Decade of Game: Ruthless Records Tenth Anniversary Compilation.* It featured two never-before-released songs by Eazy-E, as well as material by N.W.A. and other label acts. Many critics panned the album.

But the legacy of N.W.A. lives on. In late 1998, Priority Records produced *Straight Outta Compton 10th Anniversary Tribute.* Included on the release are Bone Thugs-N-Harmony, Mack 10, WC, Big Punisher, Cuban Link and Fat Joe.

Eazy-E definitely left his mark on the music industry. His passing also greatly impacted Andre, forcing him to contemplate and interpret many of life's experiences differently.

Andre never again took life for granted. And just when he needed the most help coping with the death of Eazy-E, a bunch of guys from Jersey pulled him out of his sadness.

35
BON JOVI BEGINNINGS

August 1995

Los Angeles, California

"ANDRE, THE PHONE'S FOR YOU!"

Walking in from the bedroom to the den, Andre smiled at his wife as she handed him the cordless phone.

"Hello." Andre makes those two syllables sound like one.

"Andre, how are you?"

He recognized the voice immediately as that of Kiss' Gene Simmons.

Gene got right down to business. "Shannon and I would like to go to the Bon Jovi concert Friday at the Forum. Can you take us?"

"Sure, Gene. My pleasure."

"We'll meet you at the Forum Club entrance at 8 p.m."

"See you there."

With that, the abrupt conversation ended.

Gene and *Playboy* Playmate Shannon Tweed drove themselves to the venue in Gene's black Range Rover. They needed Andre to escort them through the concert area. Even though Gene's celebrity status had started to wane at the time, he was still recognized and approached. Plus, Shannon's movie career and dazzling appearance got her more than a few stares when she ventured out in public.

Andre arrived at the Forum around 7 p.m. to pick up the tickets and passes. Good thing he got there early. He needed the extra time to rectify a ticket screw-up. Andre remembers being surprised. "I got there, and there were only two tickets and two passes at will call. I found that a little odd. How in the world was I going to escort Gene and Shannon to the show if I couldn't get in?" But ticket and backstage-pass screw-ups at will-call windows are almost considered standard operating procedure.

Good thing Andre has connections; he was able to obtain a ticket and a laminated backstage pass for himself. A few minutes later, Gene and Shannon arrived. It was about thirty minutes before Bon Jovi was scheduled to go onstage and Gene wanted to go back and say hello.

"I noticed Gene was carrying a copy of *Kisstory*." Andre recalls. *Kisstory* is the band's official history, containing hundreds of photographs and text in a hard-bound, oversized-book format. Die-hard fans would eventually pay $158.95 (plus shipping and handling charges) for the book.

That's nice. Gene brought Jon a gift, Andre thought.

As the three made their way backstage, the area was very open and quite festive. Record company execs, caterers and support staff all milled about, sharing stories and laughing. Most of the pre-show work was done; the rest was now up to the band. All bands have their own personalities that tend to spill over into a perceptible backstage vibe. This particular backstage area felt very comfortable to Andre.

The first person Gene, Shannon and Andre saw was Big Jon, Bon Jovi's security guy and an old friend of Andre's.

"Hey Big Jon!" Andre exclaimed.

And big he was. Almost Andre's height, Big Jon was a little thicker, with powerful arms and the neck of a defensive lineman. He wore a headset and a laminated backstage pass.

Big Jon smiled, as he and Andre shook hands. There is a real sense of brotherhood among the people who do this sort of work, an understanding of what each other is going through – the stresses of the road and the craziness of the industry.

"How've you been, Andre?" Big Jon asked.

"Great." Andre responded. But he could tell something was up with Big Jon. Maybe it was the look in his eyes or perhaps the slight sag in his shoulders. Andre would have to find out the reason later; right now he had work to do.

"Big Jon, I'm here with Gene and Shannon," Andre continued.

Big Jon looked past Andre's right shoulder to see the couple standing several feet behind, talking quietly to each other. He nodded as if to say he understood their celebrity status.

"They'd like to duck in to see Jon quickly, before the show," Andre continued. "Can you check?"

Big Jon excused himself for a moment and disappeared into the dressing room. He was back in seconds with the OK. Andre held the door open for Gene and Shannon to go inside.

"Those two entered the room, and I followed behind, just wanting to get a glimpse of how crowded it was and who was back there," Andre says. "Gene and Shannon said hello to everyone, and once I saw things were OK, I turned and walked out."

Andre continues his recollection. "We were standing in this long, narrow hallway, Big Jon with his back on the door and me on the wall across from him. There was just barely enough room for two people to walk side by side. Dave Davis, Bon Jovi's tour manager at the time, came by. Big Jon stopped him and said, 'Dave, this is Andre. This is a guy that you need to know.'"

Andre was a little confused by the comment but didn't show it as he exchanged pleasantries. "After Dave left, I asked Big Jon what he was talking about. And he told me the story. Apparently, Big Jon and Jon Bon Jovi had a falling out. I immediately knew that's the vibe I was picking up on earlier. There's nothing worse than trying to fill this function and not getting along with your artist. No wonder his heart wasn't in it."

Big Jon proceeded to tell Andre the details. After ten minutes, he wrapped up the conversation with, "So they're going to need a new guy, and I think you would be perfect." Andre nodded slowly, thankful for the referral and the potential of more work, but sad that his friend now had to find another gig.

Big Jon stopped and looked distant. Andre immediately recognized that someone was communicating to him via the wireless. Big Jon turned his head and spoke quickly into the headset. "I'll be right there." He and Andre nodded to one another, and Big Jon ducked back into the dressing area.

As if on cue, Dave Davis passed by. Andre, now knowing more, could better guide the conversation. Andre gave him a card, and Davis promised he'd call.

Meanwhile, Gene was making his own connections. Andre got the impression that Gene wasn't just giving Jon a copy of *Kisstory*. Rather, he was trying to interest Jon in a similar project for Bon Jovi. Apparently Jon didn't bite. So far, no such book has materialized.

Gene and Shannon had seats on the side of the stage, about 10 or 12 rows up. People recognized them, but in Los Angeles, no one makes a big deal about seeing celebrities. Although wildly successful in terms of their market with existing fans, Kiss had disappeared in the general public's eye.

"Dave Davis called me the Sunday after that show," Andre says. "We talked tour specifics, personal preferences and salary parameters. He was still being cool about the whole arrangement and made a point of telling me they were still interviewing two other people. Bon Jovi was scheduled to be on the *Tonight Show with Jay Leno* the next day, so Dave invited me down to hang out and spend some time with the guys."

Gene and Shannon had seats on the side of the stage, about 10 or 12 rows up. People recognized them, but in Los Angeles, no one makes a big deal about seeing celebrities.

By this time, the New Jersey-bred band was well past its prime. Bon Jovi's commercial zenith came with the group's third album, 1986's *Slippery When Wet*. It sold 12 million copies and stayed atop the *Billboard* charts for eight weeks. Songs like "Livin' On A Prayer," "You Give Love A Bad Name" and "Wanted Dead or Alive" gave *Slippery When Wet* a huge boost.

In the early Nineties the hair band grubbed up and mellowed out a bit but continued to churn out such radio-friendly tunes as "Keep The Faith," "Always" and "This Ain't A Love Song." Bon Jovi's 1995 album, *These Days*, established the group as one of the few survivors from the Eighties' pop-metal scene.

In early 1999, Bon Jovi would record a song for the film EdTV, and all of the band's albums were remastered and reissued. A full-length album reportedly was in the works for later that year.

Back in 1995, Andre still didn't know if he had the Bon Jovi job or not. He took Davis up on his invitation and visited the NBC studios the next day. Andre and Davis spent less than two minutes talking, and then the tour manager gave Andre an itinerary! He mentioned that the band was going to try Andre for a few weeks. If the personalities and everything worked out, he would be in for the rest of the tour, which included Australia and South Africa. They wrapped up the meeting and Davis asked for Andre's passport so he could prepare travel documents. Andre knew he was in.

36

TORD'S WILD RIDE

Bon Jovi

"SO WHEN ARE YOU GUYS GOIN' OUT?" RON SCOGGINS ASKED into the cellular phone, his car moving easily through the Vegas afternoon traffic.

"Tomorrow, " Andre replied quickly. "I'm packing now."

Scoggins could hear him shuffling papers in the background. "The family and I are going out for dinner tonight." There was a twinge of sadness in Andre's voice.

In the music industry, the term "goin' out" means just that: going out on tour. It means planes, buses, and Town Cars. It means hotels, restaurants and late-night room service. Very often, the term evokes mixed emotions.

There is a constant dynamic tension for people in this business. For family types like Andre, it can be especially difficult. Goin' out means income. It means providing for your family and your loved ones. It also means being away from them. Andre, thankful for the work but emotional about leaving his family, feels this tension every time he hits the road.

Scoggins moved the conversation along. "How long will you be out?"

"Not long." Andre replied, his voice positive with the thought of a short and successful tour. "A couple of months."

"How are they?" Scoggins was curious. He and Andre had started in this business together, but their paths had taken two different tracks. Scoggins remained on the rap side of the music business, while for the last several years Andre worked almost exclusively with rock acts.

"Great," Andre replied. "You know, a bunch of guys our age from Jersey."

Scoggins continued his probe, "How is *he?*"

Andre knew exactly what Scoggins was asking. All groups have someone who gets the most attention; the guy considered the star. And those are usually the ones with the biggest egos.

"He seems like a great guy," Andre said, referring to Jon Bon Jovi. "But I'm going to have to watch it. He is so recognizable that we may need to keep him under wraps. They even have a nickname for him."

"Really, what is it?"

"Bubble Boy."

The Next Day

"Andre, you've been here before. What's it like?" asked Richie Sambora, Bon Jovi's lead guitarist.

He and the members of Bon Jovi had been in the air for hours, heading to South America for a series of gigs on the Keep The Faith Tour. Several other members of the entourage strained to hear Andre's response over the drone of the plane's engines. His answer was brief and puzzling.

"Toad's Wild Ride," he said.

"What?" Richie asked. "What do you mean? Isn't that a ride at Disneyland?"

Andre nodded, then turned his gaze out over the plane's wing.

"Toad's Wild Ride," he muttered again.

Richie shrugged and went back to reading his magazine.

> Based on the tales of J. Thaddeus Toad in Kenneth Grahame's classic children's book *The Wind in the Willows*, Toad's Wild Ride at Disneyland captured the adventures of Toad's escape in a stolen motorcar from the Tower of London and the resulting chase by the London Police. For Mr. Toad, it is a harrowing adventure. The ride starts quickly, carrying passengers in old-time motorcars. The first part of the track passes almost entirely in the dark. Then, loud music, black lights and fluorescent backdrops assault riders as they screech through the streets of London. All the while, Toad tries to escape the police and their constantly blowing whistles. Toad, not the best driver, careens through incredibly sharp turns, faces many near misses and crashes into haystacks and doors. Debris flies.

Finally, the car crashes, sending the occupants straight to hell, where laughing red devils and a deranged pitchfork-wielding Satan taunt them for eternity. Toad's Wild Ride is a dark and exciting thrill.

Richie had no idea what it had to do with Bon Jovi and South America.

The plane's tires chirped as they hit the Buenos Aires airport tarmac.

Andre performed a great deal of advance work for this tour and exchanged faxes and phone calls for weeks with several local contacts prior to Bon Jovi's arrival. When traveling to a place like Buenos Aires, doing such advance work is paramount. Andre visited the country with Aerosmith and knew things could get dangerous.

Once on the ground, the members of Bon Jovi made their way through the throngs of officials to waiting vans on the runway tarmac. Andre's communication paid off with a police escort.

"Kind of reminds ya of the old days, don't it?" drummer Tico Torres said to no one in particular, referring to Bon Jovi's outrageous U.S. success between 1986 and 1989.

As Andre moved band members into the their respective vehicles, he addressed the group of people milling about. Obviously promoter types, they wore flashy clothes and lots of jewelry. Some carried notebooks.

"May I please have the drivers over here?" Andre shouted to be heard over the louder-than-usual runway din.

Tour manager Dave Davis slid into the back seat of the second vehicle, and Andre shut the door. The rest of the band members were already seated in the vehicles. He turned to the group standing near the vans.

"Drivers?"

"Si! Si! We are right here!"

A small man wearing glasses stepped up from the back of the group, pulling two others with him. Andre eyed the three. The smaller man who called out wore chinos and a nice shirt. The other two men were dressed in chauffeur outfits, one too small and the other too big.

"Who are you?" Andre asked suspiciously. "We only have two vehicles."

"I am the interpreter."

"The *what?* I specifically requested English-speaking drivers."

"I am sorry, Mr. Andre, but these are the only two drivers we have. Their English is not so good, so I translate for them."

"When you say 'not so good,' exactly what do you mean?"

"Just not so good."

Andre turned to the one wearing the too-big chauffeur's uniform. "How much English do you understand?"

"Si." He nodded his head in violent agreement.

"How much?"

"Si." Another enthusiastic head bob.

Andre turned to the interpreter. "They don't speak a word of English, do they?"

"Si. Not a word, Mr. Andre," smiled the interpreter.

"Greeeeeeaaaaaaaaat." Andre strung the word out as if it was a paragraph.

The cab ride to Coco's gym with Joe Perry in the Eastern Bloc quickly flashed through Andre's mind; he knew the implications of not using English-speaking drivers. The trip from the airport to the hotel could be dangerous. Quick and clear communication with the drivers would be imperative.

Well, at least we've got four armed and uniformed police officers on motorcycles leading the way, he thought.

"OK. Let's go," Andre ordered, pointing to the driver in the too-small chauffeur's uniform. "You. Drive that car and follow us. Do exactly what we do."

Andre then turned expectantly to the translator. It took him three minutes to communicate those simple instructions to the driver. Andre hated working with translators.

"You two come with me." Andre pointed for the translator and big-suited driver to get in the first van. Andre put the three of them on the long front bench with the translator sandwiched in the middle.

"Let's go," Andre directed as he slammed shut the door. "The Hyatt."

The van Andre rode in contained Jon, Richie, Tico and keyboardist David Bryan. The second carried Davis and the rest of the entourage. The cars eased out from the airport property into the afternoon Buenos Aires sun.

Andre squinted until his eyes became accustomed to the brightness. The cops hit their lights and rolled easily onto the highway. Andre's senses flared. This felt too easy.

His instincts, as usual, proved correct. Within seconds, the race was on. A pair of older Fiat-type cars — one rust-colored, one white — immediately pulled up next to the van, one on each side. They were filled with teenaged Argentine boys who were waving, screaming, taking pictures and shouting, "Bon Jovi, Bon Jovi!"

Immediately, Andre's driver started speeding up. Andre glanced at the speedometer and rapidly calculated the difference between kilometers and miles per hour.

"Tell your boy to slow down," he growled at the translator.

After a brief exchange, the message got through.

Several minutes later, two more "chase" vehicles joined the race. Similar cars carrying similar passengers. These small cars apparently were the vehicle of choice among young Argentines.

Now with two vehicles on each side, Andre instructed the translator to tell the driver to move a little quicker — an instruction the driver seemed to really understand. The van's kilometer-marked speedometer crept higher and higher: 120 - 130 - 140.

"How far to the hotel?" Andre asked, his hand gripping the front dash.

"Going this fast?" the translator asked, now looking as if he wanted to be somewhere else. "Not long." He slid lower into the seat.

Great! Andre thought. *A comedian.*

Thud - Thud - Thud.

Andre sat straight up. He heard the unmistakable sound of flesh against the van window. When traveling with big-name artists, that sound is a familiar one, although it's typically reserved for a parking lot, when the vehicle is creeping through a crowd while leaving a venue — not on a busy Buenos Aires boulevard doing 140 kilometers per hour.

"Look at this kid!" Richie screamed from the back. Andre turned to look over his right shoulder and saw a skinny guy, about nineteen, with his white T-shirt flapping in the wind, hanging out of a dangerously close vehicle.

Thud - Thud - Thud.

Andre watched as he pounded on the van window. "Bon Jovi! Bon Jovi! We love Bon Jovi!"

The band members looked horrified.

Tires squealed as the tiny car veered to the right and the teenager almost fell. Laughing, he slid back inside the tiny car. Andre shook his head. The kid could have been killed.

Andre looked in the rear-view mirror. He saw the second van right behind them — and two more chase cars, bringing the count to six. The police added their sirens. Flashers and sirens almost ensured that the number of chase cars would increase. And it did. Two more cars shot out of a side street from the left, driving right in front of the cops' motorcycles and skidding to a stop. The cops swerved to miss the cars, and Andre's van screeched to a halt right in front of the two newcomers. Andre glanced quickly at the side-view mirror just in time to see the second van come screeching to a similar stop, inches from the first.

Cars surrounded the halted vehicles. Kids poured out and pressed against the tinted windows.

"What should we do?" asked an anxious Jon Bon Jovi.

"Wait for the police," Andre replied calmly.

The cops turned their motorcycles around and headed back toward the scene, where they began to settle down the kids. Traffic started to back up behind the incident.

"What now?" the musicians asked.

Andre grinned. "Want to say hi to some fans?"

"Yeah!" came the surprisingly enthusiastic response.

Andre told the translator to let the other driver know the plan. They would do a quick meet and greet on the streets of Buenos Aires and then travel to the hotel, now only blocks away. Within seconds, the members of Bon Jovi were out of the vans, shaking hands and hugging their Argentine fans.

The guys didn't mind. They were just glad to be finished with the harrowing ride. About five minutes later, Andre instructed the translator to tell the fans that the band had to leave because Bon Jovi was running behind schedule. This is a popular excuse given to move celebrities away from clinging fans.

After the last photo was snapped and the final hug exchanged, the members of the group climbed back into the vans.

Richie Sambora was the last to enter the first van. As Andre held the door open for him, Richie started to get in and then stopped. He shot a glance at Andre and said, "Toad's Wild Ride, huh?"

"Toad's Wild Ride." Andre winked.

This wasn't the only close call in South America that Andre would have with the boys from Jersey. Jon's nickname eventually would prove to be very appropriate.

13

BUBBLE BOY

Bon Jovi

November 1995: Buenos Aires, Argentina

THE BAND, FIRED-UP AFTER THEIR WILD RIDE FROM THE AIRPORT, chatted excitedly as they poured into the lobby of the Buenos Aires Hyatt. Drummer Tico Torres, very vocal, teased Andre about an in-flight card game of "in between," in which Andre lost $20.

"Hey, Andre, want to come to my room and play some more cards?" the drummer grinned. "I could really use the extra money for some shopping later."

"Very funny, Tico, very funny," Andre replied. "Would you like to get to your room, or do you *really* want me to show you why I was drafted by the Jets."

For this Jersey-based band, the New York Jets were beyond legend, and the friendly reminder of Andre's pro-ball career quickly humbled the drummer. Tico mumbled something unintelligible as he followed a bellhop to his room.

It had been a busy couple of hours. The madness of the airport and the crazy ride to the hotel reminded Andre of just how passionate South American fans could be when it comes to U.S. rock stars. For the moment, at least, Andre and the group had found sanctuary.

"The Hyatt in Buenos Aires is one of the nicest hotels I have ever seen," Andre says. "It's converted from an old presidential residence, and the place is simply magnificent. There are actually two separate, but connected, sides to the hotel. On the second floor, across the walkway is the presidential area. That's where all the big names stay."

Andre describes the set up. "One floor has three or four rooms. That's where Richie, Tico, keyboardist David Bryan and others stayed. Then there is another area where there are only two rooms on the whole floor. One contains a huge suite, where Jon stayed — but not because he had an overactive ego. It was a necessity. The guys in Bon Jovi, and especially Jon, are all very down-to-earth. They experienced enormous success but were still regular guys. Because Jon is just so recognizable, we needed to keep him out of the way."

Andre remembers them all as playful. "Dave used to tease Jon a lot, saying things like, 'Jon, we are going out to grab a bite at a local restaurant. You want to come with us?'" Jon's answer would always be the same. 'No, I'm just going to lay around the hotel, work out, maybe get some sun, have lunch. I'll be OK.'"

"OK, Bubble Boy," would be David's consistent response.

Jon, the "boy in the bubble", could never travel in public with the rest of the band because he always got mobbed. Consequently, he rarely participated in any activities outside of the hotel.

"That was just one of the limitations of his success," Andre explains. "He was always recognized and did not want to put himself in jeopardy by being mobbed or creating a scene."

Laying low and hiding out is one of the huge drawbacks to stardom. Jon Bon Jovi is far from the first to experience this kind of seclusion.

Probably the best-known rock 'n' roll hermit remains Elvis Presley, who used to rent out entire movie theaters so he and his friends could go watch a movie and not be mobbed. Another well-known Elvis maneuver included making arrangements to shop after a store had closed. One of his favorite stops was the Harley-Davidson dealership in Memphis.

Jeanie Morrow, long time manager of that store, remembers what it was like. "It was a little sad," she says. "Many people thought Elvis did those kinds of things because he was a star. But the fact is that the poor guy just couldn't do it otherwise."

What some perceive to be an ostentatious show of wealth is really an attempt at normalcy. And like the superstars before him, Jon Bon Jovi is a bit imprisoned by his celebrity status.

"As a result, when we were on the road, the only thing that Jon would do is work out," Andre says. "At the Buenos Aires Hyatt, there is a great health club where Jon could lift weights and go for a run. He is a serious runner. Jon's trainer, Steve Thaxton, helped keep him in top form. He would work out with Jon on the weights, treadmill and bike. Thaxton is also a chiropractor, acupuncturist, massage therapist – a complete training specialist — the whole nine yards."

One day at the Hyatt, Bubble Boy decided to try his luck at making an appearance in public. Steve was off doing some mid-day shopping, and Jon wanted to go for a run. The rest of the guys were tanning on the sundeck by the pool. Jon stopped by the pool on his way out.

"I'm going for a run," he declared, as if he went jogging outside everyday.

As Andre worked with Bon Jovi, he discovered his security predecessor, Big Jon, made an occasional faux pas that didn't sit well with members of the band. Andre found out very early in his career that tact and decorum were just as important, if not more important, than being a skilled security director, road manager or tour manager.

When working with Bon Jovi, Andre felt comfortable and relaxed. He fit in well, and his personality, as usual, complemented the tour. But in South America, especially, Andre's security duties needed to come first. Andre didn't want to make a social gaffe, but he didn't want anyone to get hurt either.

Bon Jovi may have been past its prime in the United States, but in South America, Andre needed a police escort for Bon Jovi everywhere the band went. Armed police officers, many on motorcycles with Uzis strapped to their backs, usually kept the thousands of screaming fans at bay.

And now Jon wanted to go for a run unescorted!

A couple of the band members didn't move; perhaps they were sleeping. Tico looked over his sunglasses as if to say, "You're what?"

Andre quickly got up from his chair. "Uh, Jon, do you think that's a good idea?"

He approached this conversation cautiously, not wanting to overstep his bounds.

"Yeah, I'll be fine. I'm wearing this baseball cap."

Andre eyed Jon in the hat and took off the kid gloves. "Jon, I gotta' tell ya, man, you're not going to get more than a quarter-mile before they spot you. Hat or no hat."

"I can do it. I'll be fine."

"Alright, then. I'm going, too."

The pool separated two sides of the hotel. The Bon Jovi guys stayed in an area secluded from other guests. To get to the street, Jon and Andre went down a hotel corridor to some steps, which put them at the side entrance to the hotel, just off the main street.

Andre pushed open the door and held it with his foot. "I'll be right here, waiting for you."

Andre quickly surveyed the situation: no other exits or entrances in the area. If the door closed, both Andre and Jon would be out on the street with no escape route. Andre didn't like it. His top rule when working with artists is to always have multiple escape routes. This, at best, would be a single route.

He tried once more to appeal to the singer's better senses.

"Jon, if you want we can ... "

Jon stopped Andre in mid-sentence. "I'll be fine," he assured him.

Andre couldn't tell whether he was trying to sell Andre or perhaps himself on that notion.

Andre scanned the street. There were just a few people out and about — an older man walking his dog, two middle-aged women carrying packages – not enough for Andre to invoke "security privilege" and squelch the excursion.

Jon started his run more quickly than usual, probably anxious to see what would happen. He moved his 170-pound frame easily down the side street. Andre couldn't help but notice how easily Jon moved. He had become quite the athlete, and running seemed to be a very natural movement for him.

A girl in her mid-20s suddenly appeared from around the corner. Andre came alive. This would be the test. Jon looked down at the street, perhaps concentrating on his run, but more than likely trying harder to hide his identity.

The girl looked up at Jon, then looked away. The recognition only took a couple of seconds. She leapt in front of the running musician, stopping him in his tracks.

"Jon Bon Jovi! Jon Bon Jovi!" the girl shouted at the top of her lungs. She started to hug and kiss him repeatedly.

See I told you so. Andre smiled as he shook his head.

And then his smile faded. A Fiat-style car filled with kids, mostly teenage guys, screeched to a stop. There must have been four or five of them; Andre couldn't see how many as they broke out of the car and surrounded Jon.

Andre frantically looked for something to prop open the door. Nothing. No trash can, brick or piece of wood in sight. If he ran to help, the door would shut and Jon would have no escape route. Adherence to this rule has protected more than one of Andre's artists. If the door closed, the nearest hotel entrance was 500 yards around the building — exposing Jon and himself to even more of the public and perhaps a much more dangerous situation.

Andre helplessly watched the scene unfold down the street. Five more seconds and I'm getting him. As if Jon heard Andre's thoughts, the star looked up. Relieved to see Andre, Jon smiled and held his hand up to let Andre know he was OK.

The fans shouted excitedly, shooting pictures and shaking Jon's hand. After just a few moments, Jon said good-bye, turned and resumed his running — right back toward Andre and the open door.

"Hey, Jon." Andre smiled holding the door open for the frazzled runner.

"Don't start," Jon said in a playful tone. "I'm going to the hotel health club."

Andre smiled, but inside he felt sorry for Jon and the fact that he and others in his position must sacrifice their private lives. Andre wondered if it was all worth it.

For Andre, working with Bon Jovi was definitely worth the trouble Bubble Boy's popularity occasionally created. He wouldn't trade his time spent with Jon for anything, he says.

38
TALES FROM THE ROAD

Bon Jovi

WHEN ASKED ABOUT BON JOVI'S GUITARIST, RICHIE SAMBORA, Andre simply smiles and says, "Paris."

MTV was hosting an awards show there, and Bon Jovi – slated to perform – wanted to *really* enjoy the experience. It was a Tuesday afternoon.

"Andre," Richie hollered into the telephone receiver from his Parisian hotel room. "Get down here now!"

His words were terse, but Andre could tell he was smiling. Andre brightened as well. He certainly enjoyed these Bon Jovi guys.

"I'll be right there, Richie."

Andre had no idea what was up. But he knew if Richie Sambora was behind it, it had to be good. That's just his way. As Richie opened the door, Andre walked into the hotel room. "What's goin' on?" he asked playfully.

"I know you're not usually into this," Richie began. "But this is special."

The guitarist pulled an odd-shaped, green-tinted bottle out of a brown paper bag. The ancient label – old, dirty and deteriorated – peeled at the edges. At the same time, Richie wore a grin the size of New Jersey.

"Ah, cognac," Andre exclaimed.

"It's almost 100 years old." Richie beamed, holding the bottle reverently.

He quickly pulled out two bulbous brandy snifters and poured the antique libation into them.

After both men considered the glasses, they looked at each other, smiling. "To friends!" they said simultaneously. It seemed hard to believe – cognac bottled before the turn of the century, before mass-produced cars, and before anything resembling today's music industry even existed.

"Somehow, the guys in Bon Jovi found a collector of rare and vintage cognacs," Andre remembers. "He was known in collectors' circles as having one of the premier cognac collections on the planet. [Bon Jovi tour manager] Dave Davis and Richie were having lunch at this guy's restaurant. Afterwards, he invited them down to his wine cellar, where he kept his fine wines and cognac, and Richie brought some back for me. He appreciates quality — from his collection of guitars to how he and [wife] Heather [Locklear] decorate their home."

Andre's work with Richie continued outside of Bon Jovi in spring 1998, when Andre accompanied him on European promotional tours to support Richie's second solo effort, *Undiscovered Soul.*

Andre also had the opportunity to work with both Richie and Heather when he escorted them to see the Rolling Stones Concert at the MGM Grand in Las Vegas, not too long after the couple appeared on the cover of *People* magazine in November of 1997.

Another Bon Jovi member to find his way into the pages of *People* magazine in 1998 was drummer Tico Torres, who showed off his painting abilities – a relatively new endeavor for this hard-rocking drummer.

But back in 1995 on the Keep the Faith Tour in Bogotá, Columbia, one day, painting was the furthest thing from Tico's mind.

"Kidnapped!" the drummer exclaimed. "I can't believe it."

"Yeah," Andre chuckled. "Authorities are saying tourists should remain in their hotels."

Kidnapping is a fairly common occurrence in Colombia. So common, in fact, that the following warning is regularly issued by the U.S. Government:

> The Department of State warns U.S. citizens against unnecessary travel to Colombia. Violence by narcotic traffickers, guerrillas, paramilitary groups and other criminal elements continues to affect all parts of the country. U.S. citizens have been the victims of recent threats, kidnappings and murders. U.S. citizens in Colombia are currently targets of kidnapping efforts by guerrilla rebels. Colombian groups have been known to operate in the border areas of neighboring countries, creating similar dangers for travelers in those areas. Since it is U.S. policy not to pay ransom or make other concessions to terrorists, the U.S. government's ability to

assist kidnapped U.S. citizens is limited. U.S. citizens of all age groups and occupations have been kidnapped, and kidnappings have occurred in all major regions of Colombia.

Reuters News Service reports that "the country is plagued with the highest incidents of crime anywhere in the world." Police statistics show a total of 328 kidnappings during the first quarter of 1997 alone.

The particular kidnapping to which Tico was reacting hit close to home for Colombian officials.

Andre may very well have been in Bogotá when the mysterious "Dignity for Colombia" group kidnapped Juan Carlos Gaviria, brother of the former Colombian president, Cesar Gaviria. According to press reports, kidnappers contended that Juan Carlos should stand trial for his corruption and immorality benefiting from the presidency of his brother Cesar. It threw local authorities into a flurry of activity.

But that day in Bogotá, Tico would not be denied.

"Fuck that! I'm a drummer in a rock band. Why would someone want to kidnap me?"

Tico grabbed his room key from the table and turned to Andre. "Let's go."

Andre laughs as he remembers that exchange between him and the drummer. "Well, the situation may have been dangerous, but the officials there apparently weren't familiar with Tico's appetite for buying antiques. He was redoing his house, and everywhere we went, we would go looking for just the right stuff for his project. A door here, a chair there — all really cool and really unique stuff. Apparently, Bogotá was known for having cool stuff and that really appealed to Tico. He had already done his homework and had several addresses of places to go and names of people he wanted to see. He was very organized. And he wasn't about to be stopped."

"Come on, Andre! Let's go," the drummer commanded again.

"OK, Tico. This kidnapping stuff doesn't bother me," Andre replied. "But I just want to be sure you've thought this through. It's a different country, known for being a rough place. I don't want you to make any rash decisions."

"Andre, are you kidding me, man? Kidnapping? Rebels? They don't know tough. I'm from New York. Let's go!"

As Andre closed the hotel room door behind them, he suppressed a chuckle.

"That's Tico," Andre sums up. "A confident guy who gets what he wants."

By the way, the two spent a great day shopping for antiques and encountered no trouble.

Confidence and machismo aren't the only common interests shared between Andre and the Bon Jovi guys. They also enjoy a good card game — one in which Andre usually loses big money.

"Tico, what are you going to do?" Jon asked one day in mid-flight on Bon Jovi's private jet. They were in between gig cities somewhere over the United States.

Tico, pensive, tapped his cards.

"Well?" Jon prompted.

The pressure was on, and Tico knew it.

The airplane's engines droned as the plane shook with some heavier-than-usual turbulence. No one seemed to notice.

"I'm in," Tico responded.

The group clustered around the table shouted their approval. The pot was now up to $1,200.

On private flights in the band's personal jet, Bon Jovi would get tired of watching movies and reading magazines. Card games passed the time. Among the band's favorites: poker, black jack and "in between" — a game in which players lay down two cards and bet that the third one's number will fall in between the other two.

"After a few rounds, the stakes would start to get high," Andre says. "There were a couple of times when the pot was up to $250, and Tico had to throw in $500 a time."

Tico wasn't the only rocker to pay the price, though.

"When the stakes got to $500 or $1,000, everyone was sweating bullets — even these big rock stars," Andre continues. "You hit the pot, and the next thing you know, you're looking at $1,500 in your pocket. You would think that for those guys, this would be no big deal, but it was. It wasn't just the money; it was the challenge of the game. It could have been $2 going up to $4, but the guys would still be sweating! Competition is a funny thing."

39
JOVI IN THE JUNGLE

Bon Jovi

December 1995: Durban, South Africa

"HEY, BIG GUY, ARE YOU WATCHING THE GAME?" JON BON JOVI
asked over the telephone.

An NFL football game made the dark continent and another hotel room feel more
like home.

"Yeah, I am. Where are you?" Andre asked a little suspiciously.

"In the suite. Did you see that last play?"

"Yeah," Andre answered, relieved to know his artist's whereabouts.

"Well? What'd ya think? As an ex-pro, you're probably tearin' your hair out."

"Yeah, they're not doing very well. You could say they are ... "

"If you say 'Livin' on a Prayer,' Andre Augustine, I'll come down there and tackle
you myself."

"That I'd like to see."

Both men laughed.

"Hey, Andre," Jon started again. "Wanna do something fun?"

"Like what?"

"Up for a safari?" Andre could hear the twinkle in Jon's voice.

Away from the bustle of overzealous fans, life on the road takes on different tones,
depending on the artists. When touring with George Thorogood, Andre attends baseball
games. The members of Aerosmith prefer to do their own thing. Steven Tyler shops, goes to
movies or heads out for a night of local music. Joe Perry works out or spends time with his

family when he can. Brad Whitford, Joey Kramer and Tom Hamilton — all car freaks — like to go to racetracks and car shows.

Bon Jovi likes to soak up the local color of the city in which the group is playing. So going on safari in South Africa made perfect sense to these guys.

The pilot of the puddle jumper circled the small village on safari day and eventually sighted the airstrip, which looked more like a driveway than a runway.

The entire band was along, including Dave Davis and Jon's wife, Dorothea.

"There was this little village with no fences or barriers, just a series of buildings in the jungle," Andre says. "It is the weirdest thing to see, because you don't realize when you're down on the ground that you are in the middle of the jungle."

The roofless, metallic-gray Humvee that carried Bon Jovi and company through the jungle sported bench seats in rows that were adjusted to different heights so everyone could see. The driver was a friendly English-speaking African native. To his right was a man who served as the tracker and didn't speak English, but the band understood his nonverbal communication. With a wave of his hand, he could make the group sit up and be quiet.

We should have this guy work with some of the promoters, Andre thought.

"The tracker would watch the road and the tracks in the dirt, and he could tell by smell and by looking at the tracks where certain animals were," Andre explains. "We saw everything: rhinos, cheetahs, elephants, giraffes, birds, dung beetles. We even saw a lioness with a kill."

The Humvee crawled along slowly. The area was wide open except for a thick patch of jungle on the right. Suddenly, the tracker raised up his hand, and the brakes squealed the big vehicle to a stop.

"What is it?" the driver asked, concerned.

The tracker replied in his native African tongue. The rockers didn't understand the words, but they got the inflection. Something big was about to go down.

The tracker sniffed loudly, then again. He muttered something. This time, his tone was a little more relaxed. Suddenly, the party in the Humvee felt the earth shake. It reminded Andre of the scene in Jurassic Park just before T-Rex made his entrance.

In seconds, a herd of elephants in a thunderous stampede rushed by the awestruck group. It was an incredible sight.

As they headed back toward human civilization an hour or so later, the members of the safari entourage were quiet and contemplative.

"You know, when you leave on that little airplane and see nature in all her glory, it's very humbling," Andre explains. "The experience is one that'll stick with me — especially when I'm starting to feel too confident in my abilities. There's a much bigger world out there beyond the rock and rap stage."

Andre returned from the Keep the Faith Tour to a message from Kiss' Gene Simmons, asking him to call. He sounded serious.

"Andre," the message began. "Gene. We're goin' out. Call me."

Thus began Andre's role in what some industry observers call the most anticipated and successful rock 'n' roll comeback of all time. For many Kiss fans, the Alive/Worldwide Tour would be as close to a religious epiphany as they'd get. For the band, it probably felt more like time travel.

With the makeup back on and the set lists dusted off, The Demon, The Starchild, Space-Ace and The Catman prepared themselves to recapture the arena-rock crown.

40
DÉJÀ VU

Kiss

Spring 1996: Los Angeles, California

THE BUZZ ON THE STREET ABOUT THE KISS REUNION TOUR COULD be heard around the world. Gene wanted Andre to help helm a Kiss comeback tour. Gene, swamped in production details, gave Andre a number to call for specifics: Doc McGhee. Now Kiss' manager, McGhee prepared for a reunion tour unlike any other. Andre finally would get his chance to work with McGhee and to meet the other Kiss originals: Ace Frehley and Peter Criss.

Andre, whose role on the Alive/Worldwide Tour was security director and road manager, made his way through the L.A. traffic and headed toward Cole Studios in West Hollywood, California. He had finished his other work for the day and wanted to meet the rest of his traveling companions for the next several months. For the first time, he was going to be in the same room with all four of the original members of Kiss.

Andre knew his way around Cole. Almost seven years had passed since he and Ron Scoggins first met N.W.A. there, and the place held special significance for him.

Andre entered the foyer to the foot-stomping rhythm of "Deuce." He moved cautiously into the studio, trying hard not to attract undue attention. He sat on the couch, not moving. As the band rehearsed, Andre closed his eyes and listened to the music, letting a flood of memories wash over him.

"I closed my eyes, and it was like high school all over again," he says. "Friday night parties, laughing with friends, listening to music, meeting girls."

Before he could control himself, tears welled up in his eyes. "It was strange," Andre continues. "All of a sudden, I started misting up. Imagine me – an ex-jock, security director, road manager – misting up after hearing these guys do 'Deuce.' Shivers ran up and down my spine. I knew when Ace, Paul and Gene formed a line and started rocking back and forth with their guitars and reenacting the choreography they perfected twenty years ago that this tour was going to be huge. If it affected *me* like that, think what it would do for millions of fans who'd waited years for this."

Andre's intuition was right. When the Alive/Worldwide Tour (Andre's highest-profile gig) came to a close in July 1997, Kiss had played in front of two million people and grossed nearly $90 million, according to industry sources.

"Up until that point, I wasn't real sure how all this was going to come together," Andre continues, recalling that rehearsal day in April 1996. "Would it be well-received? Would Kiss sell any tickets at all? But after I heard that one song in the rehearsal studio, I knew it was going to be big." Immediately, Andre knew he would need additional security help. He called his old friend Tony Morehead and invited Morehead on the tour as well.

Not only was the old Kiss magic back, but Doc McGhee's management style and expertise would guide the boys through music-business whitewater and make this the comeback of the decade.

Doc McGhee, incredibly determined and driven, has never taken less than the best. His creativity and knowledge of the inner workings of the rock-music industry landed him Kiss' Alive/Worldwide gig, which garnered mixed reactions from some promoters.

Promoters – the rough-and-tumble characters that make the touring business possible – put up the money, take the risks and reap the rewards. Promoters are the ones who actually make the shows happen. C.K. Lendt, former accountant for Kiss back in the Seventies and early Eighties, provides a great overview of the booking process in his 1996 book, *Kiss and Sell:*

> Promoters "buy" shows from the artist's booking agent. They are responsible
> for guaranteeing a certain minimum fee for the act to perform, plus a percentage of
> the gate or the show's profits if it does well. The promoter has to make all the
> organizational arrangements – local transportation, staffing, stagehands, production,
> catering, building rental, tickets – and advertise and promote the show. If the
> promoter doesn't keep his costs under control, or if the show sells fewer tickets

than he predicted, the promoter will lose money. Most shows are gambles. And business judgments that put tens, if not hundreds, of thousands of dollars at risk are often made on nothing more than gut feeling.

As Lendt also points out, promoters in the late 1970s made huge amounts of money booking Kiss. By contrast, in the late 1980s, Kiss' lack of drawing power was the reason many promoters over-speculated and went out of business.

This prompted many promoters to react apprehensively toward the reunion tour. When approached about the Alive/Worldwide gig, some suggested McGhee try out smaller venues to "see how it goes over," Andre says. McGhee refused to book a bunch of sheds, so he gambled on arenas and stadiums and sold the promoters on why this tour would work. And it paid off.

The tour, which eventually won eight *Performance* magazine Readers Poll Awards, including Best Rock Act, Best Arena/Amphitheater Tour, Best Stage Manager, Best Creative Stage Set, Best Tour Accountant and Best Road Crew, kicked off in Detroit on June 28, 1996. Tiger Stadium sold 38,000 seats in 47 minutes.

The tour covered more than 210 cities in 26 countries and was seen by an estimated two million people. More than $7 million of sound, lighting, video, pyrotechnics and staging equipment were assembled, according to *Metal Edge's* "Official Kiss Alive Worldwide 1996/1997 Tour" magazine, and the touring convoy consisted of eleven semis and six tour buses. The touring and production staff totaled more than sixty people (plus 220 local people at each venue). Additional mind-numbing figures compiled by *Metal Edge* estimate that 58 pounds of theatrical makeup, 358 pints of regurgitated stage blood, $170,000 of stage outfits and 6,000 condoms were used on the tour.

"Unless you are a Kiss fan, you don't get what Kiss is about," Andre says. "But Doc gets it. Most of the industry people who put him down in the beginning didn't have any of the foresight to realize what was going to happen when Kiss put that makeup back on and went on tour. Doc knows about Kiss fans. He knows what turns them on and how Kiss relates to them."

Incidentally, Gene Simmons also credits McGhee with the concept behind 1998's 3-D Psycho Circus Tour. "He's always wanted to do something 3-D in the past with other bands he's worked with. But it never fit with anybody else," Gene told *Guitar World* in October 1998. "As soon as we heard the 3-D idea, we went, 'Oh, that's Kiss.'"

"Doc McGhee works harder than any manager who I have ever been around," says Andre, adding that he himself worked harder on the reunion tour than ever before. "The tour was a high-maintenance one. But Doc hung in there and made it work. I probably learned more on that one tour from Doc than in my whole career with anyone else. He taught me. He pushed me. He had faith in me. Doc ranks as one of the best coaches I ever had, in sports or any professional endeavor."

And coach he did. On the Alive/Worldwide Tour, McGhee would gather Gene, Paul, Ace, Peter, Morehead and Andre in a huddle before each performance and recite something inspirational, usually along the lines of "Let's go kick some ass!" Then, much like a football team prior to a play, they would place their hands on top of each other's and cheer, "Goooooo!" before Kiss hit the stage.

McGhee's professional and personal demeanor taught Andre that if a touring gig isn't fun for him and everybody else involved, it's not worth doing.

Andre also observed McGhee play hardball when securing financing for the Alive/Worldwide Tour, driving up guarantees for promoters and negotiating cover stories in such magazines as *Entertainment Weekly* and *Spin.*

But before the tour started, all of the success seemed much less certain. But Tiger Stadium set the stage for the future ... literally.

41
OPENING NIGHT
Kiss

June 28, 1996: Show Day
Alive/Worldwide Tour
Tiger Stadium - Detroit

PEOPLE EVERYWHERE. SOME, IN THEIR TEENS, WORE THE LATEST
baggy-style fashions and looked around them with wide and excited eyes. Others, in their
late 20s, 30s and even 40s, appeared to be fans from the original Kiss Army that formed back
in the Seventies.

Some of these fans obviously had moved on in life and found respectable jobs. They
wore short and corporate hair, clean jeans and polo shirts. The fashion calendar for others in
the older crowd must have stopped somewhere around 1978. They wore tight and faded Kiss
T-shirts, feathered back their long hair and dangled chain wallets from their waists.

They milled about in mixed groups. Corporate hairs and the '78-ers, laughing and
sharing stories of when they saw Kiss back in the day. And then there were the hard-core
fans, whose ages knew no bounds. They were young, old, short, tall and all pledging their
allegiance to Kiss.

Some came alone, like the guy dressed up as bassist and singer Gene Simmons from the
Dressed to Kill album cover. He wore a tan three-piece suit, a thin black tie and white dress
shoes. His makeup was perfect, and his hair was pulled into a "Pebbles"- type tussle on the
top of his head. The three-piece suit made a great departure from the typical makeup-
adorned and stage-costumed fans.

Others came in groups, perhaps because they felt there was strength in numbers, or maybe because they thought it made the biggest statement. One of the best was a foursome of two guys and two girls — obviously a double date. Each one dressed as a different member of the band, and their outfits were spectacular. One girl, dressed as guitarist Ace Frehley, sported a great torso-V. Her date came as drummer Peter Criss, with emerald accents on his makeup. The other couple was dressed as Simmons and guitarist and singer Paul Stanley. He was the perfect demon with a red-lined cape and impressive platform boots; she looked so much like Paul that many fans did a double take. The star over her eye was perfectly proportioned, and her lips were as red as her date's cape.

Adding to the spectacle were huge 40-foot-tall inflatable figures, one for each member of the band, towering just outside of Tiger Stadium's main entrance.

Homemade banners hung everywhere, draped across vans and dangling from concrete walls. Some were crudely created from bedsheets and spray paint, while others were professionally made canvas signs. Some just featured the Kiss logo and others shouted, "Kiss! Alive!" and "Kiss Reunion Tour!!!"

The entire scene played out like a cross between carnival and chaos. The crowd funneled through the arena's doors and turnstiles, and anticipation hung heavy in the air. The crowd noise picked up a notch, with screams of "Gene! Gene! Gene!" and chants of "Kiss! Kiss! Kiss!"

The world was about to see what these people had believed for years: Kiss simply is the greatest show on earth. Filled to capacity, the 38,000 seats in Detroit's Tiger Stadium created a human panorama as the crowd noise rose to deafening levels. Fans had waited almost 17 years for this moment.

"It just got louder and louder," Andre remembers about that first time he led the four original members of Kiss to the stage. "I've never seen such energy from a crowd."

And that energy – nervous energy, really – propelled the band, too. The limo ride from the Ritz Carlton in Dearborn felt longer than it actually was for Andre and his traveling companions that evening, Gene and Paul. When Kiss' limos arrived at the performers' entrance, the band (already in makeup and costumes) stepped out of the vehicles, and looked around at their surroundings and nervously at each other. They could hear the crowd cries, and for the first time, they realized the significance of this performance.

Andre scanned from left to right as he walked. Black anvil crates lined the walls and passageways. Huge coiled cables sat neatly in corners throughout the area. Technicians wearing tool belts and carrying walkie-talkies moved about with machine-like precision.

As Andre and the four rock legends neared the stage, the house lights went black. Some fans in the front row could make out figures moving behind the curtain. Gene noticed some fans seated just behind the curve of the curtain and cocked his head from side to side, glaring at them like a creature from the underworld who had just been disturbed. He then pointed his finger and swept it across the group of onlookers, fanning out his bat-like cape as if to warn them.

Meanwhile, in the darkness, the crowd grew more raucous by the second. As the final strains of The Who's "Won't Get Fooled Again" vanished into the June night sky, a voice from the blackness announced: 'AALLLRIIIIGHT DEEETRROOIIIIIT!!! You wanted the best, you got the best! The hottest band in the world ... Kiss!"

The crowd's roar shook the stadium. Still in total blackness, the band played the first several chords of "Deuce." Smoke poured from underneath the curtain as the rhythm of the music rocked the building's foundation.

Then, the world detonated for the first time in nearly two decades. The curtain fell with a flash of light and a deafening explosion. In an instant, Kiss was revealed, looming like skyscrapers amid the dry ice, fire and smoke.

Gene prowled the stage as though looking for victims. Paul danced like a gazelle. Ace, his human form merely a vehicle for some cosmic musical force, played flawlessly. And Peter looked like he was driving the world's most powerful Mack truck. The moment was truly surreal.

Two hours later, after Kiss blew up the stage, breathed fire, spit blood, launched rockets from guitars and played the classic anthems of a generation, the band and its army left no doubt that they once again were about to conquer the world.

Andre was in for the ride of his life.

42
‡PA(E-A(E

Ace Frehley

July 26, 1996: Show Day

Kiss Alive/Worldwide Tour

Madison Square Garden – New York City

THE FINAL CHORDS OF "FIREHOUSE" ECHOED THROUGHOUT Madison Square Garden. Kiss had sold out four nights at the legendary venue, an almost unheard of accomplishment for any group; a staggering one for four guys arguably two decades past their prime.

It was July 26, 1996, night number two. Paul Stanley grabbed the microphone.

"Alllllrrrrright. How do you like it so far?"

The response was deafening.

"Is this what you came for tonight, people?"

The crowd thundered its approval.

"Good." Paul continued with his simple stage chatter. "'Cause we're just getting started. Ace wants to say something to you. Ace?"

Ace was wandering around by the amp line. Paul turned, trying to get the guitarist's attention.

"Ace wants to sing you a song," Paul exclaimed, buying Ace a little more time. "Ace! Come here!"

Ace spun around and looked as if he suddenly realized it was his turn at the microphone. Both men laughed as Ace stumbled towards Paul.

Paul threw his arm around Ace's neck and pulled him close. "What song are we gonna do?" Ace whispered in Paul's ear.

"Oh, it's a secret!" Paul responded sarcastically, rolling his eyes. He smiled, slapped Ace on the back and moved out of the spotlight.

Ace leaned in towards the microphone, and the crowd became still. Every fan in the Garden knew what came next, but they held their breath in anticipation anyway. Ace paused for a moment. Then, not wasting any words, in his trademark nasal-thin voice, he shouted, "Shock me!" The crowd roared, the drum line kicked in and the infectious guitar intro began.

Ace let loose with the opening lyrics. "Your lightning's all I need ... " The audience sang every word with him.

Before the song ended, Ace's guitar would fly to the rafters, pour smoke as if on fire and launch rockets at the catwalks. One rocket even took out a spotlight. The spectacle was a regular part of the show.

For Andre and millions of fans, Ace Frehley defines Kiss.

But Ace, born Paul Frehley, wasn't always welcome in Kiss. After his departure in 1982, he formed Frehley's Comet. With virtually no support from the band's label, Megaforce, Frehley floundered, playing small clubs. So small, in fact, that Ace's head almost touched the ceiling at some venues.

The unexpected happened for Ace while on tour in Canada. "I was on tour with Peter Criss when Gene approached my manager about doing *Unplugged*," Ace told *Guitar* magazine in April 1996. "We thought it would be good for Kiss and great exposure for me and Peter. I was excited, so we jumped at it. Even prior to *Unplugged*, me and Paul and Gene had sat down a couple of times over dinner and discussed the old times and basically buried the hatchet. With that out of the way, we were able to talk about doing business without any worries. Plus, I cleaned up my act; they didn't have to worry about me walking in after drinking three bottles of champagne. ... I couldn't see anything negative about getting back with Kiss."

Ace's sobriety, coupled with a cleaned-up Peter Criss, cleared the way for Kiss to heal old wounds and start fresh. The reunion tour was modeled after the group's 1977 Love Gun Tour. Costumes and the set list incorporated only songs written and performed by the original members until 1978. As the U.S. shows wore on, "I Was Made For Lovin' You," from 1979's *Dynasty*, was added, and "Shandi," from 1980's *Unmasked*, was part of the Australian set lists.

Back at Cole Studios during pre-production rehearsals, where Andre met Ace for the first time, the security director had heard all the songs many times before. In fact, "Deuce" was in the set during the Revenge Tour. But he never heard it quite like this. "Bruce and Eric played the same songs, but they put their own twist on them," he explains. "They are professional performers with a crisp, sharp, technical precision to their playing. But I had never heard the music performed the way it was with Ace and Peter. Those two were the missing pieces."

"I had never heard the music performed the way it was with Ace and Peter. Those two were the missing pieces."

When the original Kiss finished "Deuce," they nodded their approval to each other. Gene took off his bass and put it gently in the stand, and then he walked over to Andre.

"Want to meet the other guys?"

"Sure."

Andre remembers the moment. "The first time I met Ace was in the rehearsal studio before the reunion tour. I had seen pictures, heard stories and watched videos, but Ace still blew me away. He didn't talk much; he just played his heart out."

Gene made the introductions. "Ace, have you met Andre yet?" Ace shook his head.

"He's our guy," Gene gloated. "He is our security director, road manager, he does it all."

Ace smiled, approached Andre and said in a heavy New York City accent, 'Hey, man. How ya doin'? I'm Ace. I heard a lot about you. It's nice to meet ya."

Andre shook the guitarist's hand. "It's good to meet you, too, Ace."

Andre has met a lot of musicians, but meeting Ace Frehley was one of his proudest moments.

Unfortunately for Ace, and the rest of the Kiss entourage, Ace had very few proud moments leading up to the tour's opening night in Detroit and during the first several shows with his old bandmates.

Production Rehearsals – Kiss Alive/Worldwide Tour

June 1996: Cobo Hall, Detroit

Detroit held magical memories for Kiss. That's where much of the band's breakthrough album, *Alive!* was recorded, and that record unquestionably launched Kiss into superstardom.

The group's three previous albums – *Kiss, Hotter Than Hell* and *Dressed to Kill* – never made much of a dent in the charts. But Kiss' live act drew crowds and attention from the media. Even though they received marginal industry support, Kiss started headlining large venues, prompting the recording of *Alive!*

Released in 1975, it sold 4 million copies in the United States and catapulted Kiss from underground cult status to commercial giant and household name. *Alive!* actually saved upstart Casablanca Records from bankruptcy, according to some reports. It also gave many fans their first taste of Kiss.

The band planned to recreate the famous opening of *Alive'*s first spine-tingling moments, with its deafening crowd noise and those now-timeless words of Junior Smalling introducing "the hottest band in the land," by opening with a pulverizing version of "Deuce."

Because of the success of *Alive!* and the rabid Kiss fan base in Detroit, Gene Simmons and Paul Stanley wrote the anthem "Detroit Rock City" in their honor. For Kiss, Detroit proved very special indeed.

Now, some 20 years after *Alive!*, they returned to rekindle that flame. At Cobo Hall, Kiss made final preparations for their long-awaited reunion tour, scheduled to kick off at Detroit's Tiger Stadium. Rehearsals were in full force – pyrotechnics, lights, the whole works. But some other not-so-magical moments were about to be relived, as well.

"Where's Ace?" growled Gene, ready to rehearse in his typical black leather-like pants and Revenge Tour T-shirt, with the sleeves cut off. Gene always acted less diplomatic than Paul when it came to dealing with a rusty and often difficult Ace Frehley and Peter Criss, who had not played many Kiss cuts since the early Eighties.

"Some of the earlier rehearsals became nightmares for Ace and Peter," Andre recalls. "Those guys were tortured. They were so out of shape and their chops were so bad that they had to be thinking, *How are we going to pull this off?"*

"Being a musician is like being an athlete," Andre continues. "There's a certain amount of skill and dexterity that you lose just because of age."

Andre remembers that the band often had to start songs over. "For the most part, Paul would have to show them how the chords went. He would grab Ace's guitar and say, 'No, Ace. This is how it goes.' Paul knows every part – what the lead guitar should be doing, what the rhythm guitar should be doing, what the bass should be doing and what the drums should be doing."

Paul also assumed the role of keeper of the craft during the tour. Even after being out on the road for a full month, Kiss still needed to work out the rust. And sometimes the band did it on the stage. During the July 27, 1996, show at Madison Square Garden, fans watched as Peter – horribly off beat on "Watchin' You" – needed Paul's guidance. Shaking his head, Paul clearly mouthed the words, "Stop! Stop!" Then he got Peter back in time with a calculated head nod.

But that June day in Detroit, Paul, Gene and anyone else associated with the tour had a right to be upset. Everyone was present except Ace. About to embark on one of the most anticipated reunion tours in history, they didn't want anything to go wrong. Fans had waited for this event for years, and Kiss wasn't about to let them down.

An unseen opponent compounded the pressure. Kiss was not only up against the rigors of getting the band together and touring, but they needed to take on a much larger and more ominous foe: The myth of Kiss.

Few bands of the rock era can boast Kiss' impact. The band has sold more than 75 million albums, toured as an entity for more than 25 years and performed in front of millions of adoring fans worldwide. Artists as diverse as Garth Brooks and Hootie & The Blowfish list Kiss as a major influence. Plus, the group was (and remains) one of the most merchandised bands in history. The fans are viciously loyal, and they have one of the most recognized and remembered names in music: The Kiss Army.

"When we sat down together, I said to the guys, 'We're training to fight Tyson,'" Paul told *Spin* magazine in August 1996. "And if we can't go in there and whip his ass, we better stay home, because false bravado and any illusions we have about who we are will go right out the window the first time we step up there and meet the enemy."

Taking on this challenge was a daunting task, and nothing could be left to chance. All personnel involved cautiously examined every aspect of the tour: the lighting, the set lists, and even the behavior of band members. And already Ace's actions proved unacceptable.

"Where's Ace?" Gene growled for a second time.

"He missed his flight," Andre responded. "Twice."

Gene was livid. "He what?"

"He missed his flight."

"Who's with him?

"His tech."

Just before the reunion tour got underway, Ace spent time in a Los Angeles apartment, preparing to put his belongings in storage for the duration of the tour. Apparently he got carried away, and the task took Ace longer than he anticipated.

But the rest of the band members didn't let Ace's unavailability stop them. They cranked up the amps, choreographed the moves and started without him. Still, Ace's absence was conspicuous and disconcerting.

When Ace finally arrived in Detroit three days later, the guys heard scuffling, some banging and then the familiar nasal tone coming from a hallway.

"Hey, what's goin' on?" Into Cobo Hall stumbled Ace, wearing his black-and-white skull-and-crossbones shirt and burdened with about nine pieces of luggage.

"Ace, where've you been?" Gene asked. "And what is all this stuff?"

Ace eventually pared his travel gear down to six bags, five of which were filled with computer equipment. The entourage tried to convince him that he had way too much luggage, but Ace stood firm. He told the others that the computer stuff would keep him occupied, so he wouldn't drink or dope, which he was not allowed to do.

In fact, Ace talked about the tour's contract rider with *Metal Edge* magazine's Gerri Miller before the tour began. "We used to have a case of champagne, a case of beer," he said. "We've eliminated the alcohol. Now we do the show, we go back to the hotel."

He also told the magazine that since he'd gotten sober, he'd gone on a health kick. "I only [work out] an hour a day, but five days a week, it adds up. The first week was murder, but now I'm into it. I'm like a junkie for it. It releases the endorphins. I don't need the chemicals anymore, none of that junk."

Was Ace sober on the tour? Pre-tour press hyped the fact that both he and Peter were clean. For media-savvy Kiss fans, the topic was one of much conjecture. If Ace appeared sluggish on stage or slightly off-key, which was often the case, the news instantly was reported in the daily concert reviews located on the popular Web site Kiss Asylum.

> From St. Louis (July 2, 1996): "Ace was stumbling around, as usual."
>
> From San Antonio (July 7, 1996): "The overall song was slow. The tempo was way down. The tempo did bring a lack of energy from all four members. Since Ace starts the song, I'll have to point the blame on him. Ace, pick up the pace!"
>
> From Chicago (July 16, 1996): "Gene and Paul carried the show, while early on Peter and especially Ace sometimes seemed a bit ill at ease back in their old roles. In fact, the two Kiss mainstays seemed a bit perturbed at times with Ace, who simply went through the motions until he took the microphone for "Shock Me."
>
> From Pittsburgh (July 22, 1996): "Ace was just a bit hot and cold on this night. Certain parts of [the 'Shock Me'] solo were clean, but he was missing notes at times. He seemed a bit sluggish. ... By the time Ace played the Beethoven's V part, he seemed to be accepting the mediocrity, because he did not nail the individual notes. He played it far more accurately as chords."
>
> From Worcester, Mass. (December 28, 1996): "[At the end of the set], Ace was over on Gene's side of the stage. Then they all moved to the center to take their bow, and on the way, Ace was looking one way and walking another and kind of walked straight into the mic stand — the same one Gene bumped into earlier. He turned to see what he had run into and laughed and untangled himself. ... After they took their bow, Gene took Ace's right arm and Peter took his left arm and they sort of jiggled them up and down, and Ace laughed and went limp, and they led him off the stage like that."

Not all nights were off ones for Ace, though, as one reviewer who posted a critique of the November 6, 1996, show in Little Rock, Arkansas, made clear: "Ace was again in rare form. He was very into the show and kept the whole ball rollin'!!!!"

With the band and its crew, drug and alcohol abuse was a taboo subject. Way too much money was involved with this enterprise for anything to go wrong. Ace was an important part of the tour, and nobody wanted him to walk.

When the question of Ace's sobriety during the tour is posed to Andre, he dodges it with the skill of a White House press secretary. "I do know that Ace was running a fever of about 102 degrees for several weeks at the beginning of the tour. That would make anyone sluggish onstage."

Reportedly, Ace displayed disconcerting behavior: falling asleep at odd times, nodding off while putting on makeup. Some veterans of Kiss tours became suspicious and worried. They had seen this all before, and it never ended well.

"With a tour this big, there was no way we were taking any chances," Andre says. "We reported our concerns to Gene and he gave us specific instructions: Clear out his mini-bars. And we did." Prior to arrival at hotels, Andre would request Ace's mini-bar be cleared of alcohol and filled with extra juice and soda.

Andre continues. "There's no sense tempting fate. I learned that from the Aerosmith guys. Anyone in recovery will tell you addiction is a daily struggle and not something of which you are ever entirely 'cured.'"

At first, Ace questioned the others. "Hey, do you have beer in your mini-bar?" he asked crew members. And inevitably, someone would respond, "Oh, yeah, mine's fully stocked." So much for everyone being helpful.

"Some hotels really screwed up," Andre remembers. "Instead of adding extra juices and soda, they took everything out of the mini-bar. Soon, Ace realized what was going on and argued with the others that if he had guests over, they might want a beer or two. As usual, he got his way. After all, if Ace left the tour, there would be no more tour."

Indeed, Ace was in an envious position. He is very often the biggest variable in the group, and at the same time, Ace is the secret ingredient. His guitar-playing style, some observers say, makes Kiss songs Kiss songs. And he is the second most-popular player in the band, behind Gene, as shown in a *Billboard Online* survey published in late 1998:

> Gene Simmons' flickering tongue and dark persona still reel in the Kiss fans, concludes a Billboard Online poll. When visitors to the Voting Booth were asked to name their favorite costumed Kiss character, bassist Simmons — The Demon — was the No. 1 choice, winning 28.1% of the electorate. Lead guitarist Ace Frehley — Space Ace — came in second with 24.1% of the

vote, while guitarist Paul Stanley — The Starchild — was third
with 18.7%. Proving the old adage that no one gives the drummer
any respect, Peter Criss — The Catman — ended with 9.0% of the
votes.

"Ace is the kind of guy who doesn't realize bad things are happening to him. It's like he doesn't know what is happening until the bullet is going into his head," Andre says. "There is nothing you can do to Ace. Nothing really matters to him. It's all just a means to an end. Money is really just a way for Ace to buy more computer equipment. You've got to remember these guys have been doing this a long time. There wasn't any changing them."

And, Andre adds, it was impossible to keep Ace on target or on time. "He always started the day like everyone else – with a phone call one hour before the band was scheduled to leave. But Ace was never on time. Then I tried calling him 90 minutes before departure. Then it went to two hours. And as the time to leave got closer, Ace eventually got calls every 15 minutes to remind him!" Andre shakes his head and adds, "It's hard enough for a road manager to coordinate the activities of six or seven people, four of whom are the act, let alone handle all that extra, unnecessary crap.

"Everybody else got one phone call," Andre continues. "Give Gene his call, and he's down in the lobby waiting for you. With Paul and Peter, it's the same thing. With Ace, there were only four or five times on this tour when he was ever on time. And then he had the audacity to act put out waiting for everyone else."

One time on the "Lost Cities" segment of the Alive/Worldwide Tour – the name referred to smaller U.S. cities the group played during Spring 1997 – Ace sauntered into a hotel lobby an hour early. He paced the lobby and announced his displeasure when Andre showed up.

"Where's everybody been? I thought we were leaving at 12," he told Andre.

"We are," Andre responded.

"My watch says one."

"Ace, we changed time zones."

"How come nobody told me?"

"Ace, it's on your daily sheet."

"What daily sheet?"

"The same one you've been getting under your door for the entire tour."

In Andre's role as road manager, transporting artists to the arena on time is critical. And with a show like Kiss' Alive/Worldwide Tour, in which closed sound checks and prompt makeup sessions are crucial, timing becomes even more important.

Ace never really took his role in the success of the Alive/Worldwide Tour seriously, nor did he accept responsibility for his actions, Andre contends, although he did provide – sometimes unwittingly – lots of comic relief.

On November 21, 1996, the band was in England on the tour's European leg heading to Manchester. The van carried Doc McGhee, the band's manager; Richard "Paco" Zimmer, the tour's accountant; Tommy Thayer, the band's coordinator; the driver; Andre; and all four members of Kiss.

"When I was traveling with Kiss, going back and forth to the arena or traveling in the van, we would play Van Games," Andre remembers. "It was an alphabet game with a topic. Before you start, someone picks a topic, like male groups. For example, someone says 'A,' and the next person says 'AC/DC.' Then the next person says 'B' and you say 'Beatles.' It does get pretty hard when you get down to some letters, like V.

"All four of the guys would participate in Van Games. But it wasn't like they did it every time they were in the van, only when they were feeling particularly friendly. Sometimes they would play games like that on the plane, too. But most of the time it was a divided camp, with everybody looking over everybody else's shoulder, jockeying for position, trying to say the right thing or whatever's going to get them more power."

Ace slouched in the first bench seat of the van, resting his head against the window and dozing. It was a two-hour drive, and the rest of the entourage was engaged in Van Games. So far, the shows in England were going well.

Ace suddenly roused, sitting straight up. Turning around and looking at McGhee and Paco, he asked a question as if his life depended on it.

"Hey Doc, when are we going to Europe?"

Andre looked at McGhee, eyes wide with disbelief. The rest of the van just cracked up. Ace appeared confused.

Finally, McGhee asked, "What do you mean, when are we going to Europe?"

The whole van erupted into another chorus of laughter.

Paul tried to put an end to the confusion. "Ace, we *are* in Europe!"

And then the inquisition began.

"Uh, Ace, do you remember our eight-hour flight?" Gene asked.

"Or realize we're driving on the left side of the road?" Paul added.

"How about the show last night?" someone else asked.

In a thin attempt to save face, Ace tried to cover it up. "No, no. I meant the other Europe!"

(In Ace's defense, there are some people in England who really don't consider themselves part of Europe. It's an elitist position, though, and one not taken by many.)

"It was a nice try, but everyone knew he didn't have a clue where he was," Andre remembers. "You could clearly tell in his voice that he thought he was on his way to a show in Dallas or somewhere."

Another time, the band was "basing" in Chicago. Basing is when a group stays at a central location and then plays the venues within striking distance. For example, Kiss may stay at one hotel in downtown Chicago and fly to shows in such markets as Indianapolis, St. Louis, Topeka, Sioux Falls, Grand Rapids, St. Paul and Madison. The flights are short enough so that the band can fly to the venue, play the show and return to the base hotel.

Andre's outbound time schedule for the band when basing in Chicago and playing a show in Indianapolis looked like this:

1:30 p.m.	Band wake up
2:30 p.m.	Meet in lobby
3:30 p.m.	Take off
4:30 p.m.	Land
5:30 p.m.	Sound check
6:30 p.m.	Open doors

Some bands like to base because it creates a home-away-from-home vibe. The practice is common for larger groups, with a normal basing stint lasting from a couple of days to several weeks.

It was around 1 p.m., and Ace was running late for the band's Indianapolis gig that night. For whatever reason, he was extremely drowsy and holding things up. His tardiness, incidentally, wreaked havoc with the band's travel schedule throughout the Alive/Worldwide Tour.

Andre and band coordinator Tommy Thayer finally coaxed him out of his suite and down to the waiting Town Cars. With everyone accounted for, the cars pulled out for the quick 30-minute ride to Chicago's Midway Airport. Ace, leaning against the window, fell asleep. Shaking his head, Andre looked at Thayer. They both knew it was going to be a long day.

Within minutes of boarding the plane, the guitarist fell asleep again. The flight was short, not even an hour, but Ace slept the whole time.

"What's wrong with him?" Thayer asked Andre.

Andre shrugged his shoulders. "I guess he was up late, playing on his computer." Ace truly is a computer geek, traveling with a lot of equipment and experimenting with computerized recording and composing techniques.

Again, Andre and Thayer did the wake-up-and-relocate routine, moving Ace from the plane to another one of the waiting Lincoln Town Cars. The ride from the airport to Market Square Arena took less than 20 minutes. Ace, once more, slept the entire time.

The three cars pulled into the parking area outside of the artists' entrance. The first one pulled to the right, the second parked behind the first and the third pulled to the left side of the first. Car doors flew open and everyone grabbed their bags, jumped out and headed for the arena. Everyone except Ace.

Andre guided the group into the building where Tony Morehead, Kiss' building security director, met them. Andre then returned to the Town Cars.

As usual, the doors of all three cars were left open. Andre made it a habit to check that nothing was left behind before locking up the vehicles. This time, though, Ace was left behind.

Andre walked over to the third Town Car and noticed band manager Doc McGhee coaxing the drowsy guitarist out of the car. "Ace! We're here. Come on. Let's get going. We're at the building. Ace?"

Ace responded with a groan and finally pulled himself out of the right side of the car and rubbed his eyes. Immediately in front of him sat one of the other Lincolns with the doors wide open. He looked around and then crawled into the back seat of that car, curled up and started to sleep again!

McGhee and Andre exchanged stunned looks. The manager walked around the car, restating his message. "Ace, what are you doing? We're at the building. What are you doing? We're here. We're at the gig. Come on."

Ace finally worked up enough energy to stumble into the arena, petrifying Andre and the band manager. *How is he even going to play?* they thought. They needn't have worried; Andre later described Ace Frehley's performance that night as "brilliant."

"On any given day, you didn't know which Ace you were getting," Andre says. "You didn't know whether you were getting the clear-headed, cool guitar slinger or Space-Ace."

43
THE DEMON

Gene Simmons

October 9, 1996: Show Day

Kiss Alive/Worldwide Tour

CoreStates Center – Philadelphia, Pennsylvania

"YOU'D BETTER WATCH OUT!" SHE YELLED TO THE YELLOW-JACKETED security guard.

The attractive girl in the front row looked like a contradiction in terms. She was about 23, brunette and dressed in a Catholic-school-uniform-style plaid skirt. But her face was done in perfect Paul Stanley makeup.

She leaned over the barricade that separated the crowd from the stage and, cupping her hands around her mouth, she called out again. "You're gonna get blood *all* over you!"

This time, the yellow-jacketed security guard heard her and looked at her suspiciously. Not knowing what to make of the comment, he wrinkled his eyebrows. Obviously his first Kiss show.

The guard exchanged puzzled glances with his security counterparts. His gaze then returned to the girl, who pointed excitedly over his shoulder. The security guard spun around, mouth falling open.

It was as if Satan himself had appeared. Standing 7 feet tall and seemingly borne out of dry ice, an evil-looking Gene Simmons hunched over his bass and leaned out towards the crowd. An under-glow of green light added to the eeriness.

Simultaneously, Gene struck two particularly low bass notes and rolled his eyes back into his head, exposing nothing but whites. He cocked his head sharply to the left and then to the right. The bass notes reverberated throughout Philadelphia's CoreStates Center.

Like beetles scurrying from the light of day, the three security guards standing watch in the 8-foot-square area in front of Gene scrambled out of harm's way. Gene's eyes returned, as "blood" (reportedly made from a mixture of melted butter, food coloring, ketchup, eggs and yogurt) oozed from the sides of his mouth. He cocked his head again, letting the anticipation build.

Then the vile, plasma-like goo spewed everywhere, splashing off the stage and the microphone stand and onto some front-row fans. Gene reared back his head and shook it violently from side to side, allowing the fluid to fly free and flow down his chin and chest.

Once more he leaned into the crowd, unrolled his freakishly long tongue and let the last bit of saliva and crimson goo drip off the tip. The security guards' faces twisted in disgust.

The crowd roared its approval. The Catholic-school girl squealed with delight. It was her favorite part of the show.

Gene Simmons is Kiss. He eats, sleeps, breathes, lives and loves Kiss. Whether the man born Chaim Whitz, later named Gene Klein and finally famous as Gene Simmons is onstage or off, his Demon persona takes over.

"For me, [being onstage] is as close to being God as there is," Gene told Gerri Miller for *Metal Edge*'s "Kiss Rocks the World 1996-1997 Reunion Tour" edition. "There's a kind of feeling you get onstage that just isn't around anywhere else. ... It's like when Tarzan kills the Great Ape and bellows out that yell – it's a god-like feeling. I've walked offstage with major cuts and not known it."

Offstage, Gene is just as cocky. "Do you really think we need the money?" he asked *Hit Parader* magazine in August 1996, when talking about the much-anticipated reunion tour. "I can guarantee that we don't. We're doing this because the time is finally right. Ace and Peter have gotten their lives together, and they have always been a part of the Kiss family. On top of that, Kiss has always been about surprises, about doing what everyone thought was impossible or improbable. Everyone said this would never happen. Don't you think that's enough motivation for us?"

Fast-forward two years, when Kiss was preparing for the rock world's first 3-D tour and Gene was full of more talk. "Let's just do what we do best and the rest of it be damned," he told *Guitar World* in October 1998. And when we go out there on the Psycho Circus Tour, we're gonna raise the stakes yet again. Single-handedly. ... If you have enough money to

throw a good party, why not throw the biggest party anyone has ever seen? Costs millions? So what. We've got millions."

44

THE STARCHILD

Paul Stanley

January 31, 1997: Show Day

Kiss Alive/Worldwide Tour

Super Top – Auckland, New Zealand

ALL 11,500 PEOPLE WERE ON THEIR FEET. THEY'D JUST FINISHED singing the final verse to "Rock 'n' Roll All Nite." Hands on his hips, Paul Stanley basked in the moment. A blizzard of confetti fell on the stage. Paul, like a general surveying his troops, looked out over the audience, which was going nuts – just like the old days. The 9-by-18 foot high Kiss logo lit up the entire arena with 1,000 MR-16 lights.

Paul's fingers expertly moved to the clips on his guitar strap. With his left hand gripping the neck of his guitar, Paul undid the front and back fasteners and disconnected the sound jack. Gripping the neck with both hands, he then threw the guitar over his shoulder like a baseball bat and moved quickly to the center of the stage.

He took one giant step and swung the guitar like an ax, striking the base of the instrument against the hard, confetti-littered stage.

An explosion discharged and rockets launched from the stage. Sparks rained down, and concussion-inducing explosions detonated every time Paul struck the floor of the stage with his guitar. He swung once, twice and on the third strike, the guitar broke into three pieces.

Paul tossed the neck to the audience on the left side of the stage. He took the smaller piece of the body and threw it to the people on the right. Then, as he had done so many nights previously, Paul saved the largest and most desirable piece of the guitar for last. He practically handed it to a beautiful girl in the front row.

He moved back to the microphone and grabbed it for the last time that evening. "Kiss loooovvvvvessssss you! Good night!" He waved to the audience, then the arena went black.

Paul is the voice of reason in Kiss, Andre contends. If there is an issue to be discussed, Paul's the one to say, "No, I don't think that's the right way to go, and here's why." And, at least from Andre's perspective, he's usually right.

Onstage, Paul wears red lipstick and sports a feather-trimmed robe before the encore. "Let's face it, he's no lumberjack," Andre says. "His guitars sparkle, his outfits sparkle, everything sparkles." Paul is often considered the band's front man because he does a lot of the singing and addresses the audience. Paul also runs, dances and kicks. He slaps his body, purses his lips and runs his hands over his chest, oozing sexuality. Andre describes Paul as "the delicate star who is the center of attention."

But offstage, the singer is contemplative and considerate. Andre gets the impression that fame was Paul Stanley's destiny. "He's told stories of when he was younger, going over to friends' houses and putting on shows for the neighbors. Small plays, skits, kid stuff. But he was always the center of attention. I think he knew at a very young age that he was different. The best times were when he and I would have lunch alone. We'd be away from everyone, and we could just talk. And it could be about anything: kids, parenting, normal topics."

Understanding such nuggets about an artist's background and personality helps Andre do his job better. "People who are successful in my position spend a lot of time analyzing what a client says or how he or she behaves," Andre explains. "Then you can figure out how you should best say things or how you can respond in certain situations. You become kind of a psychologist to help yourself help your artist. It's important. It helps you respond appropriately in certain situations – what to say, when to say it, what NOT to say ... ever."

One of the topics Andre learned not to discuss was Paul's birth defect. Among the first published pieces to mention it appeared in C.K. Lendt's 1996 *Kiss and Sell*, the band's story as told by a former employee. "He [Stanley] had what looked like a cauliflower ear that was always carefully covered by his huge mane of shoulder-length hair," Lendt writes. " ... he would undergo a series of operations to have the deformity corrected."

As a result, Paul, who was born Stanley Eisen, can't hear out of his right side.

"Even with his hearing limitation, Paul Stanley is an excellent singer and songwriter," Andre says. "And to me, it's amazing. If someone is out of tune, Paul is the first one to know. The only way I can explain it is that he was given a gift."

And music isn't his only gift. "From what people tell me and from what I've read, Paul used to be quite a ladies' man," Andre says. "He was always with the most beautiful women. Nothing but the best would do. They had to be funny, smart and drop-dead gorgeous. I never knew him back in those days. I only know him as a caring and committed husband and father.

"Gene and Paul started out together, two young guys in New York City," Andre continues. "They were competitive and hard working. Their hard work paid off and they found success. And when you get past money and fame for two testosterone-driven guys from New York, the tally of success changes. It becomes about who gets the coolest chicks."

Both men have had relationships with high-profile women. Most of these romances were well documented in the press. Paul was linked to British pop singer Samantha Fox and actresses Lisa Hartman and Donna Dixon.

Gene, was involved with Cher and Diana Ross. Today, the father of two is in an "open" relationship with former *Playboy* Playmate Shannon Tweed.

But the competition for women between the two founding fathers of Kiss has changed dramatically. Paul is now a stable family man. Gene is, well, still Gene. As proof, Andre offers an example.

A Kiss show is a well-planned rock 'n' roll assault. Explosions, the release of dry ice and fireworks are programmed down to the second, and there are also specific times throughout the show when band members take short breaks.

During these breaks, they touch up their makeup or get something to drink. Because they are the main players and the most active during the show, both Paul and Gene have small dressing-room tables just offstage and to the side. Technicians also stand watch there, in case of an equipment malfunction.

As the show rocked an arena one night, Andre scanned the crowd from his post. After trying several configurations, Andre had found his "show spot" for the tour: stage right, Gene's side, at the top of the short stairs that led off and out from the stage area. From there, Andre had the best perspective on the crowd and could also help with extra assignments.

Being on Gene's side was a job and a half, Andre recalls. He had to pay constant attention not only to the crowd, but also to Gene, who plays an integral role in each performance. Fire breathing, blood spitting and rafter-flying require a lot of coordination and sequencing. But that's not everything working Gene's side requires.

"Andre," Gene called quickly during a break one evening. "Blond, about twelve rows back, on the left."

He looked where Gene pointed, quickly identified the object of Gene's desire and nodded. He moved swiftly down the stairs, through the barricade and out into the audience.

This wasn't the first time Andre made such a journey. He never stuck around long enough to hear the conversation, but he knew Gene wasn't interested in the chosen woman's views on global warming, Andre says. Not wanting to be judgmental, he did as he was asked.

"I didn't feel it was my place to say, 'No, Gene, I don't think that's appropriate behavior from a moral perspective,'" Andre says. "I mean, it wasn't like he was asking me to do anything illegal, like get him drugs, which he doesn't do, or beat someone up. He's a grown man and my employer, so he has to make his own choices.

"For Gene, the whole thing was a crap shoot," Andre continues. "Sometimes, the girls would like the idea of being invited backstage by Gene Simmons and get all excited and giddy. But others would recoil in disgust and say, 'Gene Simmons? Me? No way!' In those cases, Gene would just find someone else."

The blond in the twelfth row this night did not recoil. In fact, she willingly came to the side of the stage, and Gene made his way down a few steps to whisper in her ear. Andre then sent her back to her seat and returned to his position at the top of the stairs. The whole exchange took no longer than four minutes.

Which was plenty of time for Paul to notice Andre missing in action. Immediately, he knew what was happening. He'd seen Gene on the prowl thousands of times during the past two decades.

As the music played on, Paul danced over to Andre and immediately lambasted him. "Don't you ever leave those steps! It's not your job to get chicks for Gene. If I ever see you out there doing that again, you're going to be out of here so fast, that it's not even ... "

He stopped for a second and then continued. "It'll make your head swim!" Paul then pranced back to the center of the stage, as if nothing happened.

Andre got the message. "Paul wanted to make sure I was watching for stage jumpers, not playing matchmaker."

In an attempt to keep all of his employers in the loop, Andre mentioned the incident to Gene, who had been unaware of the exchange between Paul and the security director. Gene simply responded casually. "Oh, really? He did? He said something? Hmmm."

Andre prevented any future clashes by telling Gene he couldn't get involved in his personal life. Gene, always ingenious, decided to send his tech from that point on.

Was Paul really concerned about Andre protecting the band from stage jumpers? Or was it something else?

"It's almost as if there was some internal struggle going on," Andre says. "And you can see it in Paul's performances or wherever there is a camera. When a magazine comes out, he's the one who looks at the magazine to see how many pictures of everybody are in there. If you take a look at photos that are staged, Paul is either on top, leaning in or leaning forward. These aren't things I just sit around and ponder. If I am aware of personality traits and preferences, I can do a better job and treat Paul the way he wants to be treated."

45
THE CATMAN
Peter Criss

October 18, 1997: Show Day

Kiss Alive/Worldwide Tour

Rupp Arena – Lexington, Kentucky

THE PRE-RECORDED PIANO AND STRING ACCOMPANIMENT FILLED
Rupp Arena in Lexington, Kentucky, as the crowd swayed back and forth, singing and waving
flickering lighters. It felt like 1976 all over again, and Peter Criss loved it.

Sitting on a small, round drum case, towel around his neck, Peter crooned "Beth," one
of Kiss' most popular and atypical songs. Originally released as the B-side of the single
"Detroit Rock City" from Destroyer, the song reached No. 7 on the *Billboard* charts.

Initially titled "Beck," "Beth" was written by Peter Criss and Stan Penridge in 1970
while they were in the group Chelsea. That band had a guitar player named Michael Brand,
whose wife, Rebecca, would call incessantly during rehearsals. The song was initially
penned as a joke.

As detailed in Dale Sherman's 1997 book, *Black Diamond*, many of the lyrics came from
what Peter and Penridge overheard during phone conversations. During the recording sessions
for *Destroyer*, Peter brought the song to the table, where producer Bob Ezrin renamed it
"Beth," for which he received a co-writing credit. Ezrin also added the orchestration. The
performance of "Beth" has always proved to be a highlight of any Kiss show.

Now, as the canned violins and piano reached a crescendo, Peter sang the closing lyrics
in his gravelly voice. "Beth, I know you love me. And I hope you'll be all right. 'Cause me
and the boys will be playin' aaaaaaallllll niiiiiiight." The crowd went nuts.

Peter stood up and thrust his fists victoriously into the air. He looked at the audience and, with the utmost sincerity, thanked them. "God bless each and every one of you," Peter said before stripping the towel from around his neck and flinging it into the throng. He smiled as he moved quickly offstage, waving once again before disappearing into the darkness.

Peter Criss, the Catman who always wears the number "3," seemed embarrassingly thrilled to be back with what he calls his "family." Peter's last official live performance with Kiss, prior to the reunion tour, came in November 1979; he officially left the band a year later.

Kiss was and is the best thing to ever happen to Peter, he's told numerous interviewers. And now that he was sober, he wanted to enjoy every minute of the reunion.

"You gotta hit the bottom to see the top," Peter – in typical jumbled fashion – told Gerri Miller for *Metal Edge* magazine's "Official Kiss Alive Worldwide Tour 1996/1997 Tour" edition. "How could you get that low? By getting that high. I hit the bottom in 1982, and went to rehab. It was a nightmare. It was the best thing I could have done for myself. I went once. That was enough of a lesson for me not to want to go back. It's hard. It was no picnic. I pray for anyone who gets out of that snake pit. You know what? Every day above ground is a good day."

"I met Peter on the first day of the Kiss Convention Tour in June 1995," Andre remembers, referring to the gig that eventually brought Peter Criss and Ace Frehley back into the Kiss family and set the stage for MTV's *Unplugged* special later that year. It also paved the way for the reunion tour. "Gene called and invited Peter. He sent a limo for him and treated him like gold, brought him up onstage to great fan reaction, fed his ego. And things just took off from there."

Andre actually escorted Peter from the limo to the convention that first day. The fans immediately recognized Peter and greeted him warmly.

On the other hand, Andre didn't hit it off so well with Kiss' original drummer, who got to know Andre better during reunion tour rehearsals at Cole Studios. "At first, he had a real macho attitude," Andre says about Peter. "I don't know whether it was because he didn't trust me or whether that was his everyday demeanor."

Perhaps that macho attitude stemmed from Peter's days on the streets of New York as a struggling musician and a member of Brooklyn's Phantom Lords. Born Peter Criscoula, the drummer has publicly acknowledged more than once that Kiss saved his life. After his

departure from Kiss, he released two unsuccessful solo albums that didn't follow in the musical footsteps of his Kiss work and sounded more like the early rhythm-and-blues inspirations from his 1978 self-titled solo album.

Peter's 1993 CD, with a band called Criss and titled *Cat #1*, never reestablished himself the way he had hoped. Mercury Records reissued Peter's first two releases in April 1998, hoping to cash in some more on the success the label received the previous year when it issued remastered versions of the first 13 Kiss albums (plus the four 1978 solo records), including original artwork. But music buyers didn't seem to care; the Criss reissues bombed.

Peter still has Kiss, though, and he's reportedly still clean and having a blast being part of the band that made him a rock 'n' roll icon. But Peter wasn't the only one having fun ...

46
BLACK N' BLUE

Tommy Thayer

HE LOOKED DAZED. SWEATING, SHIRT UNTUCKED AND BUTTONS torn off, it was obvious he was exhausted. Tommy Thayer's hair stuck straight up in some places and was matted down in others. He needed help. His attacker was wild, about 5 feet, 10 inches tall, with dark hair and tearing into Thayer like a Tasmanian Devil.

"I can't see Tommy! I can't see him!" Andre cried.

Tony Morehead responded quickly. "Neither can I."

"Should we go help him?"

Gene Simmons suddenly appeared, standing over the two men. "Leave him alone. He'll be all right."

It wasn't a fight; it was a lap dance. When the song ended, the girl left a very dazed, confused and stimulated Tommy Thayer behind. Gene, Andre and Morehead (Kiss' venue security director) roared. He looked as if he had fought a war.

The Kiss crew was out for an evening in Las Vegas. Thayer's attacker was of the tall, leggy variety, and the attack wasn't unwarranted. In fact, it was requested.

"On the Alive/Worldwide Tour, a couple of us went to a strip club in Vegas," Andre recalls. "Tommy met this dancer, became smitten and requested a private dance. It was amazing he survived. She was going crazy. Flips, handstands, you name it. We couldn't really see Tommy, just the frenetic activities of this girl. She went nuts."

Some would say Tommy Thayer, now in his late-30s, is living a dream. Standing just taller than 6 feet, he is clean-shaven with spiky brown hair. Andre describes him as "long and lean." He is talented and multifaceted, and he made his way into the Kiss camp after playing Ace Frehley in the tribute band Cold Gin.

"I met Tommy Thayer at Gene Simmons' house," Andre recalls. "We were getting ready to do the Kiss conventions, and Gene called a planning meeting at his guesthouse. It was a very low-key affair, which involved Gene explaining his expectations for us and reviewing our individual and shared responsibilities."

Thayer is a lifelong Kiss fan and a talented guitar player in a rock band called Black N' Blue. According to Sherman's *Black Diamond*, the group opened for Kiss on the Asylum Tour. Thayer also co-wrote two songs with Gene ("Betrayed" and "The Street Giveth and the Street Taketh Away") for Kiss' 1989 *Hot in the Shade* album.

The strategy of enlisting talented fans is common in the music industry. It enables bands to find talented and extraordinarily productive people driven by their passion for the band. Often, they work for very low salaries.

Thayer performed admirably as the Alive/Worldwide Tour's band coordinator, a role that required him to accomplish any task thrown at him – carrying bags, coordinating local media interviews, handling personal mail and messages. He also coordinated the tour's check-signing process, in which Gene and Paul personally signed every paycheck. Thayer would then distribute or mail them.

Kiss thinks very highly of him, as evidenced by Thayer's year-round employment, a rare benefit in the industry. Thayer also wrote, produced and directed *The Second Coming*, a video released in November 1998 that documents the Alive/Worldwide Tour.

Despite all this glory, Andre got the sense that in the beginning Thayer might have been a bit naïve about the inner workings of the rock 'n' roll world.

Near the end of the tour's first U.S. leg, the members of Kiss, Thayer, Andre and McGhee were on the band's plane heading to another gig somewhere in the Midwest. A day or two off was scheduled, but because of the timing and location, there just wasn't enough time for everyone to go home.

Paul Stanley, anxious to see his wife and young son, planned to privately charter a plane and blast home for the day. Management, including Thayer, knew he was going, but the rest of the band did not. Not wanting to disrupt group dynamics, Paul decided to keep his quick trip home a secret.

Thayer and Andre sat facing Paul and McGhee, while the rest of the band's entourage was nearby. Ace sat alone in another set of four seats. Peter Criss and his companion, Gigi, sat with Gene in the couch area of the plane.

As the engine noise droned incessantly, Andre, McGhee, Paul and Thayer talked and read magazines. Thayer, who speaks in a loud voice to begin with, upped the volume to compensate for the jet's noise.

"So Paul, what time are you leaving for L.A. tomorrow?" he blurted.

Andre ducked behind his magazine, then snuck a peek out over the top and caught Paul giving Thayer an icy stare.

Thayer apparently didn't get it, so he asked again. This time he used even more volume.

"You're still going to L.A. tomorrow, aren't you, Paul?"

Paul, with a strained look on his face, insistently mouthed the words, "Quiet. They do not know I am going."

Thayer still looked perplexed, and Andre knew he had to intervene. He leaned over and whispered in Tommy's ear. "He doesn't want anyone to know he's going."

Tommy sat back as if he'd seen a ghost. He stayed uncharacteristically quiet for the remainder of the flight.

47

TIPS, TRICKS &
TECHNIQUES

THROUGH THE YEARS, ANDRE HAS GAINED ALL SORTS OF
different skills and abilities from working with various performers. Among the most useful is
learning how to treat artists the way they want to be treated. It's a subtle skill, but one that
has kept Andre in demand. One of the most important tasks remains escorting famous
people in and out of ordinary places.

"Hey, are you ready?" Paul Stanley asked into the phone receiver one October 1996
non-show day in Chicago during Kiss' Alive/Worldwide Tour.

"Sure Paul, I'll be right up," Andre responded.

Non-show days during the tour were coveted, and Paul liked to make sure he got some
shopping done. One of the most personable aspects of Paul Stanley, Andre says, is that he
enjoys participating in real-world activities, like picking up CDs at a local music store, going
to movies or shopping for hair-care products.

"Some of the artists I've worked with don't do that kind of stuff, but it's interesting that
Paul does," Andre says. "One of the things I never get tired of is watching people's
expressions when they are walking down the aisles at Walgreen's and notice Paul Stanley
checking out the latest shampoos."

Paul and Andre entered Walgreen's. Andre walked a little behind him and on Paul's left
side. A few college-age guys noticed Andre and Paul, but they just sort of nodded at the two
and walked right past them. Andre turned around and saw them high-fiving each other, no
doubt ready to tell their buddies, "Hey, we saw Paul Stanley buying toothpaste."

As Paul continued to peruse the health-and-beauty items, Andre kept his body between Paul and other shoppers in the aisle, constantly scanning people's faces, trying to read whether they'll pull out a camera or reach for a pen and piece of paper.

"A lot of times, I don't even think Paul realized what was going on around him," Andre says. "He's been doing this for 20 years with someone like me. He's either so confident that I will take care of any situation that comes up or he's oblivious." This shopping trip went off without incident, although sometimes Paul and Andre weren't so lucky.

More often than not, Andre will notice a small group of females who have recognized Paul and are beginning to squirm and point.

"I go over there, try to calm them down and say, 'Hi, girls. How ya doing?'" Andre explains. "Because Paul is a friendly guy, I'll ask the girls if they want Paul to sign something for them. Then, in a very non-conspicuous way, because I don't want a big scene, I'll ask Paul to sign something for them. I may even take the piece of paper out of their hands and hand it to him, signaling to them that this is nothing more than an impromptu autograph session. We're not there to chat. Paul may ask their names, or I may even encourage the girls to talk. He'll just sign it, 'To Alice, Paul Stanley.' Then he'll draw a line and sign, 'To Julie, Paul Stanley,' and then hand it back to me to give to them. I'll say something like, 'Thank you, ladies. We'll see you at the show.' And I send them on their way."

Gene Simmons has his own strategy for keeping fans at bay. "Gene would go out occasionally to a club," Andre remembers, "and Paul would either go out to dinner or to a movie. They would never go anywhere together. Often when we were staying at a hotel, Gene would go downstairs and have lunch by himself. He would call me and say, 'I'm going downstairs to have lunch and I'll be back in my room in ninety minutes.' That was his way of saying he didn't need me just then.

"Eating out, Gene will request a quiet part of the restaurant and kind of keep his head down. If someone recognizes and approaches him, he will politely say something along the lines of 'I tell you what. When I'm done eating my lunch and reading my paper, I'd be more than happy to sign whatever you'd like.' People usually get the hint and wait until he is finished to approach him."

But the bottom line is always safety. Regardless of what a particular artist wants, it's up to Andre to assess who would be most in the public eye and therefore in the most potentially dangerous situation.

Working with Steven Tyler, for example, requires more extraordinary skills and 100 percent supervision. Because of his bubbly and gregarious personality, Steven truly likes to socialize with fans. Andre has found a fine balance between catering to the celebrity's desires and keeping them safe.

Gauging fan interaction with Steven Tyler is tough. Andre usually alternates between walking on either side of Steven. "It's not like I'm leading

"You can tell [Steven Tyler] genuinely enjoys going out and being seen. He also adores his fans. I love that about the guy."

him or protecting him," Andre explains. "Rather, it's like he and I are just two normal guys out for a walk." Andre says he always wrestles with the decision of whether someone should approach Steven and how long to let them near him. "It seems like sometimes, if I let him, he would talk to people for hours."

For Andre, Steven is probably the most fun to protect. "You can tell he genuinely enjoys going out and being seen. He also adores his fans. I love that about the guy."

If anything, Steven and other rock stars might even be a little naïve, Andre contends.

"On the last Aerosmith tour I was on, the guys told me, 'You know, we see the same people following us around for autographs,'" Andre recalls. "I'd been telling them for years that these people were selling their signatures. They asked me how I knew that. I told them, 'Because you sign 25 things for the same person. That person in New York was the same as the one in Chicago. Don't you look at these people?' They just then realized that people sold their autographs. Some of these guys have started to curb their signing activities within the last few years. But it was a good run for all those people who were selling autographs for a living."

Sometimes Andre and his artist combat autograph hounds by moving rapidly through crowds, announcing that they have no time to sign at the moment or telling fans they don't want to be disturbed while dining. Many big-city waiters and waitresses are accustomed to

turning away autograph-seeking fans from their celebrity-filled tables by telling them the restaurant's policies include no autograph signings.

Still, some crazed fans – usually under the influence of alcohol – insist on interrupting their favorite stars' meals.

"That's when I take it to the next level," Andre says. "I tell them they're being rude and ask if they'd like some stranger to come over while they're eating dinner and try to start up a conversation. If that still doesn't work, and I can't reason with somebody on an intellectual level, we have to get physical. I tell them, 'Well, you're not being reasonable, so I'm not going to be reasonable. I just have to tell you once more that the answer is no. And if you don't want to accept that, then you'll just have to go through me to get to them. Is that the kind of confrontation you want, pal?'"

Any takers on that offer?

"Are you kidding?" he laughs.

At the opposite end of the fan-behavior spectrum are Japanese fans. Andre recalls several times when fans greeted Aerosmith at a Bullet Train station and presented band members with gift-wrapped presents, including notes.

A member of the touring entourage usually accepts the gifts, Andre says, and the recipient opens them later in private.

"Japan is a whole different scene with the fans because of the cultural differences," Andre says. "People there are very mild-mannered and respectful. So there's usually no danger of physical harm."

Regardless of what part of the world George Thorogood is visiting, he's one of those artists who just prefers to keep to himself a lot more than someone like Paul Stanley or Steven Tyler.

Andre has described George as an "old-time blues man stuck in a popular musician's life." George likes the fact that people enjoy his music, but after he's shared it with them on the concert stage, he rarely wants fan contact.

When George is at home and not on the road, he settles into even more of a routine, and he's one of the few artists Andre has worked with when not touring.

A typical off-the-road day might look like this:

12:30 p.m.	Pick up George at home
1:00 p.m.	Head to gym for workout
3:00 p.m.	Lunch
4:00 p.m.	Rehearsal studio to work on new material or rehearse
5:30 p.m.	Head home

Much like George Thorogood, it often seems as if Joe Perry is energized by the sheer joy of making music. Andre has said that Joe sometimes forgets he's playing lead guitar for Aerosmith in front of 18,000 screaming fans and just becomes engrossed in his music.

Maneuvering Joe though a crowd is never really much of a problem, Andre says – certainly unlike traveling with Steven Tyler. He is friendly and approachable in public, but he also keeps moving. There usually isn't much of an opportunity to stop or engage him.

Other security skills – usually the ones used during a performance to take care of stage jumpers or unruly fans — are more conflict-oriented. Andre calls his three most common moves the "Forearm Rip," the "Hook" and the "Back of the Belt." He uses them when someone's behavior endangers themselves or others.

- **The Forearm Rip:** Bend one arm at a 90-degree angle and raise it above your head in a sweeping motion with a clenched fist. "You may not be trying to hit anyone, but just by putting your forearm out in front of you like that, you can defend yourself and keep someone from slamming into you," Andre says. "Meanwhile, your other hand and arm are free."

- **The Hook:** Wrap your arm around the neck or chest of a charging fan to stop him in his tracks. "I usually like to get people from the back, so that I'm behind them with my whole arm around them," Andre says. "Hook your other hand around their waist or clothing and just kind of ride them out. You raise them up a little bit on their toes and their momentum just carries them wherever you want them to go."

- **The Back of the Belt:** Simply grab the offender by the back of the pants or belt and just pull that person toward you. "They have no control if you're pulling from the back," Andre says. "It's usually the best way to gain control because they can't see where they're going, and they have less strength going backward than they do going forward."

Andre also gets to practice his first-aid skills occasionally. Things can get quite intense onstage with the noise, the occasional jumper and objects flying around.

One time, while on the road with Aerosmith, "Dude (Looks Like a Lady)" had just ended with Joe Perry and Brad Whitford riffing wildly at the end. They play well off one another and enjoy jelling at the end of songs. The rowdy crowd that night ate it up. Amidst banners, bras and beer cups strewn all over the stage, Steven puffed out his chest, pouted his lips and engaged the crowd.

Then, from about ten rows back, stage left, an object came careening towards the stage. Someone launched a large butane lighter that smacked Steven in the face. Andre shot out from the side of the stage.

Steven's hands covered his face. He headed back towards the drum riser, where Steven knew there would be towels. Drum tech Andy Gilman had one ready.

"Get me a fuckin' towel!" Steven screamed, blood pouring down his face, as though he had gone a round with Evander Holyfield. Gilman handed him a towel just as Andre arrived. He put his arm around Steven and walked him to the side of the stage.

"Keep pressure on it, Steven," he advised.

At the side of the stage, Andre relied on his sports background to help him nurse Steven back into "show shape" and finish the show.

Other skills are more social in nature. To be successful, it's important to converse about a wide variety of topics when you're on the road for months. Sports, politics, world events and just about any other subject is bound to come up. To properly prepare for such conversations, Andre tries to watch cable television news twice a day – once in the morning and late at night, if he can.

He must also communicate security messages and philosophies to other security personnel, management people and local law enforcement officials. Social abilities, control skills, patience and flexibility are just some of the skills needed to work with so many different artists. And each artist has his own quirks – especially the members of Kiss.

THE RICHARD ZIMMER GROUP

HOTEL _____

_____

_____

PHONE _____ FAX _____

Kiss signs into hotels using aliases. These sheets would be circulated internally. Can you tell who is who?

	ROOM #	PHONE #	BAG #
RICHARD ZIMMER	_____	_____	10
ANDRE AUGUSTINE	_____	_____	6
TOMMY THAYER	_____	_____	8
GEORGE B. SHAW	_____	_____	2
BUCK RAM	_____	_____	3
ROBERT WEST	_____	_____	4
TONY MONTANA	_____	_____	5
DOC McGHEE	_____	_____	1
GEORGE SEWITT	_____	_____	9

_____

_____

THE TIM ROZNER GROUP

HOTEL _____

_____

_____

PHONE _____ FAX _____

	ROOM #	PHONE #	BAG #
	_____	_____	7
TIM ROZNER	_____	_____	6
ANDRE AUGUSTINE	_____	_____	8
TOMMY THAYER	_____	_____	2
JERRY BUTLER	_____	_____	3
BUCK RAM	_____	_____	4
RANDY WHITE	_____	_____	5
JACK KELLY	_____	_____	1
DOC McGHEE	_____	_____	9
GEORGE SEWITT	_____	_____	

George Shaw/Jerry Butler: Gene Simmons

Buck Ram: Paul Stanley

Robert West/Randy White: Ace Frehley

Tony Montana/Jack Kelly: Peter Criss

48
CELEBRITY DYNAMICS

IT'S NO SECRET THAT THE KISS CAMP HAS BEEN DIVIDED FOR years. Gene Simmons and Paul Stanley founded the band and have stuck with Kiss through good times and bad, as if rock 'n' roll spouses. Peter Criss and Ace Frehley left for personal reasons in 1980 and 1982, respectively. But the MTV special and subsequent reunion tour brought everyone back together again.

Although band members have been quoted explaining how the reunion of Kiss came together naturally, not everything went smoothly once the tour idea became reality.

"I'm definitely one of the laziest guys in the band, and sometimes during rehearsals, the other guys would have to give me a kick in the ass," Ace told *Guitar World* magazine in September 1996. "It's funny, because when I first got to rehearsals, I came in wanting to play these old songs relatively note for note. I'd been playing these songs for years, and I was playing them maybe 60 or 70 percent correct. And Gene and Paul had to tell me, 'C'mon – either shit or get off the pot, Ace. Let's get these right.'"

"I had to sit for hours and watch old videos of us and listen to the music over and over," Peter told the magazine in that same issue. "I'd forgotten a lot of that stuff over the 17 years. I really had to get reacquainted with the whole thing, and it was a struggle for me."

The struggles Ace and Peter had to overcome did not always sit well with Gene and Paul, but the band persevered to pull off one of the biggest victories in rock 'n' roll history.

"I felt very comfortable, emotionally and otherwise, just really plowing into Ace and Peter about whatever my point of view was," Gene admitted in the April 1996 issue of *Guitar* magazine. "But clearly, if anyone ever said anything bad about Ace or Peter from the

outside, I'd kill them. I have the right to have an emotional point of view about Ace and Peter. Outsiders have nothing to say about it."

Despite Andre's attempts to be friendly, it took Ace and Peter some time to warm up to him. After being in the music industry for so long, they'd seen a lot of security and management hacks, so who could blame them? Andre remembers the specifics. "Ace and Peter had their own manager and they were just leery of people who worked for Kiss during the Bruce [Kulick] and Eric [Singer] (previous Kiss members) era. They didn't trust anyone, as evidenced by their behavior.

"At first, everything was questioned and scrutinized," Andre continues. "It was important to be very careful about what was said or how things got done, so that it wouldn't be misinterpreted as one-sided. And it could be anything from disseminating information, arranging telephone interviews with media, or carrying someone's favorite chewing gum."

For a long time, Ace and Peter looked at Andre as one of the "new crew," he contends, which made Andre's job more challenging. Andre had to make sure he treated everyone equally.

Swag (free merchandise) also proved challenging on the Alive/Worldwide Tour. Fans can be quite generous. Gene automatically wants one of everything for his collection, Andre says. He's been collecting Kiss material from the beginning, and if it says "Kiss," Gene wants it.

Paul, who didn't really care about collecting memorabilia in the past, now finds the practice more appealing, Andre says. "He's starting to keep stuff now because he never kept anything from the old days. Paul probably wants to have some things for his son, Evan, to see from his earlier accomplishments. So the implication was, you better give one of everything to everybody, even if they don't ask for it, even if they don't want it, because it'll be construed as you're taking care of Gene and Paul better than you're taking care of Peter and Ace."

That's not all.

"Peter would comment about how there were rarely ever pictures of him in newspapers or magazines," Andre elaborates. "After more than 20 years of being a drummer, you would think he would know that the media doesn't want pictures of drummers. Too much stuff in the way."

Peter and Ace would often ask, "How come Gene and Paul do all the interviews?" Gene in an attempt to be fair to everyone, started assigning the interviews among the four original

members. When Gene told Andre about the new policy, Andre's thoughts shifted immediately to Ace. *Sometimes we can't even get Ace to the show without an act of Congress. How are we ever going to get him to do interviews?*

Andre didn't have to worry about that for long. The practice of Ace and Peter sharing interview duties lasted only a week or two.

Onstage or off, Kiss' personalities came with its members. Gene, Paul, Peter and Ace stated from the very beginning, in the early 1970s, that their makeup and onstage antics represented their alter egos. Andre confirms that this is still the case. "Even when they take the costumes and the makeup off, it never comes completely off," Andre says. "These onstage personalities really follow them off the stage and into their everyday lives in different ways."

Andre must be aware of these traits at all times, regardless of what group he's touring with. To help him keep the characteristics of so many artists straight, Andre tries to fill in the blanks to sentences like this: "When working with so-and-so, I always do such-and-such."

Since Andre entered rock 'n' roll and began working with so many major bands, he's kept a mental scorecard to help him sort out the characteristics of so many diverse artists. Here's his roster:

Gene Simmons:	" ... carry condoms."
Steven Tyler:	" ... carry a Sharpie."
Joe Perry:	" ... bring my workout clothes."
Paul Stanley:	" ... have $1,000 in my pocket."
Brad Whitford:	" ... keep my handcuffs ready, because Brad likes to wander off."
Ace Frehley:	" ... carry a spare room key."
George Thorogood	" ... find a nice quiet bar."

49

'WE'RE WITH THE BAND, MAN!'

THE ANTICIPATION OF THE KISS CONCERT, JUST TWO HOURS AWAY, had fans on an emotional high. A group of about 30 people crowded around the backstage security gate at Milwaukee's Bradley Center. The crowd consisted of just as many guys as girls – all in their late teens and early twenties.

"Come on! Let me in!" one guy pleaded, clinging to the gate, like an orangutan drunk on Jack Daniels. "I haaaaave to talk to Ace!"

The security guard behind the gate chuckled and said, "Look, you don't have a pass. You're not a chick. You're not getting in." Simple enough criteria.

"Pllleeeaassse," the persistent fan continued. The guard just shook his head.

Two guys pushed their way to the front of the group and got the guard's attention with a not-so-subtle "Yo!" One pulled aside his untucked shirt to reveal a stick-on backstage pass affixed to his jeans and said confidently, "We're with the band." His friend nodded and smiled, flashing his own pass. The guard behind the gate signaled his approval and motioned to another guard, sitting in an enclosed Plexiglas office, to open the gate.

A buzz, a click, and then the gate slowly started to open. The guard kept the crowd at bay while the two guys slipped through the opening.

"Hey, are you guys with the band?" one girl called out.

"Can we come with you?" yelled another.

"Pllleeeaassse, tell Ace I haaaavvvvve to talk to him!"

Being "with the band," a catchphrase of the 1960s and later a regular punch line on *Saturday Night Live skits,* has become a full-blown obsession with fans.

Andre has been involved in several conversations with fans that include those words. Listen to one of the calls he received while Kiss was in New York City on its Alive/Worldwide Tour:

"Andre! How are ya', man?" It was 10 a.m. and it sounded like the caller had already downed several margaritas.

"Who is this?" Andre barked into the receiver.

"Its Joe, maaaan! You remember me?"

"Oh, yeah. How could I forget?" Andre's eyes rolled. Maybe he remembered; maybe he didn't.

"Hey, can I get some tickets to see my good buddy Paul tonight?"

"I'll have to ask."

"Can I come back and say hi. You know, maybe get some passes?"

"I'll have to ask."

"Can you have Paul call me?"

"I'll have to ask."

"Wow. It's been great talking to you, man."

"Yeah, terrific."

It's the same with every band Andre has ever worked with, in every city they have ever played: the "we're with the band" syndrome. People will try anything to score free tickets and get backstage to be near the artists.

"I can't understand it," Andre says. "Besides, being backstage isn't that cool." But the twinkle in his eye lets you know he's seen things backstage that only he and the artists will ever know.

Probably one of the toughest roles Andre plays as a security director is "gatekeeper," the middleman between the artists and their so-called "old friends." Sometimes this can lead to uncomfortable situations.

New York and Los Angeles shows can be especially difficult. These are the high-profile gigs, heavily attended by industry types. Hometown areas also complicate the matter with lots of family members and friends. For Kiss, it's New York. For Aerosmith, it's Boston. For Bon Jovi, it's New York or New Jersey. For the rappers, it's always New York and Los Angeles.

And then there's the media. The guest list can be huge. Hundreds of people may be on a guest list, all angling to get backstage and spend time with the artists. Managing this requires sophisticated pass systems, allowing the appropriate people access to the appropriate places. A typical pass system looks like this:

- **All-Access Laminate:** Allows you to go anywhere in the venue at anytime. Backstage, artists' dressing rooms, out in the house – anywhere. It's reserved for artists, close family members, security, and record-company and production people.

- **Colored Tour Sleeve:** Access to artists and dressing rooms. It's typically reserved for security managers, wardrobe people and guitar techs.

- **Support Sleeve:** All access, but with exceptions. It's usually for the crew and opening act.

- **VIP Laminate:** Allows the wearer backstage before and after the show. It does not allow all-access privileges but is more prestigious than a stick-on VIP pass. They usually are reserved for special guests.

- **Stick-On Passes:** Passes given to radio station contest winners or local media. They get people backstage – most likely to a meet-and-greet session – and that's about it. The colors change every day to avoid misuse or counterfeiting.

Fans use anything to try to get backstage. One of the most common remains the "yesterday's pass" approach. Andre explains: "Fans will win backstage passes on a radio promo, come backstage and enjoy the show and the scene. Then, if we are playing within driving distance the next night, they will show up and try to use the same pass twice. We change pass colors all the time so that it's tough to do that. But the 'yesterday's pass' people often get backstage for a little while, because someone at the door will just see a pass and let them in. But they're usually not there for long." Andre grins.

The most creative approaches come from fans who actually create bogus passes. The most frequently counterfeited pass is the all-access laminate.

"Fans have been pretty ingenious," Andre says. "They scan, photocopy or create a bogus pass on their computers. If an artist is touring behind a product, such as an album, they use the artwork from the CD cover, then take it to a copy shop like Kinko's, laminate it, put a hole in the top, run a shoestring through it and presto! Future record-label executive!

"Some of the bogus passes have been pretty good. Others are just sad," Andre continues. "Like trying to use 'yesterday's pass,' these bogus passes may get you by the $5-an-hour Rent-a-Guard, but you won't last five minutes backstage."

By far, the most common method used to get backstage is the friend, family member, long-lost-love routine.

Friends and Family

Oddly enough, family and friends can be among the most challenging of all pass holders. These may be people who aren't accustomed to hanging out backstage or even attending concerts. Andre and his crew always try to make them comfortable and welcome, but it can be tough.

"Often, because of who people know or think they know, everyone feels that they should have a personal audience with the artist," Andre explains. "I just can't let that happen. The people I work with are performers, and there is a lot of mental preparation before a show. I have to respect and protect their desire for privacy."

The biggest offenders are the "old friends" or business acquaintances. Typically, these are people the artists see only when they're in town. Because of past associations, a particular person sometimes is given tickets or passes as a friendly gesture. Occasionally, the

artist's management contacts the person, but more often than not, the person contacts the management company or Andre to get tickets. Sometimes, situations get tricky.

"I usually review the guest list with the artists, and we go through a who-gets-what routine," Andre says. "Usually people are very reasonable with their requests, but some are not. There have been times when an artist will say 'Yeah, I know him. He's a pain. Give him some tickets, but no passes,' or 'Give him tickets and after-show passes only.'"

Many artists skip the after-show appearances, which take place in a separate room and are similar to pre-show meet-and-greets.

Artists usually receive a ticket allotment for each show. For example, they might get ten tickets per show to use however they want. That may not sound like much, but consider: ten tickets per show at an average price of $50 per ticket, multiplied by all band members and then multiplied again by as many as 225 dates or more, and that's a lot of revenue that goes into free tickets. And extra comp tickets for hometown shows mean more money out the window.

When it comes to ticket allocation, Andre is often the bearer of news – be it good, bad or both. That day in New York with Kiss was no exception.

"Yeah," came the less-than-enthusiastic greeting on the line's other end.

"Joe. Andre Augustine calling from Kiss."

"Hey! Andre, what's goin' on, man? How are you doing?" The voice perked up immediately.

"Here's the deal. You can have four tickets, then buy four tickets. And, unfortunately, there are no passes to be had."

Silence.

"Joe?"

"I can't get eight tickets, huh?"

"You may have four, but you have to buy the other four."

"Buy four?"

"Buy four."

"And no passes?"

"No passes."

You could hear the dejection in Joe's voice, and Andre couldn't figure out why he was surprised.

"The only time he comes around or tries to contact the artists is when they are in town," Andre says about Joe and countless others like him. "And the only contact he tries to make are to mooch tickets."

Andre shakes his head.

"Every time I see this person, he is in the band's food room, eating everything, making sandwiches to take home. Why would he think the band would want him and his companions around? And even though I know they have been to dozens of shows, because I've seen them there, they act as if each one is their first one."

Andre wrapped up his conversation that day with Joe the same way he concludes thousands of such conversations.

"Your tickets will be at the will-call window."

"Will call? Where is that?"

"Window, at the main box office."

"Will call?"

"Will call."

Despite Joe's dilemma, Kiss made free tickets a fan-relations triumph on the Alive/Worldwide Tour.

50
'YOU WANT TO GIVE US WHAT!?!?'

ANDRE'S FAVORITE PART OF KISS' ALIVE/WORLDWIDE TOUR CAME each night an hour or so before show time, when he would upgrade seats for a few very lucky fans, an oft-repeated scene.

"Excuse me, how would you folks like to sit in the front row?" Andre stopped some concertgoers and asked them.

"What?"

"How would you like to be guests of Kiss and see the show from the front row?"

"You're kidding right?" The man walking the concourse at the Dane County Coliseum in Madison, Wisconsin, pulled his two young sons near and eyed Andre suspiciously.

"Nope."

The father scanned Andre from top to bottom. Seeing the headset, permanent backstage pass and wad of tickets in his hand, the young father's gaze stopped on Andre's face. Looking into Andre's eyes, the man knew he was sincere.

"Sure, we'd love to!"

The father kneeled down and explained the conversation to the two boys. They let out an enthusiastic scream, and both boys threw their arms around their father. Andre smiled. He felt warm as he witnessed the family moment. But then he was overcome with sadness, as he thought about his own three boys. It had been a long time since he felt their arms around him. Being on the road is never easy for a loving father.

Handing out tickets to deserving fans and gauging their response is Andre's favorite part of the day and usually makes any downside of his job worthwhile. He smiles as he remembers the experiences. "I have to be honest – when I do that, I feel a little like Santa Claus."

Ticket giveaways are fast becoming a standard in the industry, and Andre and fellow security man Tony Morehead did a lot of giving away on Kiss' Alive/Worldwide Tour.

An interview with production manager Tim Rozner in *Metal Edge*'s "Kiss Alive/Worldwide 1996/1997 Tour" edition elaborates on Kiss' concept of giving away tickets:

> "Before the opening act starts, I and other people on our staff will take some of these tickets and find Kiss fans up in the rafters, kids sitting behind a post – the kind of Kiss fans that are really excited to be there – and we'll trade their tickets for the good ones.
>
> "It's gonna happen at every show. It not only reinforces the fact that this band takes care of their fans, it also stops the scalpers and the people who can afford these tickets but who aren't Kiss fans from having those seats. ... The band can see quite far, and you can see who's down front. It's a big difference when it's solid Kiss fans, people who know all the words. They feed off the crowd, so they love to have that contact."

On a typical evening during the Alive/Worldwide Tour, Andre and Tony would eat dinner in the catering area and then head out to walk around the venue, seeking out "interesting fans," as Andre calls them, and upgrading their tickets.

These "interesting fans" could be just about anyone, but Andre did have some parameters. "We might find some real die-hard fans in the nosebleed sections, or maybe a husband and wife," says Andre. "If someone looked as if he spent his last nickel to come to a show, or maybe a young guy who looked like he worked for a month to be able to bring his date to a show, we would upgrade them."

When fans were selected, their responses ranged from screams, hugs and jumping up and down, to a big smile and a simple, "Thanks."

Andre pauses a moment, looks up, and smiles slightly. "My favorites are the families. A husband and wife with children, or single fathers with children. After the first few seconds of the concert, I go to the front to check on them. They usually are in a trance, staring at the stage, or they see me and start freaking out all over again. Ticket giveaways are definitely the best part of the job."

One aspect of the ticket giveaways that got blown out of proportion on the Alive/Worldwide Tour was the notion that they were strictly for attractive women who might want to spend time with the band, Andre says.

David Browne, a critic and writer for *Entertainment Weekly,* fueled the fire when he wrote a cover story for the magazine's August 16, 1996, issue, entitled "Sex, Drudgery and Rock & Roll." The article, which chronicled Browne's brief stint as a roadie on the Alive/Worldwide Tour, included a section about Andre and Browne giving away tickets prior to a show at Cleveland's Gund Arena:

> "Look at that ass," says hulking, stone-faced Andre Augustine, Kiss' personal security guard. We are surfing the arena's concession areas in a nightly ritual: the ticket swap. At each venue, Kiss set aside roughly 10 front-row seats, and just before show time, Augustine offers lucky ticket holders the chance to switch. There's only one catch.
>
> "Can we have backstage passes?" cajole three frat boys. Augustine smiles faintly. "Nah – your tits aren't big enough," he says. The swap makes for a comic sight: a six-foot-plus bruiser propositioning petite, scantily clad blondes with the line, Are you alone tonight? (Another front-row requirement.)
>
> "Excuse me, ladies," intones Augustine to two leather-clad babes, who keep walking. "They don't wanna talk," he sneers. "They got dates." Trying to assist, I point out two girls in T-shirts and Kiss makeup – not model material but clearly fans. Augustine gives them a dismissive glance and goes on scoping the crowd.

The piece only told half the story. "That guy who wrote that took my comments totally out of context," Andre contends. "He made it seem like we were only out to get girls. Let's be honest. Sure, we wanted to find some attractive people. But we also gave tickets away to couples and families that night. You'll notice he never made any mention of that. I would be lying if I told you we didn't pick some pretty girls, but we don't do it just because we think some girl is going to flash the band. It really has a lot to do with guiding the dynamics of a crowd. Imagine that you've just played 100 dates and been on tour for months, and you have months more to go. One way to keep energy in the show is to have well-placed, enthusiastic fans positioned so the artists can feed off of their energy. That's what we tried to

do. What we didn't want is for the artist to have to look at some toothless guy chewing tobacco and spitting all night. Or worse, a row full of record-company stiffs!"

Guiding crowd dynamics is an important role in giving away seats. Contracts with promoters usually specify how many tickets are reserved for the band. But the one thing those contracts almost never spell out is where those seats are located. They are always good seats, but not all are in the front row and spaced evenly across the stage. Sometimes as many as fifteen seats may be on one side of the stage.

"Not only is it impossible to determine who's going to sit where," Andre says, "but occasionally, it can be difficult to give these tickets out! Some people are under the impression that it's louder in the front row. But that just isn't so. Most of the speakers throw the sound from the sides. The front row is actually one of the quieter places – relatively speaking, of course."

Then there is the trust factor. "Some people just don't trust being approached by a stranger at a concert," Andre says. "Even with all my official credentials, passes, tickets and headset, some people still think I'm pulling a scam. And I only have so much time before I've got to get backstage. So if someone doesn't think I'm legit, I don't spend too much time trying to convince them otherwise."

Despite these minor inconveniences, Andre loves ticket giveaways. And whether the tickets go to families, interesting fans or pretty girls, the result is always the same: a night the fans will never forget.

51

IN THE GARDEN OF GOOD AND EVIL

Kiss

July, 1996
Kiss Alive/Worldwide Tour
Madison Square Garden – New York City

ANDRE WATCHED THE ACTIVITY IN THE STREET. CABS AND PEOPLE
buzzed everywhere. Manhattan is always electric. But this week, there was something extra.
Kiss sold out four consecutive shows at Madison Square Garden. The boys were back in town.

Anytime Kiss plays New York, the crowds get just a little crazier. New York is the band's
hometown, and Gene Simmons, Paul Stanley, Peter Criss and Ace Frehley always want to
perform at their best. So do the fans.

Tim Rozner, the show's production manager, kicked off the second of the four shows as
he did every night. "You wanted the best ... " The 18,000 people shouted the words right
along with him. " ... You got the best. The hottest band in the world ... KISS!"

As Andre looked out over the screaming fans, something didn't seem right. The locally
hired security people weren't positioned in their proper spots. It was early in the tour, and even
Andre and venue security director Tony Morehead were still deciding how to best work the
show security posts. In fact, for whatever reason, everyone on this tour was still feeling their
way around, finding out how to work together as a team three months after the tour opened.

Andre had alternated his post between Gene's side and Paul's side of the stage
throughout the tour (he eventually settled on Gene's side), but he worked Paul's side in New
York because the singer had expressed concern about the crazy crowds.

The Garden is a tricky place. Built like a bowl with a concourse level that cannot be accessed by the floor, the Garden features a lip on the outside of the stage through which a particularly creative fan can gain access to the stage. And that's exactly what happened that night – twice.

"The guys were about halfway through the show and suddenly I saw a man walking behind the amp wall on Paul's side of the stage," Andre recalls. "As I bolted across the stage to keep him from going out front, I remember thinking, *Where the fuck did this guy come from?*"

The shirtless jumper was about 5 feet, eight inches tall, weighed around 190 pounds and looked about 26 years old. He was stocky, built low to the ground and wore black jeans tucked inside his boots. The top of his boots sported shiny silver spikes. Some people in the crowd began to notice the commotion.

Andre reached him and applied his patented "back of the belt" grab. For the first time in Andre's career, he couldn't budge a jumper. "The guy planted. I grabbed him and he didn't move," Andre remembers. "I knew he was messed up on something, and that really complicates the situation. Plus, the crowd was watching us now, not the band. I had to be careful that I didn't thrash him too badly in front of 18,000 fans."

The scene started to move in slow motion. The jumper let out a growl and his eyes flashed. Andre suspected angel dust and realized he was going to have to get tough. He had seen guys on dust before who acted so violently they had to be taken out by four cops. But Andre also had to keep in mind he was in front of a sold-out arena.

The man leaned forward, so Andre grabbed his waistband with his right hand first and then switched to his left hand, freeing up his right arm to hook under the jumper's right side. The security man got him in a half-nelson and tripped him.

"So he's down," Andre picks up the story. "I grabbed him by the top of his boot, but he had those spikes. So I let go and grabbed him in his pants pocket. His pants ripped from the pocket to his crotch. I grabbed his waistband instead, slung him around and his head hit the stairs at the side of the stage. There's no talking involved in this situation. It's all physical."

By this time, Morehead arrived on the scene, grabbed the jumper by his hair and dragged him, face-first, down the steps, his head thumping against each stair.

Meanwhile, Ace continued to wail on his guitar while Gene stalked the left side of the stage.

After all this, the guy continued to flail, Andre says. A few Garden security workers grabbed him from Morehead, took him into an isolated area and "explained" to him the dangers of stage jumping.

Less than five minutes later, "Flower Child," as Andre calls her, emerged onstage from the same area as the spiked jumper. Decked out in hip-huggers, with no shoes and blonde hair, the twenty-something girl began dancing towards the middle of the stage.

Andre ran out, grabbed her by the waist and walked her down the stairs to the backstage area.

"Would you put some people behind this curtain!" Andre yelled at one of the Garden's security chiefs after escorting the dancing hippie away from the stage area. "I just had two people actually saunter onto the stage. I'm sick of this, man. Help us out!"

Despite the near-misses with jumpers, Paul and Gene remain reasonable about fans who run onstage, Andre says. "They figure that if somebody jumps on stage, that person doesn't really want to harm them. That person wants to just get up on stage, show their presence, maybe hug them.

"Peter and Ace, on the other hand, think somebody jumping the stage wants to hurt them," Andre continues. "Well, my reaction to that is, 'If somebody wants to get you, why are they trying to get up next to you and do it in front of thousands of people? They would just buy a nice seat on the side of the stage, take a gun with a scope and blow your brains out. Was the hip-hugger chick going to *dance* them to death?'"

Throughout his career, Andre says, most of the dozens of stage jumpers he's escorted to the door have been rock fans. Rap crowds don't take the stage, he says. "It's a different mentality, an altogether different vibe. There was a lot of attention given to security measures because of the violence that was associated with those shows back then. Would you jump on stage with Ice Cube?"

52
SOUTH AMERICAN SCARE

Kiss

March 11, 1997: Santiago, Chile

"ACE! GET UP."

Andre pounded on Ace Frehely's hotel room door. He and band coordinator Tommy Thayer had been trying for the last 45 minutes to get in touch with the lead guitarist. He hadn't responded to any of the dozens of calls placed to his room, and after 15 minutes of pounding, he hadn't yet answered the door. Thayer and Andre grew accustomed to having a tough time rousing Ace, but that day felt different.

More than three-quarters through the tour, Ace's behavior deteriorated. He was later than usual, groggier than usual and seemed less in control. Every so often, he received a "special delivery" package, and Andre suspected he was drinking.

Plus, there was the occasional mini-bar receipt listing more than a beer or two. Andre would often find bottles behind the TV or mini-bar. Concerned, he sought advice from tour accountant Paco Zimmer.

"But, Paco, how can Ace play the shows if he's messed up?" Andre asked in the midst of one of these sessions.

"Easy, Andre, easy." Paco had seen it a thousand times before. "Sometimes musicians just go on autopilot. They have played those songs so many times that it becomes second nature."

Venue security director Tony Morehead, who has been sober for 17 years, was worried, too. He and Andre wondered how their friends in Aerosmith might have responded if faced with a similar situation.

"The Aerosmith guys would have stopped the tour and sent him to rehab." Andre theorizes. "But I guess this tour was just too big. Maybe some people thought this might be Kiss' last shot.

"In retrospect," Andre quips, "I get the impression that if Gene and Paul would have knocked on Ace's hotel room door and found him dead, they would have looked at each other, shrugged their shoulders and said, 'Well, at least we got eight good months out of him.' But I think as far and Gene and Paul knew, it was just the occasional beer or two. They were unaware of anything else. And let's be real. It would be silly to stop this tour and lose millions because a grown man wants to drink a couple of beers after a long night at work."

But the situation with Ace escalated, Andre gripes. "The routine of trying to get him to the gig on time and move him from hotel to hotel continued to worsen. And it really pissed me off. I don't know what his problem was, but it was reaching the boiling point ... with many people."

Although he had no proof that Ace was using, the thought of a drug-related accident on his watch turned Andre's stomach. Andre hated drugs. He had seen it ruin families and lives. From Andre's perspective, drug use resulted from nothing more than self-centeredness.

"A lot of people depended on this tour," Andre points out. "The crew, the vendors and all the ancillary management people derived income from this gig – money to pay their rent, feed their families and build their futures. And the band needed this tour. Of course, there was the money, but more importantly there was the accomplishment factor. Gene, Paul, Ace and Peter were well into middle age, and they wanted to see if they could do it one more time. I'll be honest. It became a real source of pride for all of us that this tour was going over as big as it was. And I wanted to do my part to make sure it continued."

Andre rocks back in his chair, throws down his pen and punctuates his thought. "But above all, the fans needed this tour. They were the ones spending hundreds of dollars to buy tickets, programs and T-shirts. They needed this tour because it gave them something to look forward to, a break from an otherwise monotonous routine. Plus, it proved that the things they held close in their younger years, the ideals promoted by Kiss, were still valid. The fans really needed and deserved this tour."

And Kiss delivered. As band manager Doc McGhee told *Performance* magazine in February 1997, Kiss' success philosophy is simple. "If it's a $10 ticket, we give 'em a $20 show, and if it's a $50 ticket, we give 'em a $100 show. That's the show Kiss puts on."

This tour brought a night or two of escape from the 60-hour workweek and provided fans a short trip down memory lane to a less complicated and perhaps happier time in their lives. Besides, the Kiss Army had waited a long time for this reunion.

What if they got inside and found Ace Frehley dead on the floor of his hotel room?

Andre brings his focus back to Ace. "Ace's career has been one in a million, he's made rock 'n' roll history, and he's responsible for thousands of kids picking up a guitar and learning to play. It's heady stuff."

But that day in South America, Andre wasn't nearly as reflective. Andre just hoped and prayed Ace had not done something stupid. He continued pounding on the door with greater and greater intensity.

How could Ace throw it all away? Andre asked himself. *He has so much to be thankful for.* He started to viciously kick the bottom of the door, which strained and flexed under the force of every strike.

"Where's the damn hotel guy?" Thayer asked urgently, his eyes pleading for a resolution to this agonizing situation. Ace was Thayer's musical inspiration, his whole reason for pursuing a career in music. Thayer's face twisted with concern for the guitarist who held a special place in his heart. As both men continued pounding, Ace's room remained eerily silent.

"I don't know," Andre looked over his shoulder and down the hall. "But if he doesn't get here soon, we're kickin' this fuckin' door down."

Andre had contacted the hotel office, and the manager on duty was supposedly headed up with a passkey. But Andre and Thayer weren't waiting for him. The pounding continued. Other guests started looking out of their doors to see the ruckus.

Thayer turned white. Neither one had mentioned it, but both he and Andre thought the same thing: *What if they got inside and found Ace Frehley dead on the floor of his hotel room?*

"If he's dead, I'm really going to be pissed," Andre said through grit teeth, perspiration starting to seep through the orange and white Harley-Davidson logo on the back of his black T-shirt. "That's it. I'm breakin' the fuckin' thing down."

Just as Andre stepped back to get a running start at the door, the hotel manager appeared. Horrified at the scene, he stood there for a second, dumbfounded. Andre saw him from the corner of his eye.

"Come on, man! Get us in!" Andre ordered.

The shaking hotel manager slid the passkey into the slot and opened the door. It stopped abruptly. Chain locked. Andre moved quickly to the door, shoving the hotel manager out of the way with his shoulder.

"Ace!" Andre shouted through the opening. "Ace! You motherfucker! You better be in there, Ace!"

Then the men heard groaning coming from inside the room. After several seconds, Ace fumbled with the chain lock and cracked open the door.

"Ace!"

"Huh? What?" he said groggily, removing the chain. Thayer and Andre pushed the door open and walked into the room, brushing past the guitarist.

"Ace, we've been trying to get you for an hour," Andre huffed. "We thought you were dead." Andre scanned the room looking for anything out of the ordinary.

"Dead? Huh? What? I was sleeping, man," Ace replied.

Andre wanted to smack him. Just grab him by the neck and knock some sense into him. It took every ounce of control not to lay a hand on him.

"Sleeping! Ace, we've called you dozens of times, and Tommy and I have been frantically pounding on your door for a half-hour. What's wrong with you, man?"

A dazed Ace looked at Andre, shrugged his shoulders and sat on the bed.

"I'm a deep sleeper," he offered.

It sounded more like a question than a statement.

53
'YOU GOTTA DO WHAT YOU GOTTA DO'

April 5, 1997: Show Day

Kiss Alive/Worldwide Tour

Civic Arena – Columbus, Georgia

THE DAY BROKE DARK AND OMINOUS. A STEADY RAIN FELL, AND thunder rolled through the city of Atlanta. At about 7:52 a.m., the ringing of the phone in Andre's hotel room cut through the clamor. Andre picked up the receiver and before he could say a word, the voice on the other end began.

"Andre, we need to go."

He recognized the voice immediately as David Killary, Kiss' number-one pilot. Almost without taking a breath, Killary continued, "There's a bad storm coming through."

The weather forecast predicted a large storm front heading for Atlanta, and it was going to get nasty. To make the next show in Columbus, Kiss had to move fast.

"When?" Andre asked, clearing his throat.

"Now."

"OK. Let's do it."

Kiss had been based out of Atlanta's Ritz Carlton for several days. The hotel catered to the band's wishes: mid-afternoon omelets, 24-hour room service, and for Doc McGhee and tour accountant Paco Zimmer, great golf courses. Everyone enjoyed the hotel, except Gene Simmons. Not because he didn't like the hotel, but because he doesn't like basing.

Gene prefers staying in the city where the band plays or simply moving on to the next town right after a show. "It's part of his personality," Andre explains. "Gene is the king of

hang. He likes to go to new places and hang out. Part of this may be Gene's ability to make new friends wherever he goes. He really is a *friendly* guy."

This personality trait, however, makes Andre's job a little more challenging. It's not like Gene Simmons can just go out in public unescorted — some would say it wouldn't be safe for the general public.

Having members of the band travel individually exerts pressure on the road-management team. It fragments the group and makes the unit short-staffed. But if the strategy keeps the artist comfortable and happy, who cares? Andre just considers that another part of the job.

That particular time, Gene stayed in Chapel Hill, North Carolina, and was to meet the band in Columbus, Georgia, the next day for the show. He would fly first-class commercial with Tony Morehead.

April 5 was not a scheduled "move day," when everyone packs up and moves on to the next city. But with the storm coming, it was now Andre's responsibility to get the band, the jet and the entourage in its entirety to Columbus. The incredibly tight schedule got tighter by the day. More shows and, more cities meant every moment counted, and there couldn't be any disruptions in the schedule. The weather reports indicated Atlanta could be a problem for a few days. Kiss would now move to their next base city a few days early. But moving at a moment's notice is no small task for a band like Kiss.

Kiss had arrived back in Atlanta early that morning from the show in Chapel Hill. The gig went well. Fans who reviewed the concert on the Internet even commented about how the band just seemed to be playing better and better together. Andre, taking care of the last bits of business from the previous day, didn't get to sleep until 2:15 a.m.

After hanging up the phone, he rubbed the sleep from his eyes and looked around his room. It was not neat. A fax machine, cell phone chargers and a pile of memos cluttered the desk. On top of the dresser lay walkie-talkies, keys and his pager. Several pairs of sneakers littered the room, and clothes were strewn everywhere. Andre quickly got up, trudged through the mess and went to work.

He checked his list of people to notify. Although Andre had this list memorized, he always checked off his calls on paper to ensure against mistakes.

As his left index finger ran down the page, his mind worked fast. All sorts of unexpected arrangements needed to be made. Hotels, transportation and additional logistics were now added to his already full day. List in hand, he sat down and set about making his calls.

When traveling with Kiss, Andre always calls Paul Stanley first. Regardless of the situation, Paul is always the most pleasant. He usually says, "Good morning" and "How are you?" With Paul (and Gene, if he's around), there are no complaints, no comments, no questions. "Let's face it," Andre says. "When you've been in the rock 'n' roll game as long as these guys, everyone learns the mantra. You gotta do what you gotta do. That's all there is to it."

Andre then called Ace Frehley, Peter Criss, Doc McGhee and Paco Zimmer – in that order.

Next, he focused on the tasks necessary to execute the move. His immediate responsibility was to get the band to Columbus so the show wouldn't be jeopardized. But the weather wasn't the only obstacle putting the show at risk.

In the lobby of the Ritz Carlton, the scene played out on cue. Bags were carried downstairs, room charges and mini-bar bills were tallied and paid, and members of the band and entourage milled about the lobby. Because it was still early by rock 'n' roll standards, everyone looked a little groggy. But generally, it was business as usual. One thing, however, wasn't typical: Peter complained about pain.

"My arms are killin' me," he announced, dropping his gig bag at his feet in the lobby. "I can't raise them over my head."

Andre was used to the occasional complaint from the guys about being tired. But this hinted at something more. Andre could actually see Peter experiencing physical discomfort, wincing when he raised his arms.

Peter had gotten a massage from a physical therapist the night before – certainly not a superfluous luxury, given the athletic-like performance required to play a Kiss show. But now he stood with his arms hanging limply, as if pulled towards the ground by some gravitational force. He continued to complain about the pain.

We'll get a little food and a little coffee in him, and he'll be fine, Andre thought. He couldn't have been more wrong.

The wind blew as the band made their way from the white Lincoln Town Cars to the private jet parked on the tarmac at Atlanta's Peachtree Airport. Upon entering the plane, immediately to the right were two sets of seats facing each other. Just beyond them was a

table on the right-hand side with another group of four seats. And behind that section were the couches, which ran the remaining length of the plane.

A door separated the main cabin and the pilots, but it was rarely closed. The guys liked to keep it open. That way, if anyone needed something, wanted to ask the pilot a question or just felt like seeing the view from the cockpit, they could.

Ace proved the most comfortable with flying. The rest of the Kiss travelers were by no means white-knucklers, but Andre never got the impression that they took flying lessons on their days off.

Conversations during the short trip turned unusually somber. Peter didn't feel well, and everyone, concerned about his health, waited to see how he felt when the plane landed. The mood seemed agitated by a sense of urgency to get to Columbus.

As the group deplaned in Columbus, Andre could tell Peter's problem was serious. Peter tilted to one side as he walked, then to the other. No one talked to him; they wanted to give him some space.

The band moved quickly to the hotel, a Sheraton. Nothing exceptional, just a plain, sterile, standard hotel. It wasn't like the Ritz Carlton in Atlanta, or the Righa in New York, or the Ritz in Chicago. But these guys had seen a lot worse, so no one really complained.

Besides, more important matters were at hand.

As the band settled in, McGhee took action and instructed Andre to summon the "rock doc." Fast.

"Rock doc" is an industry term for physicians who work with local promoters. These doctors are considered "on call" when the promoter has a band in town. Usually general practitioners, they treat everything from laryngitis to the flu. They also have access to prescription medicine 24 hours a day.

Andre called the local promoter, but drawing from his sports background, he knew Peter didn't need just any doctor. He needed someone with a background in sports medicine; someone used to getting athletes back into action in a hurry. He specified this to the local promoter.

When the doctor arrived, he was a young man with glasses, tall, slender and angular, sporting brown, short-cropped hair. Andre thought he looked like an athlete himself. As the doctor examined Peter, the rest of the group set up camp in their rooms.

Rock docs have a tough job. They must make a diagnosis without the help of sophisticated equipment or clinical surroundings. And they may not be familiar with the dynamics of putting on a show or the costs involved. When they casually prescribe two aspirin and a day's rest, they may not realize they've just written a $400,000 prescription.

After only a few moments, the doctor concluded Peter's exam. The diagnosis: "Arm fatigue," he said, "with the possibility of more damage with continued use." His prescription was for Peter to use ice and to rest. Or risk serious injury.

No kidding, Andre thought. *I could have told you that.*

The next decision was among the toughest the band ever faced. What should Kiss do about the show? The crew, which resembled a small army, had spent all day setting up eleven tractor-trailers worth of gear. The show in Columbus was now considered "in and up." Once the equipment and staging is in and up, sunk costs soar. Some estimates put these costs at $250,000 a night for the Alive/Worldwide Tour.

But the most important consideration was the fans. Some were traveling from miles away, and thousands were already in transit. The band did not want to disappoint anybody. Andre recognized another problem potentially more deadly than disappointment. Thousands of fans and a canceled show, especially one as big as this, would be a security nightmare. Enraged fans might riot, damage property, inflict injuries or worse.

He recalled a 1992 incident in Montreal during a Metallica/Guns N' Roses double bill. Metallica lead singer James Hetfield seriously burned himself in a pyrotechnics stunt gone awry, and Metallica had to stop short its portion of the show. Rather than be upstaged by the drama their touring compatriots faced, Guns N' Roses hit the stage for 50 minutes and then split. The move incited thousands of fans to riot and destroy millions of dollars in property.

Back in Columbus, Kiss had another sold-out gig to consider the next night in Nashville, which is a larger market with even more fans, media and pressure. Rock 'n' roll is a business, and it would haven been irresponsible for the band's management not to consider these issues.

Finally, far from being the last consideration, there was Peter Criss himself. No one had ever replaced Peter behind the drums on tour as long as he was an active member of the band. Peter had some heavy thinking to do and not much time to do it.

McGhee and Peter discussed the dilemma at length. The final decision rested with Peter. If he would permit it, Eddie Kanon, Peter's drum technician and friend, would sit in for Peter. He knew the songs and was considered a more-than-capable drummer. Eddie had even played for an occasional sound check while Peter rested on the tour. Eddie Kanon was the best and only choice.

In one of the toughest decisions Peter ever made, he conceded. If he didn't, he might jeopardize the rest of the tour.

Eddie Kanon, then 26 years old, would be the only other person in history to don "The Cat" makeup and drum with Kiss. Even Peter's replacement in the early Eighties, Eric Carr, portrayed a different character with different makeup. It was an agonizing decision.

There is some discrepancy about when this controversial decision was actually made. But by most accounts, by 4:30 p.m. on April 5, 1997, Eddie Kanon was officially named Peter Criss's fill-in for that night's show.

"The guys weren't worried about Eddie's skills or whether he could pull off the show," Andre recalls. "They were concerned about whether the band would jell. When you've played music with a person for decades, you develop a second nature about what is going on when you're onstage. Although they knew they couldn't make up for decades in one sound check, they did want to do everything possible to make the show great."

By then, everyone was clued in except Ace. Gene arrived shortly after the others and was appraised of the situation immediately. He knew the show must go on. Plus, it was time for sound check.

Andre and Tommmy Thayer moved quickly to Ace's room. They knocked and, surprisingly, Ace opened the door right away and turned to gather his things. As he threw some items into his gig bag, Thayer attempted to make small talk and casually mentioned that Peter wouldn't be playing.

"What?" Ace immediately stopped packing.

Thayer continued. "Peter's not going to sound check. He's not feeling well and he might not play tonight."

"What do you mean, he might not play? Is the show going to be canceled? I'm not playing if Peter's not up there."

Ace and Peter were tight. In many ways, Kiss was always a divided camp: Gene and Paul on one side, Ace and Peter on the other.

Andre sensed trouble. Sometimes in this business, you can't always share everything with everyone all the time. This was one of those times, and Thayer should have known better.

Ace sat down on the bed, eyeing Andre and Thayer suspiciously. "No big deal, Ace," Andre told him. "The rock doc came down and told Pete he had to rest or he might seriously injure himself. Eddie's gonna sit in. Everything's cool."

"If Peter doesn't go on, I don't go on," Ace repeated. "Where's Doc? I need to talk to George [Sewitt, who was the personal manager for both Peter and Ace]. What room is Peter in?"

Ace called Peter. All Andre and Thayer could hear was Ace's end of the conversation.

"What's going on?" Ace's nasal tone strained under the stress.

"You're skipping sound check?"

"How are you feeling?"

"You might not play? If you don't, Eddie's going to fill in."

"Do you think this is a good idea?"

Andre shot Thayer an "I can't believe you" look. It was their job to get Ace to sound check, and now it looked like that might be a problem.

Why did the circumstances take Ace by surprise? Andre wondered. After Peter's comments at the hotel in Atlanta and on the plane ride, it seemed pretty inconceivable that Ace could be unaware of the severity of the situation.

Ace wrapped up his conversation with Peter and immediately tried reaching Sewitt. After several unsuccessful attempts, he slammed down the phone, shrugged his shoulders, grabbed his gig bag and said, "Well, all right. Let's just go to sound check."

As the three men left the hotel room, Ace had second thoughts and asked, "Where's Doc? I gotta talk to somebody about this."

Andre responded, "Everybody's waiting in the lobby, so let's just head down there."

Once in the lobby, Ace dragged his feet. Someone suggested that they get in the van and discuss it on the way. That's when the convincing from the rest of the band began.

Paul started gingerly, as if talking to a toddler. "Peter might not be able to play tonight. Eddie knows the songs, so he'll just sit in. No big deal."

"I don't know ... " Ace hesitated.

Gene immediately interceded. "Hey, Eddie's going to play. Let's just go do the show."

At the venue, Gene, Paul and Ace met privately to talk over all aspects of the situation. Everyone agreed that going through with the show was the right thing to do. The next big question was how to tell the fans.

Meanwhile, an unsuspecting Eddie Kanon was setting up Peter's drums like he did every night. Doc approached from behind. "Eddie!" Doc called out. "Gene and Paul want to talk to you."

Eddie would later confide to a friend that he "thought for sure he was being let go." And he remembers being confused about it, because he figured he'd been doing a good job.

Additional versions of the scene recount that Doc brought Eddie into a room with Gene, Paul and Ace, who reportedly approached Eddie with the classic bad news/good news story.

"Eddie," Paul started, "we have some bad news. Peter is injured and can't play tonight."

"The good news," Gene stepped in, as if on cue, "is that you're going on in his place."

Before Eddie could say a thing, band-support personnel swept him up and began putting Peter's cat costume on him.

Gene, Paul, Ace and Eddie applied their makeup backstage (yes, they do their own!), surrounded by tackle-box-sized makeup kits filled with white paint and black grease pencils on each of the four prep tables.

Eddie had been given a few quick pointers, and Gene and Paul were going to help him when he got to the intricate parts of Peter's makeup.

"Should we have Tim say something to everyone before the show?" Paul asked as he applied the white makeup that served as the base for his look and that of the other members. Tim Rozner was the tour's production manager and the voice behind their raucous opening.

"Or should we do it during the show?" Gene offered. "Regardless, we have to tell them. It's the right thing to do."

Ace quietly went about making up his face. This was typical pre-show behavior for him. He's usually quiet before taking the stage.

"Maybe we should offer a ticket refund?" Paul suggested. He then second-guessed himself. "No. How would we ever sort out the logistics with the promoter?"

Paul then paused and turned sideways, looking at the other three. "Let's give the fans a great show," he said.

And Kiss did.

Moments into the concert, right after playing "Deuce," Paul announced to the crowd: "Peter is sick and back at the hotel. But we wanted to come out here and kick your ass anyway." He said it quickly, perhaps as a result of the adrenaline that was pumping through everyone, especially Eddie.

Reviews on the Web site Kiss Asylum regarding the Columbus show varied.

Some were negative.

"I am not the first one to let everyone know about the mullet they put in to play drums for Peter," wrote one disenchanted fan. "The Eddie Kanon guy on drums had zero energy and no showmanship. He was just there hitting the skins."

Yet other reviews almost glowed.

"People need to understand that Kiss was in a no-win situation," one writer admitted. "The other option would have been to cancel, but who wins in that situation? They did the right thing. Give Kiss credit for pointing out the substitute instead of trying to trick the fans."

"He obviously knew the songs and was playing them very similarly to the way Peter was playing them on this tour," wrote another. "I got the vibe that Paul, Ace and Gene put more energy into the show to make up for the lack of Peter. ... It was indeed a very surreal situation watching a short-haired guy in Peter makeup playing with Kiss, but considering the circumstances, he did a wonderful job."

And Peter's public message displayed decent sportsmanship. "The band trusted [Eddie] enough to let him do it," Peter told *Metal Edge* in August 1997, referring to the incident. "I didn't realize that he'd have to go the whole nine yards with the makeup and the outfit, and I really feel bad for him in a way, because he said it was the scariest two hours of his life."

"I think the people who were going to get it, got it, without Paul making the announcement," Andre says now. "But there wasn't really any kind of pointing and shouting, 'Hey, who is that playing drums?' It was just a great, high-energy show."

The next day, Peter was a little depressed and perhaps a bit embarrassed. "He is probably the most emotional member of Kiss, and he's the one who will hug you, ask you

how you're feeling and really care about your response," Andre says. "But he still had his health and the rest of his career to think about. Peter was the one who was most affected by the incident – not the fans or anyone else in the organization. He's the one who really felt like he disappointed his friends and his fans."

Peter was back behind the drums for the following night's show in Nashville.

54

UNDESIRABLES

Kiss

April 28, 1997: Winnipeg, Canada

"WELCOME TO CANADA," FLASHED THE OVERHEAD SIGN IN illuminated red letters. It was two in the morning on April 28, 1997, but the cheap florescent lights made it look like midday.

Kiss had just wrapped up a concert in flood-ravaged North Dakota, where the band, in an unusual display of generosity, donated the proceeds from a specially designed T-shirt to victims of the flooding, via the United Way. The T-shirts read: "Fargo, We Will Survive, Alive/Worldwide." In an atypical concert move, Paul Stanley actually held the shirt up during the show and asked fans to purchase it.

Now, Kiss needed some goodwill to get them through customs.

Andre made his way past the roped-off maze leading to the customs agent and handed the officer the group's passports. The officer scoured the documents so intently that Andre thought he might be checking the spelling. The agent wasn't smiling.

The training center for Canadian customs is located in Winnipeg. All budding new recruits receive a one-way ticket to Winnipeg to learn the position. As can be imagined, they all set out to prove they are the ultimate in their country's protection.

The situation is compounded with agents from the other end of the spectrum. It seems as though Winnipeg is also the place where older, perhaps demoted, customs agents are sent. Mixing young, budding Mounties and jaded, older agents creates attitude anyway you slice it.

"Stand over there!" the young Canadian customs officer barked.

"What exactly is the problem, sir?" Andre asked politely.

"Stand over there, please."

After several minutes, Andre tried again.

"Sir?"

"Just a moment," came the sharp reply from behind the glass.

The officer conferred with a senior officer, speaking in hushed tones and gesturing frequently toward the computer screen. Finally, the young officer motioned for Andre to approach the glass.

The officer slid several passports under the glass. "These people are free to enter the country."

Andre scooped up the passports, scanning the names and assessing the situation. Paul, Gene, Peter, venue security director Tony Morehead and Andre all were given the green light. Andre looked up at the officer just as he began to speak.

"And these are not." The officer slid more passports under the glass. Canadian officials had a problem allowing band manager McGhee, Ace Frehley and tour accountant Paco Zimmer into the country.

"And what, specifically, is the problem with these passports?" Andre asked. "Everything is current. I checked them myself."

"It's not the passports."

"Then what is it?"

"It's the people."

"The people? And what specifically is wrong with the people?"

The officer's response came quickly. "Undesirable."

"Undesirable?" Andre's voice climbed an octave. "Undesirable? What in the world makes you think these guys are undesirable?" He gestured with his hand, asking the agent to take one more look at the innocent travelers.

McGhee, Ace and Paco milled about the area. They looked tired and a little disheveled. Ace slouched on a chair, exhausted. McGhee and Paco spoke occasionally to one another and paced back and forth. Andre could barely contain a chuckle. *I guess they do look a little undesirable,* he thought.

The three in question noticed the attention and looked up. They smiled meekly at the Canadian official. It was late, and they were willing to try anything just to get some sleep.

The reasons why this trio was considered undesirable were dubious, at best, Andre claims. Ace had a few old driving-while-intoxicated charges on his record. Most of those well-publicized events happened in the United States years ago. With Canada's reciprocity agreement, however, all U.S. offenses get taken into consideration. But the sticking point for Ace was just one offense, which unfortunately happened in Canada and appeared to make the agents a little uneasy.

Meanwhile, McGhee's name had come up in some "undefined context," Andre says.

The most ridiculous reason for detainment was the one given for Paco. Touring with Jimi Hendrix back in 1967, Paco tried to enter Canada with a Benzedrine tablet in his possession. As a result, Canadian officials deported him.

According to a registered pharmacist at U.S Pharmacopeia, a drug information company, Benzedrine was the brand name for amphetamine sulfate marketed by SmithKline French. It was available over the counter in the late 1950s and early 1960s in tablets and extended-release capsules. In 1964, regulators ruled that Benzedrine could only be distributed by prescription – making Paco's possession of the tablets without a prescription in 1967, illegal.

Paco didn't think it was an issue. Since that time, he had traveled in and out of Canada dozens of times while working with Canadian pop singer Bryan Adams. But he apparently never had to pass through the "exceptional" custom agents in the Winnipeg office.

Gene, Paul, Peter and Morehead made their way to the exit and the waiting vans. For them, room service and soft beds were within reach. Morehead turned and winked at Andre. He followed the artists quickly to assume any security responsibilities. For Andre and the others, the wait would be a little longer.

As the reunion tour's security director/road manager, one of Andre's responsibilities was to make certain everyone in the entourage passed in and out of customs. As Andre watched Morehead escort Gene and Paul, he caught himself thinking that just doing security is easy. He stopped and shook his head, knowing he was kidding himself.

Andre set out to prove that his group was not dangerous to Canadian national security by pointing out multiple Canadian stamps, indicating that other Canadian customs officers had shown good judgment and let the men in question enter the country. Andre also made

several references to "ancient history" and how it was important not to hold these people unnecessarily for events, which in some cases, happened decades ago.

"Besides," Andre proclaimed in his closing argument, "we're part of a rock band, not some terrorist organization! And we promise not to blow anything up while we're here."

The customs officer nodded his head. He was coming around.

"Except maybe the Winnipeg Arena." Andre grinned.

The officer shot a concerned look at Andre and then realized the big guy was joking. He smiled at a grinning Andre and nodded his approval. McGhee, Ace and Paco eventually were allowed to enter the country. All it took were a few hundred dollars to purchase specially issued Minister's Passes, provided by immigration officials to allow non-admissible people to enter Canada under certain circumstances.

"Welcome to Canada." Andre muttered, as he handed the money to the smiling customs agent.

Andre wasn't in Canada very long.

At 11:45 p.m. on April 29, 1997, Andre received a telephone call in Winnipeg from his home in California. Kiss was making a run through North America's upper regions before heading to play dates in Germany, Austria, Serbia, Switzerland, Prague, Sweden and Spain. Andre had a family emergency and needed to leave immediately.

In the touring business, the Family Leave Act doesn't exist. There were other competent security people anxious to fill Andre's slot on the high-profile tour. When Andre broke the news about his family to McGhee, the manager's comments were short and to the point. "Your family needs you. When are you leaving?"

Andre looked at him, puzzled.

"Andre," McGhee continued. "What we're doing out here on the road isn't really important. Family is what's important."

Andre, still conscientious of his tour responsibilities, relayed to McGhee his concerns about picking up and leaving the tour. McGhee quickly assured him that things would be handled. "Tommy will help, Paco will help, and I will jump in wherever necessary. You go take care of your family."

Andre left Kiss' Alive/Worldwide Tour on April 30, 1997, at 7:30 a.m. and headed home to do just that. For family reasons, he never returned to the tour.

Meanwhile, Doc and the members of Kiss and their entourage called Andre frequently to check on everything, and – despite well-documented examples of the band's financial stinginess – they kept him on the payroll through the end of the tour on July 5, 1997. It was an unprecedented act of support from the band and Doc McGhee. "He told me that I'd worked really hard on the reunion tour and that it was a difficult situation," Andre recalls now with a smile. "He's this stocky, little guy, with a huge heart."

55
REFLECTIONS

ANDRE'S CONCLUSIONS DRAWN FROM HIS WORK IN RAP AND ROCK 'n' roll are as interesting and eye-opening as his experiences. Here, he shares his thoughts about becoming friends with Jon Bon Jovi, Jam Master Jay and George Thorogood; why most rock stars have few friends; how racism pervades the music industry; and what really matters in life.

Rock Stars as Friends

"It's almost impossible to have a rock star you work for be your friend," Andre says. "You are never really his peer."

But how can you not call yourself a friend of someone you've spent years traveling the world with and sharing meals, laughs and pictures of your kids?

"It's the game," Andre explains. "Has Paul Stanley called me and asked me to go the movies with him? Sure. But it probably wasn't because he wanted my company; it's because he needed someone to be with him at the movies."

Andre continues. "First of all, I don't do what they do. I'm not a musician. I've never stood onstage in front of 40,000 people and played a guitar or sung a song. I'm different, and therefore considered an outsider. Plus, I simply can't be friends with Paul Stanley. I'd like to be, but I can't. I can't go to exclusive restaurants seven days a week. He's a rock star; I work for rock stars. I don't have the same social status."

That's why, unless an artist still spends time with someone he grew up with or attended high school or college with, chances are he doesn't have many close friends. "Very few of

the stars truly have friends," Andre explains. "You and I can be successful, and we can be friends. I'm not your friend because of what you do; I'm your friend because of you."

Unfortunately, the invisible lines dividing society get wider when it comes to the entertainment business. The cavernous space between the haves and have-nots increases every year. Yet Andre still feels blessed to have the close relationships that he does with many artists.

For example, he hangs out with George Thorogood and watches baseball games with him at home and at the stadium. He and the guitarist also enjoy talking with each other about their families – one of Andre's favorite topics.

Andre also considers the members of Bon Jovi special. Close to Andre in age, they consider themselves "just a bunch of guys from Jersey," Andre says. "They see themselves more as a team and never really took themselves too seriously when I worked with them. They took their music and their performing seriously, but not themselves. That's one of the differences between Bon Jovi and Kiss. I think the Bon Jovi guys understood relationships and have a healthy attitude toward the music business and everything that goes with it."

And, of course, Andre still remains close to everyone in Aerosmith. Whether attending a car race with Brad Whitford, Tom Hamilton and Joey Kramer; lifting weights with Joe Perry; or shopping with Steven Tyler, his experiences with Aerosmith remain some of his most treasured.

"What I really enjoy about Steven is his stripped-down, no-bullshit approach," Andre says. "It's rare for a celebrity to share that with many people. I see flashes of it in Gene Simmons, but with Steven Tyler, there are times and places when he just lets it all hang out. It's a beautiful thing."

Perhaps it's Steven's triumph over drugs and alcohol; perhaps it's his drive and his creativity; perhaps it's his recognition of his second chance at personal and professional success. Regardless of why, Steven possesses the energy and sparkle few other people do, Andre says.

"The working relationship I had with Steven was really unique," he continues. "There is more of a human and friendly quality about Steven that you really don't see very much in other celebrities."

Although often cynical about celebrities, their egos and the worship fans throw on them, Andre still realizes that not every security director can say he and his wife exchange cookie recipes with Steven Tyler or named their first-born son after Run-D.M.C.'s Jam Master Jay.

"In retrospect, there have really been some great ones," Andre admits. "Jam Master Jay, George Thorogood, Richie Sambora, Jon Bon Jovi, Will Smith, Joe Perry, Steven Tyler, Gene Simmons. Yeah, I've been fortunate."

Everybody's got an Angle

The mere fact that Andre is asked by his artists to escort them to concerts, drive them to appointments and update them on the development of his kids is a testament to Andre's ranking with his clients.

Most artists, he says, believe they can't let anyone get too close to them, physically or emotionally. "So many people have burned them that now they don't trust anyone," Andre explains. "They get used so much that they put up a protective barrier around themselves. It's sad, but you really can't blame them. A lot of artists have had more money stolen from them – by record companies, business managers, and so-called friends – than they've actually received.

"Jam Master Jay, George Thorogood, Richie Sambora, Jon Bon Jovi, Will Smith, Joe Perry, Steven Tyler Gene Simmons. Yeah, I've been fortunate."

"Their craft is music and performing," Andre continues. "The whole business of selling records and tickets is really a Catch-22. Without those sales, artists wouldn't have a vehicle to deliver their creations. But through the tours and the record deals, they get taken advantage of, especially when they're just starting out."

The music industry has responded to the artists' plight many times. Insiders cite enormous expenses to create records and tours, even for acts that never generate any income. In those cases, the overhead is spread to artists who are profitable.

"Naturally, successful artists feel as if they are carrying the weight of the world and providing a living for many people," Andre says. "Sometimes, they even see me that way.

And the truth is, I'm different. But at the same time, I'm not. They provide the concert tours, which enable me to earn a living."

And performers can't even turn to each other for consolation. While two rock giants like Paul Stanley and Steven Tyler, for example, might be interested in each other's work and lifestyles, they most likely never could be friends, Andre contends.

"Their egos won't allow it," he says. "But they would ask me, 'What are the Aerosmith guys like?' or 'Are the Kiss guys fun to hang out with? What do they like to do?' Privately, I think they are very curious about each other."

Id & Ego

Andre compares the music business and the ego-inflating high that performers get from it to sports competition.

"Think about sports and music," he says. "In sports, you have a home team and a visiting team. When you're the home team, the crowd loves you. When you're the visiting team, no one loves you. In music, most of the time anyway, you're always on the home team. When an artist walks onstage in front of a sold-out 20,000-seat arena, everyone is there to see him and cheer him on. It's not like he's got several thousand people in the 700-level seats giving him a hard time and calling him names.

"But that's not reality," Andre continues. "Being on the inside, we see these guys in such a different light than music consumers do. We see them as they really are, and sometimes that's sad. Because, for many of these really popular artists, their day-to-day existence is really an incredibly lonely one. Successful musicians fill a very small segment of the general population. But imagine what it does to your self-image when you're surrounded by nothing but people who adore you."

After a few years, the whole adulation thing can really twist artists around, adds Andre, who's worked with several aging performers. "Look at Paul Stanley," he says. "He has been so successful for so long that he is considered by many in the business to be a legend. I don't know how he keeps it together. You always have to be on. That's got to mess with your head."

Style is Everything

Andre admits he doesn't like the lack of personal time on the road. The never-ending, hectic pace can be soothed a bit, though, by receiving feedback from his artists.

"Artists, just like businesses, have their own style, their own culture," Andre explains. "The Aerosmith guys were always very open with their praise. I can remember them saying stuff to me like, 'Hey, I saw how you stopped that guy who was trying to get onstage. That was cool!' Or we'd be doing an in-store appearance and I'd give a young kid a Joe Perry guitar pick. Joe would make it a point to notice and tell me thanks, 'That really helps send a great message.' George [Thorogood] is like that, too. He always says please and thank you. It's just like in the real world. Some people give praise freely when it's deserved. Others don't."

Andre, however, remains a realist. "I know this is my job. That's why it's called work. You can't expect a lot of praise in this industry. In fact, if you need a lot of positive feedback, you're definitely in the wrong business. You will starve if you live on praise alone."

As pragmatic as he is about artists' feedback – positive or negative – regarding his professional performance, Andre always acknowledges the true champions of the tour circuit: The techs responsible for loading the stage and gear in and out, day after day and night after night.

Unsung Heroes

"The crew are really the backbone of music touring," Andre says. "They never live the glamorous life on the road. In fact, not only is it the least glamorous job in touring, it's probably the most dangerous one with the least rewards. These guys do back-breaking labor – moving amps, rigging, lighting the whole stage. It's monstrous. The real challenges are the strings of three, four or five shows in a row, with no time off."

Injuries to crew members are all too common. Tales about victims of lighting rigs, pyrotechnics and other equipment run rampant on the tour circuit.

"These workers – almost always male – go to sleep at 2 or 3 in the morning and are up at 6:30 a.m., getting ready for the next show," Andre says. "Crew members work all day, ride on a bus, sleep on that bus and pretty much exist on pizza and bad catering. The toughest

part is the close proximity of the living quarters, where a dozen people might be crammed on a tour bus for months at a time."

So what drives these people?

Andy Gilman, drum tech for Aerosmith's Joey Kramer for more than a decade on some of the biggest and longest tours in recent rock history, sheds some light on the motivation:

"For me, even after a thousand shows, when those house lights go down and the crowd roars, that moment of anticipation right before the curtain falls ... is magic. I get chills every time."

Rock Fans vs. Rap Fans

Andre's observation of music fans also provides insight into the fundamental differences between rap and rock fans. "I think they just see things differently," he says. "Sure, some white, middle-class suburban rock fans may fantasize at times about being like the musicians onstage. They may even learn to play an instrument and join a band for awhile. But at some point, most usually realize they must do something else to earn a living. And they have many different career options.

"Black, inner-city youth, on the other hand, have a different outlook. Many only see three ways out of their situation in life: sports, rap or dope. So they fantasize about being the rapper onstage, too, but they hang their future hopes and dreams more seriously on becoming the rapper on that stage."

But remember, he says, that the audiences for the early rap shows in some areas were mostly white, middle-class kids. Styles from the street have always been popular with kids, regardless of their background.

Andre also notes gender differences. "A lot of times, there would be more guys than girls hanging around backstage. With Bon Jovi, though, you had nothing but screaming 16-year-old girls. With Kiss, the split was about half girls, half guys. Backstage with the rappers, you saw almost all guys. Those guys wanted to see their heroes, and the rap artists couldn't understand it. 'Where's the women?' was the question they usually asked."

Although he never grew up in a negative inner-city environment, Andre was exposed to some negative experiences. "I've got some cousins with checkered pasts with the law," he says. "They were in and out of jail a lot. When I was 12, we were at a barbecue at my aunt's

house. One of my cousins, about 21 at the time, was smoking PCP and getting high. He started tearing my aunt's house up, and she called the police. When the cops arrived, it took about five of them to subdue him. That was a strange thing to happen at a family function."

Andre's story helps explain the impact rap culture has had on the dynamics of management within the genre.

"It's an old story," he says about the backgrounds of many black rap fans. "He or she is in a gang, never finished high school, and is a derelict drug dealer who got a bad start in life." Some of these kids become rappers, but very few attain the long-term success of old-school Eighties rappers like Run-D.M.C., who still performs at clubs, or Public Enemy, whose albums still sell well.

"It's the same story with lots of major sports players," Andre continues. "The guys coming out of the inner cities, especially the basketball players, have the same backgrounds as the rappers. They just happen to be 6-feet, 8-inches tall and play hoops. But the basketball courts they learned to play on are still down in Knickerson Gardens in the South Central L.A. projects, or in Chicago's Cabrini Green.

"One difference, though, is that the professional sports business is more controlled, more conservative. You have to behave in a certain way or the money is taken away. In music, there are fewer constraints."

Racism

One of the most difficult aspects of Andre's job – perhaps the most difficult – is dealing with the racial factor. He encounters racism in the music industry more often than you might think.

"In some arenas, I don't get the help I need," Andre contends, referring to the lack of local assistance from promoters, security crews and law-enforcement officials. "Certain parts of the United States are worse than others. But it's always bad. Sometimes information about a venue or a date is withheld, and I have a sense I'm not getting cooperation because I'm black. There's a lack of respect, a lack of trust, because of the color of my skin."

Is Andre using victim mentality here?

"Hey, I'll be the first guy to tell you it works both ways," he admits. "I've seen black organizations not give guys jobs or fire guys because they were white. The sentiments were

always that the white managers ripped them off or screwed them over. But the bottom line is – white to black or black to white – there's no place for racism in the music industry. There's enough other crap to deal with without having to worry about someone's color. We're all people."

Music: Last Bastion of the Lucky Break

One aspect of the music business that keeps kids of all races and nationalities dreaming of success remains the thought of breaking big. And the music world is one of the few places where that's still possible, Andre says. "In this business, you can still be a fluke. You can still be a kid who writes a song, creates a buzz on the street and gets a hit."

Like a race car screaming off the racetrack and through the barricades, this is when many artists spin out. "And then there is money and no control," Andre says. "That's why so many artists get ripped off by mangers or spend their newfound fortune on drugs."

Examples of musical success-from-out-of-nowhere stories abound. "Take Luke Skywalker," Andre suggests. "He independently published and distributed his music and created quite a stir with The 2 Live Crew, whose *As Nasty As They Wanna Be* was the first album declared obscene by the U.S. Supreme Court. Eazy-E hit it huge with N.W.A. Make a couple of demos, work through local radio stations and get picked up by a major record label. You can just get lucky. A person can't do that in sports. In sports, there are only a certain number of teams and a certain number of players on those teams, and you have to measure up to a benchmark of athletic performance. There can be as many rappers out there as the market allows."

Veterans like Aerosmith, Kiss and Bon Jovi – who are still going strong after millions of albums and thousands of shows – are rarities, and Andre knows he's been blessed to work with some of the most successful performers of the rock and rap era.

But for everyone, be they performer, management or crew, one day it will all come to an end. No more hotels, planes, Town Cars and room service. No more soggy cereal, cold pizza and warm beer in the back of a tour bus. The tensions and frustrations of life on the road will fade away – and all that will be left are memories and friendships.

"The only thing that is permanent is change," Andre says. "The stardom, screaming fans and sold-out shows are all temporary. One day, it's all going to end. Then the really

important matters kick in, like relationships. This game certainly isn't about money, fame or material possessions. Family, friends, colleagues – what's really important are your relationships with other people.

"When it's all said and done," Andre concludes, "what I cherish most – other than my relationship with my family and my creator – are the bonds I share with the artists and crews who travel around the world, bringing fans the greatest shows on earth."

ENCORE

The Author & Andre

February 8, 1998

NBA All-Star Game

Madison Square Garden – New York City

FOR THE PAST TWO YEARS, I'VE REALLY BEEN TOO BUSY WRITING this book to be much of a basketball fan, but the sense of excitement that permeated downtown Manhattan during the NBA's All-Star Weekend beckoned me out of my hotel room. My wife, Amy, was in town on official business. I, on the other hand, joined her for the free tickets and great seats.

Venturing out of the Crowne Plaza late Sunday morning, I noticed limousines parked everywhere. Members of the press and television crews moved about, while agent types glad-handed team representatives and spoke in confident tones to potential clients. Scenes from *Jerry Maguire* flashed through my head.

I had spent most of the previous two days working on this book. New York's street-saavy energy provided the perfect inspiration for hammering out chapters about Public Enemy, the Beastie Boys and Kiss. I must admit that I took frequent breaks and wandered over to the Javitz Center, where public basketball events shared the spotlight with amateur rap contests. I watched and listened to teenager after teenager hit the stage with stars in their eyes, attitude in their voices and dreams of becoming the next Ice Cube, Chuck D or Will Smith.

As we entered Madison Square Garden for the big game, the air crackled with electricity. Moments before tip-off, the NBA's top players took the court as the crowd went ecstatic. Upon Michael Jordan's introduction, the noise level reached that of a Kiss crowd. I

laughed at the thought. *"You wanted the best, you got the best. The hottest athlete in the world ... Miiiiichaaaaaell Jorrrrrr-daaaaaannnnnn!"*

My wife and I settled into our just-off-center-court seats, watching the parade of celebrities as they came and went from their courtside seats. Madonna and her entourage appeared relaxed; Jack Nicholson seemed to enjoy the adulation; and Matthew Broderick and Sarah Jessica Parker couldn't stop smiling.

The Garden's sound system started pumping out "1999" by The Artist Formerly Known as Prince. And then the crowd noise amplified. Amy and I looked toward the huge video display to see what the commotion was all about, and there – above center court and beaming out to all four sides of the arena – flashed images of The Artist and film director Spike Lee making their way toward their seats.

Wanting to catch the duo's entrance with our own eyes, we averted our attention to one of the floor entrances. Leading The Artist and Spike through a maze of journalists and photographers strode Andre Augustine – wireless headset positioned over his black slicked-back hair, with his long ponytail dangling behind him.

During the past year, Amy and I had gotten to know Andre quite well. We shared meals and living space, talked about our lives for hours, met countless times about this book's progress and exchanged holiday cards and family photographs. Yet, apparently, we still didn't know everything about Andre Augustine. And it occurred to me – no matter how hard I try – I will never know everything about him. Nobody will.

Suddenly, a photographer stepped in front of The Artist and Spike, raising his camera. Andre (dressed in a formal jacket – at The Artist's request, we later learned) just kept walking and slowly shook his head. The photographer understood immediately. There would be no princely photos for him that night.

After safely escorting his two celebrities to their courtside seats, Andre returned to the player-entrance tunnel, where he stood to watch over his client.

Amy and I waited a few minutes, and then we headed over to say hello to our friend.

"Yo, man!" I grinned.

"Hey!" Andre rushed over, clearly surprised to see us.

Shaking hands and hugging, we all talked quickly.

"Great to see you!" He smiled his big, warm grin. "What are you two doing here?"

"Never mind us," I said, quickly jerking a thumb towards the floor and speaking out of the right corner of my mouth. "You're working with The Artist!"

"Yeah, well ... " he began, a little sheepishly. "There are some things we just can't talk about."

Andre filled us in, mentioning that he's worked with The Artist for years – on Japanese tours, at private functions and other assignments. But an unusually strict confidentiality agreement keeps him from talking about any of the details.

The revelation that Andre has worked with The Artist sums up the core of this entire project: a series of incredible experiences that cumulatively make up a remarkable career.

Andre witnessed the beginnings of the rap movement from the inside, which paved the way for the hard-core gangsta scene and the uprisings of the hip-hop nation. He is a companion and confidant to many performers, and he still talks with Gene Simmons on the phone and sits in George Thorogood's living room watching the Anaheim Angels on television.

He also brings a global perspective to America's most cherished export, entertainment, by observing how music crosses all geographical borders and cultures, as well as how music's performers interact with and embrace their international fans.

More than an ex-jock, Andre Augustine reached these heights through intelligence and an understanding of the music business and the political and economic systems that make that business work. His insight into the human psyche – and fans' minds – helps him diffuse potential problems through planning and reasoning, rather than by brute force.

Back in Madison Square Garden at the All-Star Game, after a few minutes of talking to Andre in the players' tunnel, I noticed his eyes focusing on something in the distance. His attention turned, and Andre spoke into the tiny pea-sized microphone on his headset.

"Yeah, boss. Sure thing. No problem."

Without the slightest expression of anxiety, Andre turned to Amy and me.

"It was great seeing you guys again. We'll talk more, but right now I've got to get back to work."

We hugged, shook hands and smiled. This book project had become more than just a business deal; it really was a labor of love.

My mind reeled, thinking of what it's like to be Andre Augustine. I shuddered at the thought of working in front of tens of thousands of fans, standing as the only protection

between an artist and an alcohol-induced fan who rushes the stage. I imagined living side by side with some of rock's and rap's true legends, traveling the world and sharing in their successes and failures.

I frowned for a moment, remembering that life on the road takes Andre away from his family, tearing him from his loyalty to home life and the need to constantly provide financial security for his loved ones. By contrast, I tingled anticipating the adventures that lie ahead of Andre every time that phone rings.

I felt proud knowing the guy.

As halftime approached, we noticed Andre moving Spike and The Artist back through the crowd. One of the men sitting beside me tapped me on the shoulder and asked, "Hey, do you know that big guy with the ponytail down there with Prince?"

"Yeah," I grinned. "I know him."

"Who is he?"

I turned for a second to watch Andre part the crowd. Fans moved quickly out of his way, nodding in respect. No one even attempted to distract or touch The Artist.

"Andre Augustine," I said quietly. "Guardian of the Gods."

– Mark Rodgers

ANDRE ON TOUR

FEB. 1998 - APRIL 1998
U.S., Europe

Tour Manager

NOV. 1997 - MARCH 1998
U.S.

Personal Assistant/Personal Security

JUNE 1996 - JULY 1997
U.S., Europe, Japan, South America

Tour Manager/Security Director

JAN. 1996 - MARCH 1996
U.S., Japan

Security Director/Advance

SEP. 1995 - DEC. 1995
Japan, Australia, South Africa, South America

Personal Security

AUG. 1995 - SEP. 1995
U.S.

Security Director/Personal Assistant

MARCH 1995 - AUG. 1995
U.S.

Road Manager/Security Director

APRIL 1993 - DEC. 1994
U.S., Europe, Japan, South America

Road Manager/Security Director

Richie Sambora
Undiscovered Soul Tour

The Artist
"The Jam of the Year"

Kiss
Alive Worldwide Tour

The Artist

Bon Jovi
These Days Tour

George Thorogood
Lets Work Together Tour

Kiss
Convention Tour

Aerosmith
Get A Grip Tour

Feb. 1993 - April 1993
U.S.

Tour Manager

Arcade
Never Gonna End Tour

March 1992 - Nov. 1992
U.S., Europe

Road Manager/Personal Security

Kiss
Revenge Tour

March 1991 - Nov. 1991
U.S., Canada, Japan

Security Director

Nelson
Give Me the Rain Tour

Oct. 1989 - Sept. 1990
U.S., Europe, Australia, Japan, South America

Security Director

Aerosmith
Pump Tour

June 1989 - August 1989
U.S., Canada

Security Director/Personal Assistant

George Thorogood
Badlands Tour

Feb. 1989 - May 1989
U.S., Canada

Security Director

Eazy-E & N.W.A.
Straight Outta Compton

April 1988 - Nov. 1988
U.S., Canada, Europe, Australia

Security Director

Run-D.M.C.
Public Enemy
Run's House Tour

April 1987 - Oct. 1987
U.S., Canada

Security Director/C.S.C.

Run-D.M.C.
Beastie Boys
Together Forever Tour

PHOTO ACKNOWLEDGEMENTS

Photo number 1: Photographer unknown. Photo number 2: Photo by Ron Scoggins. Photo number 3: Photo by Ron Scoggins. Photo number 4: Photographer unknown. Photo number 5: Photo by Andre Augustine. Photo number 6: Photographer unknown. Photo number 7: Photo by Andre Augustine. Photo number 8: Photo by Andre Augustine. Photo number 9: Photo by Andre Augustine. Photo number 10: Photo by Ron Scoggins. Photo number 11: Photo by Ron Scoggins. Photo number 12: Photo by Ron Scoggins. Photo number 13: Photo by Andre Augustine. Photo number 14: Photo by Andre Augustine. Photo number 15: Photo by Andre Augustine. Photo number 16: Photo by Ron Scoggins. Photo number 17: Photographer unknown. Photo number 18: Photographer unknown. Photo number 19: Photo by Andre Augustine. Photo number 20: Photo by Andre Augustine. Photo number 21: Photographer unknown. Photo number 22: Photographer unknown. Photo number 23: Photographer unknown. Photo number 24: Photographer unknown. Photo number 25: Photo by Andre Augustine. Photo number 26: Photo by Andre Augustine. Photo number 27: Photographer unknown. Photo number 28: Photographer unknown. Photo number 29: Photographer unknown. Photo number 30: Photographer unknown. Photo number 31: Photo by George Chin. Photo number 32: Photographer unknown. Photo number 33: Photographer unknown. Photo number 34: Photographer unknown. Photo number 35: Photo by George Chin. Photo number 36: Photographer unknown. Photo number 37: Photographer unknown. Photo number 38: Photographer unknown. Photo number 39: Photographer unknown. Photo number 40: Photographer unknown. Photo number 41: Photographer unknown. Photo number 42: Photographer unknown. Photo number 43: Photographer unknown. Photo number 44: Photographer unknown. Photo number 45: Photographer unknown. Photo number 46: Photographer unknown. Photo number 47: Photographer unknown. Photo number 48: Photo by Bob Dowd. Photo number 49: Photo by Bob Dowd. Photo number 50: Photo by Andre Augustine. Photo number 51: Photo by Andre Augustine. Photo number 52: Photo by Andre Augustine. Photo number 53: Photo by Andy Gilman. Photo number 54: Photo by Andre Augustine. Photo number 55: Photo by Andre Augustine. Photo number 56: Photo by Andre Augustine. Photo number 57: Photographer unknown. Photo number 58: Photo by Andy Gilman. Photo number 59: Photo by Andy Gilman. Photo number 60 : Photo by Andy Gilman. Photo number 61: Photographer unknown. Photo number 62: Photographer unknown. Photo number 63: Photo by Mark Weiss. Photo number 64: Photographer unknown. Photo number 65: Photographer unknown. Photo number 66: Photographer unknown. Photo number 67: Photographer unknown. Photo number 68: Photographer unknown. Photo number 69: Photographer unknown. Photo number 70: Photographer unknown. Florida Fan 1992. Photo number 71: Photographer unknown. Photo number 72: Photographer unknown. Photo number 73: Photographer unknown. Photo number 74: Backstage Pass. Photo number 75: Backstage Pass. Photo number 76: Photo by Andre Augustine. Photo number 77: Photographer unknown.

Unless otherwise noted, all photographs are the property of Andre Augustine and from his personal collection.

INDEX

GUARDIAN
OF THE GODS

ORDER FORM

Date:

Name:

Address:

City: State: Zip:

Phone: Fax:

Email:

Method of Payment: ☐ check (to Monkey Boy Media) ☐ Visa ☐ MC
or Money Order

Credit Card #   Exp:

Signature:

Item	Qty x Price	S&H	Total
Guardian of the Gods	☐ x 22.95	standard shipping +	=
	Wisconsin Residents Add **Sales tax** =		
	TOTAL =		

122 Green Bay Rd. #9
Thiensville, WI 53092
1 800/666-5390
fax 414-512-1708

e-mail:
info@monkeyboymedia.com

web site:
www.guardianofthegods.com

KISS ALIVE / WORLDWIDE 96-97

Not even Andre can intimidate the Demon. Andre & Gene Simmons backstage, mugging for the camera on 1997's "Lost Cities" segment of the Alive/Worldwide Tour.

KISS ALIVE/ WORLDWIDE '96-'97 ALL ACCESS

Jam Master Jay getting one
up on Andre backstage
Europe, 1988.

RUN'S HOUSE

RUN
DMC

RUSH ARTIST MANAGEMENT

ALL AREA ACCESS

Tougher than leather.
D.M.C., Andre & Run backstage
in Germany, 1988.

Three amigos. Russell Simmons, Ron Scoggins and Andre, backstage in the U.S., 1988.

A break from the road. Run, D.M.C. and Jay at the home of Ron Scoggins' mother, enjoying good food and good company, 1988.

Andre negotiates with Russell over a pay raise Ron Scoggins, Russell Simmons and Andre backstage in the U.S., 1988.

"Guinness wasn't good enough" Run-D.M.C. shipped a pallet of Olde English 800 to Europe for their 1988 tour, for "medicinal purposes."

"I'm D.M.C. Yeah you know me" Everyone knew D.M.C. that night in Australia.

Looks like the Olde English worked! Run, doing what he does best. Onstage in England, 1988.

THE DOPE JAM TOUR
SAY NO TO DRUGS

KOOL MOE DEE
ERIC B. & RAKIM
DOUG E. FRESH GET FRESH CREW

ALL AREA ACCESS

otto

RUN-D.M.C.

PCT-1202

Working the pit at a sold-out 1988
Run-D.M.C. show. The guys would
give Andre their gold chains for
safe keeping during the show.
Would you try and take them?

"Hey man, where are the chicks?"
Waiting to be noticed, Andre, Jam
Master Jay and Run sit outside
the Como Hotel in Sydney, Australia.

D.M.C. backstage in 1988.
Notice the neat organization
of the meticulous and orderly
rapper's dressing area.

The German media loved Public
Enemy, especially at this 1988
press conference at a nightclub
in Germany.

Chuck D. of Public Enemy signing
autographs after a 1988 Germany
show in front of the barricade.
All the kids love Chuck.

Chuck D is in the foreground
as Professor Griff shows one
of his signature stage moves
to a 1988 sold-out Aussie crowd.

Home away from home. Famous
rappers are inconspicuous in this
European McDonalds. Two months
later, Public Enemy's popularity
made this impossible.

Good guys wear black.
George Thorogood and Andre
before a show at L.A.'s House
of Blues in 1997.

GEORGE
THOROGOOD

The
Tonight
SHOW
WITH
JAY LENO

George is about to show a
Dallas crowd just how bad he is.
Andre and George backstage
at Deep Ellum Live moments
before the show, 1995.

LET'S WORK
TOGETHER
TOUR

Starring

GEORGE THOROGOOD
& The DESTROYERS

AND HOT TUN

Roadie Charlie Hernandez yucking it up during the last show on Nelson's Give Me the Rain Tour.

Babes in Toyland. Backstage before Gunnar and Matt take the stage for a 1991 Nelson show.

Andre and Steven "Get A Grip"
before a 1994 U.S. show.

Taking a much-needed break during a 1990 *Saturday Night Live* taping, Tom Hamilton, Andre and Joe Perry pose for a quick shot in front of the famous logo.

Unleashed in the East. Aerosmith arrives at the Narita Airport in Japan in 1989. Pictured are Brad Whitford, Andre and Steven Tyler.

Steven loves his fans. Seen here in North Carolina in 1989, Steven takes the time to pose for the camera with this unidentified member of Aeroforce 1, under the ever-watchful eye of Andre.

Mr. Tyler on the private jet, circa 1994.

Mr. Perry on the private jet, circa 1994.

AEROSMITH TOURING

BAND

STEVEN TYLER
JOE PERRY
BRAD WHITFORD
TOM HAMILTON
JOEY KRAMER

TIM COLLINS
KEITH GARDE

ROAD S

JIMMY EYERS
JERRY GILLELAND
TRES THOMAS
PETER MERTENS
THOM GIMBEL
KAREN LINEHAN
VICTOR DAVILA
BRUCE KNIGHT
PHEY MACMAHON
WILLY TWORK
BOB CARRELL
SUZANNE SEIDEL
ANDY GILMAN
STEVE DIKUN
FRANK FELDER
JIM SURVIS
JULIE PETERSON
LARRY YAGER
SETH GOLDSTEIN
RICH BARR
STEVE CARLSON
NICK STORR
BILL HEAD
DON DOME
EDDIE KERCHER
GREG WITZ
COREY STONE
STEVEN ANDERSON
KENT SHAFFERMAN
DALE JEWETT
MARK HETIRICK
CARL KING
BOB MADISON
ANDRE AUGUSTINE
MIKE HENRY
ARLIE MANUEL
JAY BARKER
DAVE THOMAS
MARK DOWN
OLIVIER BOUCHA
JO LEE
KATE PAUL
RACHEL MILNE
ANEE BOTTING

AEROSMITH
Marcus Amphitheater
RAIN OR SHINE
NO REF/EXCH/RCRDING
FRI AUGUST 5 1994 8:00PM

"You want the band to appear at
the Playboy Mansion? Hmmm, let
me check ..." Andre fields a call.

The Bruise Brothers: Mike Henry
and Andre Augustine planning
the 1994 Get A Grip Tour strategy.

Andre and Mike Henry squeeze
some information out of Joey
Kramer.

Game face. Andre blocks and tackles his way through the crowd, guiding Steven Tyler safely through the airport in Buenos Aires, 1994.

TALENT GUES
PIERRE COSSETTE
PRODUCTIONS/
NARAS

AT RADIO CITY MUSIC HALL
NO. 017 MARCH 1, 1994

AEROSMITH

VIDEO
scrapbook

"I protect him, I don't dress him!" Andre and Steven looking cool backstage on the 1994 Get A Grip Tour.

John Kalodner, Steven Tyler, Andre Augustine, Mike Henry and Joe Perry exiting the stage area after a 1994 sound check at Rock AM Ring Festival.

Coming through! Andre and Steven shoot through the throngs on the Bullet Train platform in Tokyo, 1994.

"What do you mean I can only have one steak?" Andre, Steven Tyler, April Kramer, Joey Kramer, Billie Perry, Joe Perry and two unidentified waiters (who immediately found more meat!) in Rio de Janerio, 1994.

"You want me to climb that one too?" Andre and Steven Tyler on top of the world, January 25, 1994. Aerosmith celebrates Andre's birthday high atop one of the pyramids in Mexico.

"Work with me people, I'm trying to make a movie here." Andre captures the moment for posterity, backstage in Atlanta. Andre, Steven "Smiling" Tyler and Tom Hamilton.

All systems go! Andre leads Aerosmith to the stage.

SET LIST - JULY 12, 1994
GANEY YEHOSHUA PARK
TEL AVIV, ISRAEL

EAT
MA KIN
FEVER
DRAW THE LINE
AMAZING
RAG DOLL
CRYIN
SHADDAP
STOP MESSIN
WALK ON DOWN
JANIE
ELEVATOR
SWEET E
DUDE

CRAZY
EDGE
WALK THIS WAY

A serious moment in front
of Jerusalem's Wailing Wall.
Steven Tyler and Andre.

Andre shares "The Hook"
technique and other security
tricks with a pair of
enthusiastic Israeli soldiers.

Andre helps Aerosmith through the Grammys' red carpet entrance.

LL AREA ACCESS

"Hey Steven, want me to go after that guy who wrote on your stomach?" Actually the singer did his own body art on the Get A Grip Tour. Steven Tyler and Andre.

Good friends and good times.
Brad Whitford and Andre.

Tom Hamilton must really
like this place. And who
wouldn't, it's a restaurant
on the Isle of Capri.

PUMP

1. YOUNG LUST (ASCAP/BMI)
2. F.I.N.E.
3.1 GOING DOWN
3.1 LOVE IN AN ELEVATOR
3.2 LOVE IN AN ELEVATOR
4. MONKEY ON MY BACK
5.1 WATER SONG
5.2 JANIE'S GOT A GUN
6.1 DULCIMER STOMP
6.2 THE OTHER SIDE (ASCAP/BMI)
7. MY GIRL
8. DON'T GET MAD, GET EVEN
9.1 VOODOO
9.2 VOODOO MEDICINE
WHAT IT TAKES

Tom Hamilton and Andre in the *Saturday Night Live* dressing room.

The Last Supper? Far from it. The Aerosmith family continues to enjoy good friends and good food.

Andre at a 1993 Aerosmith in-store autograph signing in the Virgin Mega Store in Paris.

Autographs will have to wait.
Andre ensures Tom and Joey enjoy
the race at the Charlotte North
Carolina Motor Speedway in 1993.

Andre tries to sweet talk
Kyle Petty into giving him
and Brad Whitford a lift.

"All right, who locked the keys
in the car?"

"Wait 'til Joey sees these!"
Tom Hamilton and Brad Whitford
with a pair of Camaros in 1994.

BLEY ARENA   DEC.7
V.I.P
GET A GRIP
TOUR

There is nothing like a Les Paul!
Joe Perry anxiously waits his
turn as Brad Whitford tries out
a new toy.

PUMP
WORLD TOUR
1989 - 1991
ACCESS
ALL AREA

"These things come with strings,
right?" Joe Perry and Brad
Whitford make inquiries at the
Gibson factory.

Joey Kramer with his long time drum tech, and Andre's road warrior pal, Andy Gilman, moments before show time in Germany.

Mind and muscle. Legendary A&R man John Koladner and Andre.

Looks like Mike Henry has 'lost his grip', monkeying around onstage during the last show of the US Get A Grip Tour.

Andy Gilman replaces a broken drumhead while Aerosmith kept a rollin'.

"We're not worthy!" Bob Dowd, Andre and Tony Morehead on the set of Wayne's World II. Andre and Aerosmith can be seen in the movie.

1994 Monsters of Rock Festival - Donnington, England: Before Aerosmith ...

... during Aerosmith.

CHERISHED MEMORIES OF
A LOVING HUSBAND AND FATHER
JOHN HENRY
BONHAM
WHO DIED SEPT. 25th 1980
AGED 32 YEARS
He will always be Remembered
in our hearts
Goodnight my Love. God Bless.

One of the greatest drummers
to ever grace the earth:
John Henry Bonham.

After the burn. Andre and Joe Perry are glad to be finished in Busek Gym in Munich, Germany.

Walk this way! Leading the boys offstage after a 1994 Wembley Arena show.

Andre watching Jon Bon Jovi's back.

Matt BonGiovi (Jon's brother), Richie Sambora and Andre. Lions and tigers and bears, oh my, on March 12, 1995.

The ever-gregarious Paul
Stanley backstage before a
show on the Revenge Tour.

KISS
REVENGE
TOUR
1992
ALL ACCESS

"Gene? You've changed!" Eric Singer, Paul Stanley Chewbacca, Andre and a kneeling Bruce Kulick stop for a photo at Disney World.

Andre and Paul Stanley take a break from touring with this 1992 trip to Disney World.

Ever feel like someone is looking over your shoulder? Andre and Eric Singer backstage during the Revenge Tour.

RITZ
BACK STAGE
LOADING
ENTRANCE

Paul Stanley and Andre sneak out through the in door on the way to the car after a Revenge Tour sound check at The Ritz in New York City.

Gene Simmons carefully considers a question at this 7:30 AM radio remote broadcast at Hooters in Florida. Andre looks on.

Andre taking Kiss to sound check.

Paul Stanley and Andre at the Australian press conference for the Down Under Convention Tour, 1995.

Paul Stanley, Tommy Thayer
and Andre take the plunge at
Disney World, 1992.

Some fans actually thought
they could get to the band's
dressing room with this
confiscated bootleg pass.

Got dip? Kiss has some fun at
Ace's expense on the
Alive/Worldwide Tour jet.

Leaving on a jet plane. Paco Zimmer, Gene Simmons, Peter Criss, Paul Stanley, Ace Frehley and Andre.